Novels of Initiation

A Guidebook for Teaching
Literature to Adolescents

Novels of Initiation

A Guidebook for Teaching Literature to Adolescents

David Peck

Teachers College, Columbia University
New York and London

Published by Teachers College Press, 1234 Amsterdam Avenue,
New York, NY 10027

Library of Congress Cataloging-in-Publication Data

Peck, David R.
  Novels of initiation : a guidebook for teaching literature to
adolescents / David Peck.
    p. cm.
  Bibliography: p.
  Includes index.
  ISBN 0-8077-2951-5
  1. American fiction—Study and teaching (Secondary)
2. Initiations in literature—Study and teaching (Secondary)
3. Adolescence in literature—Study and teaching (Secondary)
4. Teenagers—Books and reading. 5. Youth—Books and reading.
I. Title.
PS374.I5P4   1989   88-38517
813'.007'12—dc 19   CIP

ISBN 0-8077-2951-5

Manufactured in the United States of America
94 93 92 91 90 89   1 2 3 4 5 6

To my students, early and late,
whose responses to these novels
have sharpened my own

Contents

Acknowledgments

A number of people helped in the preparation of this manuscript. Sheila Kasprzyk, Jim Sieg, and Kirsten Lagatree commented on individual chapters in progress and encouraged me to complete the work. John Maitino read the entire manuscript and gave me invaluable suggestions, especially about the introduction and individual teaching guides. Charles May, ever my intellectual mentor, pointed out a number of ways in which the final book could be better. And Randy Lewis and Darlene Campbell cheered me on toward the goal line.

Work on *Novels of Initiation* was partially funded by California State University, Long Beach.

Introduction

Novels of Initiation is a guidebook for teachers containing analyses of a dozen of the American novels most commonly read in high school English classes. I have included both adult classics that have been adopted by teenage readers (such as J. D. Salinger's *The Catcher in the Rye*) and the newer young adult (YA) titles, specifically written for adolescent audiences, that are increasingly finding their way into the junior and senior high school literature curriculum (such as Robert Cormier's *The Chocolate War*). All of the novels treated here are linked by the idea of initiation, for all of them feature young protagonists making that perilous passage from childhood to adulthood—which is one of the reasons these novels are so appealing to teenage readers.

The literary term for these novels is *Bildungsroman*, a "novel of education" in which the central character learns about the world as he or she grows into it. Some of the novels included here stress the individual psychology of this adolescent passage (Judith Guest's *Ordinary People*, Sylvia Plath's *The Bell Jar*), while others focus on the changing protagonist in the family unit (Mildred D. Taylor's *Roll of Thunder, Hear My Cry*, Robert Newton Peck's *A Day No Pigs Would Die*), and still others on the clash between the individual and society (F. Scott Fitzgerald's *The Great Gatsby*, Mark Twain's *Adventures of Huckleberry Finn*).

The stress throughout this book is on the ideas that are alive in these literary works and on the critical thinking we need to develop in students in order to help them recognize those ideas in literature. Thus the analysis of each novel stresses both the central initiation theme and the additional themes—such as tolerance and freedom—we find in it, and the teaching guide suggests ways to get at those ideas in reading, discussing, and writing about the novel.

FORMAT

Each chapter in this book focuses on a single novel, with the order of chapters based roughly on class reading level (those novels best suited for junior high appear toward the end). But chapters have also been arranged to highlight the connections among novels; thus Twain follows Salinger because of the many parallels between their two books, and is followed in turn by Cormier's *The Chocolate War*, which echoes *Huck Finn* in several crucial ways. But there are infinite possibilities for such combinations, and the last section in each chapter suggests other works to "pair" through comparisons of theme, character, and setting. The goal throughout *Novels of Initiation* has been to link books thematically, so that students can see ideas and values in some comparative context: how two works treat the theme of love, or how two different characters handle the problem of prejudice; how Huck and Holden, for example, deal with their remarkably similar societies.

All the chapters have roughly the same format. Each begins with a list of key information about the novel: author, genre, point of view, grade level, characters, and so forth. The rest of the chapter is then divided into two main parts:

1. An analysis of the novel itself, including discussions of story and setting, characters, themes, and style and language.
2. A guide to teaching the novel, including suggestions for approaching the novel, some discussion and writing topics, and "bridging" to related literary works, especially other novels.

While this book may be used in college courses on adolescent literature—where a number of the different novels treated in the book can be read and discussed— I have designed it mainly for teachers working with individual novels in high school and junior high school English classrooms. With that purpose in mind, I have tried to make every chapter as self-sufficient as possible. And in every case I have chosen recent, readily available paperback editions of the novels, so that readers will easily be able to find quotations and other page references. (Note that unless another source is specified in the citation, page references throughout each chapter are to the edition of the novel listed in the chapter opening; full facts of publication are given in the first section of the bibliography.)

Analysis of the Novel

In the first part of each chapter, I set forth the four basic elements of the novel. Under "Story and Setting" I give a detailed recap of the entire novel, describing setting and retelling major events—what happens, where, and with what emphasis. One of the problems that beginning novel readers have is that they tend to emphasize the wrong things: the scary Boo Radley story in Harper Lee's *To Kill a Mockingbird*, for example, may seem much more interesting to them than the equally important story of racial injustice centering on Tom Robinson. Students need to learn which incidents and details are thematically significant and which function more for purposes of plot (or suspense, as in Harper Lee). In the section on "Characters," I give profiles of the most important characters and describe whether characterization generally is two- or three-dimensional. Often in this section I sketch out the changes the central protagonist goes through in his or her initiation into adulthood. In "Themes," I outline the major meanings of the novel. This is probably the most important section of each chapter, for the central ideas of the novel are here laid out in some depth and detail. Finally, in the section on "Style and Language," I discuss the formal elements (irony, symbolism, personification, etc.) of the novel. Form and content cannot ultimately be separated in literary works, which means—to put this axiom positively— that we can use the one to get at the other: the discussion of point of view in the chapter on Salinger, for example. takes us to the heart of the meaning of *The Catcher in the Rye*; analysis of figurative language in the Steinbeck chapter likewise leads to a number of important ideas in *The Red Pony*.

The glossary at the end defines key literary terms as they are used in the book and directs readers to specific chapters where they are defined and discussed in context. But throughout the book I have avoided technical literary jargon as much as possible. Too often in our teaching of literature, a stress on literary terminology overshadows our focus on literary content and form, and students end up feeling overwhelmed by questions of the mechanics of literary study, to the exclusion of more important discussions of the literary works themselves. Thus I do not emphasize literary history or literary genres: the definitions for terms like *Renaissance* or *naturalism* should be working definitions only, tools to help students place works in context, not ends in themselves. Too often, students are more worried about the exact definition of a term like *tragedy* than about the more important question of what an actual tragedy, such as *Romeo and Juliet*, really means.

In the first part of each chapter, then, I summarize the form and content of the novel under discussion, and a teacher reading this brief synopsis should come away with a good understanding of the main ideas and formal elements in the novel.

Teaching the Novel

In the second part of each chapter, I turn some of the ideas and stylistic elements of each novel into teaching strategies. Here I try to make that crucial transition from what we as teachers know to what students are only beginning to understand. Surely the most important element in our teaching is how we get our students to learn; students walk out of the best English classrooms with the tools for formulating their own questions about the meaning and technique of literary works. I have tried to give teachers some strategies for developing this kind of critical thinking throughout this book.

Each teaching guide begins with suggestions for approaching the novel through its thematic or formal elements, including the special features of this work that may surprise students but that are essential to a recognition of what is going on—how to get from the meandering mysteries of *The Catcher in the Rye*, for example, to student understanding of its literary and psychological elements. Sometimes in the "Teaching Suggestions" I stress literary style as the best way to start teaching the book: metaphor in Carson McCullers, for example, or symbolism in Steinbeck. At other times I suggest the major themes and ideas: the social criticism of America's consumer culture in Fitzgerald, for example, or the pride and dignity of black family life in Mildred D. Taylor. In other teaching guides, I point out something unique about the book itself: for instance, that Robert Newton Peck's rural Vermont setting can be a vehicle for discussing the uses of the past and the importance of community. In all cases, these are suggestions meant to help teachers encourage students to start making observations themselves about the form, meaning, and significance of the literary work in question. (See the questions that conclude the "Teaching Suggestions" in Chapter 2, on *Huck Finn*, for example, or the questions in the same section of Chapter 4, on *Ordinary People*.) If students can start to ask themselves what Holden Caulfield means when he says, "I was sort of crying"—to cite but one example—they may have moved closer to an understanding of his character and, consequently, of the novel itself. They should certainly be closer to seeing the organic interconnections between the "what" of the novel and the "way" it is narrated.

The second section of each teaching guide is a list of discussion and paper topics, including ideas for both journal or out-of-class writing. The three R's are being replaced today, I think, by what we can call the three C's: critical reading, critical writing, and critical thinking. And we cannot do one in the classroom without doing the other two. Therefore, in all of the chapters, my emphasis has been, as much as possible, on writing about literature. I encourage teachers to have their students use a Reading Log, a journal or notebook that they regularly carry to English classes, as a repository for journal ideas, rough drafts of papers, responses to literature, and so forth. The best way to get at the ideas in a literary work is to read it carefully, think about it critically, discuss it fully, and write about it specifically. Thus in the teaching guide to *The Catcher in the Rye*, after discussing the ways that teachers might use its points of view, characterization, and symbolism as entries into the novel, I list a dozen discussion and writing topics that are also intended to help students move more easily toward the meaning and significance of Salinger's novel.

The first and best discussion and writing questions often elicit what we call "affective" responses: How did you like this novel? Why? What did it remind you of? How does it compare to your own life? Have you ever been in a situation like this one? Adolescent readers respond best to literature when discussion of it starts within the circle of their own experience, when they can begin their reading by relating to the work personally and emotionally. This is not the last level of response, certainly, but it is often the best to begin with, for once that affective link has been made—once students feel the connection between the work and their own lives—it is a great deal easier to get them to think about other ideas or connections in the novel. Students who have first recognized their own experiences with fear may be much more sympathetic to Henry Fleming's situation in Crane's *The Red Badge of Courage*. And students who have grasped Huck Finn's dilemma in terms of their own lives may better understand not only the novel and its relevance for today but also something about their own conflicts with society.

As part of that affective strategy, I often recommend reading the first sections of novels—a chapter or two—aloud to a class that is about to begin a novel. We have lost the art of reading aloud somewhere along our educational way, and it is time to return to it. (Jim Trelease's *The Read-Aloud Handbook* is one of several recent books urging a return to oral reading.) Students who have heard the first two chapters of *A Day No Pigs Would Die* read aloud will have a great deal of difficulty not finishing the book themselves. Students who hear the beginnings of novels read to them also hear the teacher's emphasis and explanations and *pleasure* in the reading. The rest of the novel then becomes almost a three-way experience, for the teacher's voice will continue in the students' minds as they later read silently to themselves.

In addition to suggesting the use of the Reading Log described above, I make other teaching suggestions that are rooted in assumptions about how the literature classroom should be organized. For one thing, I believe strongly in collaborative learning: students can often learn as easily from each other as from any teacher. Whenever possible, students should be organized into one-on-one and small-group work: to brainstorm literature or writing assignments, to exchange and go over drafts of papers, or to review earlier material. In the "Discussion and Writing

Ideas" section of the teaching guide to Chapter 3, for example, I suggest that teachers assign groups of students to follow the different major characters through the *The Chocolate War*, an exercise that can lead to students' recognition both of the characters' values and the importance of point of view. It may take teachers some time to organize such a collaborative classroom, but the benefits, to students and teacher alike, are immeasurable.

In the third section of the teaching guide ("Bridging to Other Works"), I list other literary works that could be used with this particular novel. Often these are novels that can be "paired" with the one under discussion, for teaching two works of similar character or setting may be the best way to get at their meaning. *A Day No Pigs Would Die* works fine by itself, for example, but when paired with William Armstrong's *Sounder*, all kinds of natural comparisons emerge, the qualities of both works are highlighted, and students can begin to see ideas in real juxtaposition: how, in similar situations, different characters act and react in different ways—how the protagonists in these two YA novels lose their animals and then their fathers but learn from these painful experiences. Often in this section I develop the similarities between the particular novel under discussion and others treated in this book. (See the thematic unit on "the individual and society" that concludes the discussion of Robert Cormier's *The Chocolate War* in Chapter 3, for example, and other sample thematic syllabi in Appendix A.)

Additional Resources

Along with Appendix A, the material included at the back of this book is provided as an extension of the teaching guides. Appendix B contains a list of other American novels of initiation, both popular adult and YA titles. The appendices are followed by the Glossary, described earlier in this introduction. Finally, there is the Bibliography, which is divided into three sections: first, the complete citations for the 12 novels that are the focus of the book; second, the primary literature cited in the text and listed in the "Bridging" sections of each chapter and in Appendixes A and B; and third, a list of the secondary sources used in compiling this study. As the Bibliography indicates, no book begins life as an orphan, and in addition to those works referred to in the text, there are three titles that have been particularly helpful in my own thinking on adolescent literature and that readers may find useful as well: Nilsen and Donelson's *Literature for Today's Young Adults*, Probst's *Adolescent Literature: Response and Analysis*, and Reed's *Reaching Adolescents: The Young Adult Book and the School*.

RATIONALE

Why do we teach novels in high school at all? The obvious answer is that we think there is something valuable for students in the act of reading, discussing, and writing about an extended piece of fiction; further, by helping them to develop both an interest in and an ability to analyze such longer works of fiction, we hope we are encouraging them to become lifetime readers. But it is also important that they learn to read critically so that *now*, and not just in the future, they can sift through material and recognize important incidents, ideas, forms, and relations among these elements. Critical readers of *The Catcher in the Rye* can come to understand Holden Caulfield's dilemma—frozen into a place somewhere between childhood and adulthood, unable to move forward or backward—and thus to understand something of the complexity of the human situation. And to understand how the imagery and symbolism of the novel (the carrousel at the end of the novel, or, even better, the ducks that Holden worries about throughout) underscore those ideas is to recognize how language in literature works and how ideas can emerge from incident and metaphor as well as from exposition.

Finally, such reading transports us imaginatively into another world where we experience events from the point of view of other human beings. People who cannot make this flight of fancy are essentially locked within themselves and may never be able to experience the world except from their own egocentric perspectives. Critical, involved readers of Harper Lee's *To Kill a Mockingbird*, on the contrary, can experience both fear and love through fictional characters and incidents in a world totally unlike their own. Novels, and especially adolescent novels, are constantly transporting us into these other worlds: think of William Golding, Scott O'Dell, Jean Craighead George, Rudolfo Anaya, Theodore Taylor, S. E. Hinton, and the dozens of other writers that young people read and enjoy.

Recommending Reading

Besides teaching these novels, we can recommend similar books to students who have just completed one novel and are ready for another. One of the things that we have lost in the last 20 years is a stress on outside, or recommended, reading. The majority of literature programs in the United States do not urge or require students to read on the outside and have given up the attempt. Too often, students will not do that reading: the lure of TV and movies is just too great. (The average teenager spends more time switching channels on the TV than in leisure reading.) But I think we have given up the battle too easily. Good schools still require outside reading, good teachers are still working with librarians in their communities to establish lists for summer reading, and good administrators are still helping teachers and students to find the time for such recommended reading. There are thousands and thousands of books that we could recommend: each "Bridging" section merely lists a few of the novels that students might like to move to if they enjoyed reading this particular one, and the list in Appendix B includes others. (Many English classrooms contain some kind of card file where students can recommend good reading to one another—or warn others of particular hazards.)

One of the reasons teachers do not recommend books may be that they do not know them. The average high school English teacher who has been teaching for some years may not be aware of all the books that are available for adolescents to read, particularly all the young adult novels. YA books have only been around for some 20 years, and many teachers may not be familiar with them, while others may have a negative, traditionalist prejudice about this kind of literature. A number of YA novels are excellent and worthy of literary study, as I think the three YA chapters in *Initiations* amply demonstrate. A novel like Cormier's *The Chocolate War*, to take but one obvious example, has all the literary elements of any serious adult novel: its structure, characterization, and literary style are complete and yield to the same kind of critical reading we could make of an older novel—*The Catcher in the Rye*, for example. More important, YA novels have been written for teenagers; they have subjects and themes that are relevant to that population of readers. *The Chocolate War* is about teenagers and addresses their concerns much more thoroughly than Salinger's novel, which is concerned with other, perhaps more adult, ideas. (One good plan: teach Salinger, then recommend Cormier.) Teenagers may more readily respond to Cormier's novel than to a classic novel; certainly YA titles are better recommended books than many of the more traditional novels we could list, and they make the English teacher's job easier, for we do not have to "sell" S. E. Hinton or Mildred D. Taylor the way we might have to promote some nineteenth-century writer (such as Hawthorne, perhaps) we think valuable for adolescent readers. In the "Bridging" section of each chapter, I list all the titles that I think would work well with the particular novel studied, including related YA novels. I recommend dozens of titles by such YA writers as Katherine Paterson, Cynthia Voight, Robin Brancato, William Hogan, Terry Davis, and many others throughout these chapters.

Focusing on Adolescence

Why have I stressed the initiation process in selecting novels for this book? The obvious answer is that so many of the books popular in high school happen to have that central focus: American writers are obsessed with the idea of adolescence, and young people quite naturally enjoy reading about themselves, or characters of their own age. Thus a number of American classics have ended up as staples of the secondary curriculum—*Huck Finn, The Red Badge of Courage, Member of the Wedding.* But there are other pedagogical reasons for the stress here on adolescence. The initiation process is a basic one in human development, for it takes us from the protected and ideal world of childhood into the real and often discouraging (at least for adolescents) world of adulthood, where disillusionment and disappointment are commonplace. It is in the initiation process that we discover just how limited our childhood illusions really are; put positively, through a healthy initiation process we gain a realistic recognition of those goals that we *can* achieve as adults and, conversely, those values and modes of behavior that we should discard. In every case, there is a loss of innocence and a consequent gain in experience. (Frankie Addams, for example, the heroine of *Member of the Wedding,* has to shed old illusions before she can gain a new identity in her growth toward adulthood.) This initiation process can obviously take place in a number of different arenas (religious, political, etc.), but in fiction it is usually psychological and sexual.

Adolescence is a separation from childhood and a preparation for adulthood, and often the teenager has to go outside mainstream society in order to achieve some individual identity before returning to that society as an adult human being. (*Catcher's* Holden Caulfield and Jerry Renault in *The Chocolate War* both feel like "outsiders" for most of their novels, and Jerry's return, at least, is problematic.) Sometimes the protagonist feels like an outsider and just wants to fit in (like Frankie Addams in *Member of the Wedding* or Conrad Jarrett in *Ordinary People*). At times, also, groups of adolescents band together to create their own outsider society (as in S. E. Hinton's *The Outsiders,* perhaps, or the popular film *Breaking Away*). In all these examples, the process of initiation involves different means, but the outline remains roughly the same: the protagonist has to go outside society—either alone or with others, and however briefly—before returning as an adult. And in the end, like Huck Finn, the hero may choose to stay outside.

Why is it that fiction is so often about this process? In essence, all literature is about change, and what more profound change is there than the transformation from innocence to experience? (The short story is even more obsessively about initiation: think of the adolescent epiphanies in stories like James Joyce's "Araby" or John Updike's "A & P.") Put in aesthetic terms, all literature is dependent upon plot or narrative structure, and most stories revolve around some reversal or climax; again, what more profound climax than the growth into maturation, the process by which the crysallis becomes the butterfly? The initiation story, in short, for both human and structural reasons, is perfectly fitted to literature and has been told again and again throughout history. And, of course, initiation is not limited to youth, for we go through the process of change continuously throughout our lives, and literature captures the process at whatever stage it occurs. (Think of the works on old age that also involve some initiation into a new response to life: Ernest Hemingway's *The Old Man and the Sea*, perhaps, or Katherine Anne Porter's "The Jilting of Granny Weatherall," or even *King Lear*.)

Definitions about such a complex process as adolescence may finally be self-defeating, but let me here make just a few notes on the adolescent process in the United States, particularly in recent years. We have an essentially adolescent culture—compare the relative youth of the United States to the age of European, Asian, African, or Native American cultures—and this fact is reflected as much in our literature as anywhere. Why is it that so many protagonists of so many American classics are teenagers? From Huck Finn and Henry Fleming to Nick Adams (in Hemingway's short stories collected in *The Nick Adams Stories*) and Jody Tiflin (in *The Red Pony*), ours has been essentially an adolescent literature—which is one of the reasons many of the classics in American literature can be taught in high school literature, and are. (The same thing is not true for English literature, by the way; think of Joyce, Virginia Woolf, D. H. Lawrence, et al.)

Another important thing to note about adolescence in our culture is the vagueness of its boundaries. In many other cultures, adolescence is only a brief pause between childhood and adulthood, but in ours it has been stretched out until it can consume a full decade in a young person's life, from the ages of 10 or 12 until 21 or so. The first thing to note is how early adolescence begins in the United States, often before any biological thresholds have been crossed. Another aspect of the problem in American culture is the absence of any clear demarcation to the end of childhood or beginning of adulthood; there is no significant national or cultural ritual that marks for the child, as for his or her society, that passage into adulthood. (One of the reasons for this delay is economic: advertisers try to keep us all as young as possible, for as long as possible, so that we will be consumers without responsibility; the ideal shopper is a

16-year-old with credit cards.) The adolescent in America, therefore, is often in a kind of social and psychological limbo, someone with limited economic power but no real status, treated as a child by parents and teachers, but with a social, sexual, and cultural sophistication that sometimes belies this position. It is not easy being an adolescent in America today, not only because of the increasing number of options that teenagers have but also because the very definition of their role is vague and constantly changing. Reading literature about themselves helps teenagers to define their own identity and to develop their values, for literature poses alternative lives and lifestyles and gives readers the opportunity to think about and to try out different roles and thus to determine their own status—if only in contrast—more clearly. Both *The Bell Jar* and *Ordinary People* give younger readers the experience of going through the hell of adolescence in another's shoes.

Teaching Literature Thematically

Teaching literature via the ideas and values that it carries may be the most important plea that *Novels of Initiation* makes. Somehow our secondary literature curriculum has gotten locked into historical and genre approaches that have lost much of whatever usefulness they once had. The best way to teach literature at the junior and senior high school levels is by theme, by the ideas that students will find in these and related works, and by the bridging they can do through idea and character to their own lives and to other works. (Why is tolerance such an important idea in Harper Lee's *To Kill a Mockingbird*? How different is its treatment in Mildred D. Taylor's *Roll of Thunder, Hear My Cry*? What relevance does it have to our own lives? And what relationship does it have to the idea of self-respect that we find in both novels?)

If students continue to study literature in more advanced classes or in college, then that is soon enough for them to learn the technical terms that literary critique demands and the historical connections that surveys of national literatures give us. But at the secondary level, students should be meeting literary works by the ideas they carry, the values they embody, and the choices they point to in our own lives. This is one of the main reasons why teenagers read: to find out why someone like or unlike themselves did or did not do something. (Why does Nick Carraway admire the criminal Gatsby? Would you be such a loyal friend? And why do Huck and Henry Fleming run? Would you do the same thing?) High school readers need to confront literary works as a series of affective, value-laden choices that can help them to clarify their own values and ideals and choose options. Even as historically distant a play as *Romeo and Juliet*, for example, should be met as a literary work that poses choices for adolescents and grapples with questions of love, luck, loss, and family loyalty—and not as merely another milestone (important as it may be) in the long history of English literature, or, worse, as an example of the genre of tragedy. Students need to see literary works as the embodiment of ideas and values, and they need to see the connections and comparisons to the treatment of those ideas or values in other literary works, as well as in their own lives. The teaching guides in this book try to help teachers do that job, through affective (and effective) discussion questions and writing topics: to help students understand Conrad Jarrett's guilt about his brother's death in *Ordinary People*, for example, and recognize the strategies he learns to cope; to help students see the positive steps Esther Greenwood is taking at the end of *The Bell Jar*, or the healthy values Jody Tiflin is choosing in *The Red Pony*.

Clarifying Values

Robert E. Probst (1987) has written most recently and effectively about this whole question of what we get from our reading. Literature, he notes,

> invites us to participate in the ongoing dialogue of the culture. It presents to us what others have experienced and how they have made sense of that experience, and it invites us to take those perceptions, combine them with our own, and build out of the mix the conceptions and visions that will govern our lives. Literature provides us not knowledge ready-made but the opportunity to make knowledge. And it is knowledge not about things— those it leaves to scientists and engineers—but about relationships and values and purposes. It is the kind of knowledge that each individual is responsible for. In the end, only I—and only you—can decide what *love*, *goodness*, *evil*, and *justice* mean, though I must do it in the context of the culture. ("Adolescent Literature" 27)

Values, of course, have always been an underpinning of literature (even when critics and teachers did not call them by that name), and their recent reemergence in the classroom is an important recognition of the real role they play in literary study. (See *Model Curriculum Standards*, for one example of this recent trend.) We cannot talk about a novel like Salinger's *The Catcher in the Rye* without talking about values, about the ideas and ideals that arouse an emotional response in characters and readers alike and that consequently motivate behavior in both. Holden Caulfield holds a developing value system, and readers respond to his attitudes and behavior (for example, toward Phoebe, Sally Hayes, the two nuns) whether they recognize the process at first or not, and their own values are accordingly affected—attitudes toward "phonies," to cite one value judgment Holden is constantly making. To be able to discuss this process in the classroom—to identify the attitudes or ideals that motivate behavior in characters—helps students to recognize and clarify their own values.

If we think about it, we realize that values are all about us all the time; to cite but the most obvious example, the very moment a teacher walks into a classroom, he or she is demonstrating values; for example, neatness, punctuality, respect for others, concern for learning—these are all ideals that may be exemplified by the teacher's behavior, whether or not the teacher or the students are aware of them. The chapters in *Novels of Initiation*, in both the analysis and the teaching sections, stress the search for such ideas and values in these novels, and classroom discussion should capitalize on their discovery.

If we expect students to be able to understand the increasingly complex modern world into which they are growing up, then we had better start now to teach them to think with the clarity and subtlety that they are capable of and that today's issues demand. In short, if we want an informed populace—and we know that a democracy demands it— capable of understanding today's complex issues, from American foreign policy to drugs to the homeless, then we had better start training young people now to be able to think for themselves, to recognize their own values, and to be able to see the values in issues and in people outside themselves. There is no better place for this kind of values clarification than in literature, for literary works pose values puzzles for us: here are these characters acting in these ways for these reasons—what do you think? (Why does Nick Carraway praise Gatsby? Why does Atticus Finch let his kids attend the rape trial? And how has your experience been like Rob Peck's in *A Day No Pigs Would Die* or Jody Tiflin's in *The Red Pony*?) This book tries to help teachers to get students thinking about the ideas and themes in the literary works that they are most likely to confront in their secondary education; it also tries to prepare students, through critical reading and writing and thinking, to become adults capable of working through their own values.

Novels of Initiation

A Guidebook for Teaching
Literature to Adolescents

1 "If you really want to hear about it"

THE CATCHER IN THE RYE

Author: J. D. Salinger (b. 1919)
Genre: social and psychological realism
Time of novel: two days in mid-December, 1949
Locale: eastern Pennsylvania and New York City
Point of view: first person
First published: 1951
Edition used: Bantam paperback (1986); 214 pp.
Grade level: 10–12
Principal characters:
  Holden Caulfield, a 16-year-old boy on the verge of a nervous break-down
  Phoebe, Holden's 10-year-old sister
  Allie, Holden's younger brother, who died of leukemia in the summer of 1946
  D. B., Holden's older brother, now a screenwriter in Hollywood
  Ward Stradlater, Holden's roommate at Pencey Prep
  Robert Ackley, an unpleasant boy who rooms next door
  Sally Hayes, a girl Holden dates in New York
  Jane Gallagher, a girl Holden secretly cares for
  Mr. Antolini, an English teacher at Elkton Hills when Holden attended it, now living with his wife in New York City
  Sunny, a prostitute in the Edmont Hotel, where Holden stays, and Maurice, the elevator operator, also her pimp

ANALYSIS OF THE NOVEL

Story and Setting

The Catcher in the Rye covers a "lost weekend"—from Saturday afternoon to Monday afternoon—in the adolescent life of Holden Caulfield. On the edge of emotional collapse, Holden somehow finds during this weekend the love and inner resources to free himself from childhood and start moving into adulthood. Narrated by Holden some months later from the sanitarium where he has been recovering from the breakdown that apparently occurred *after* that weekend, *The Catcher in the Rye* is the classic 1950s male initiation story.

The novel opens on a cold December day, with Holden standing on a hill in Agerstown, Pennsylvania, looking down on the campus of Pencey Prep, a private boarding school that has just expelled him for failing grades. He is on his way to visit his sick history teacher, but crossing the road to Mr. Spencer's house, "I felt like I was sort of disappearing" (5), an early hint of the fragility of Holden's hold on his own identity. Mr. Spencer warns Holden that life is "'game that one plays according to the rules'"—a piece of advice that adults are always giving him in the novel—but Holden knows that it is a game only when one is on the winning side "where all the hot-shots are" (8), where he clearly is not. Mr. Spencer forces Holden to listen to his failed examination paper on the Egyptians (Holden wrote what little he knew on the riddle of the mummies), but Holden is daydreaming about the lagoon in Central Park in New York and "wondering where the ducks went when the lagoon got all icy and frozen over" (13). Humiliated by "old Spencer," Holden still tries to make the sick teacher feel good, thus beginning a recurrent pattern in the novel. At times Holden is, in his own favorite word, a "phony," for he is nice to people whom he does not like and who are unkind to him; but Holden is a hypocrite out of love, not self-regard. "I'm the most terrific liar you ever saw in your life" (16), he warns us truthfully.

Holden returns to his dorm and, after "sad" and "depressing" encounters with his "stupid" dormmates, decides not to wait until the following Wednesday, the official start of the school Christmas holiday, but to leave Pencey now. Robert Ackley is a "nasty guy" who shows his selfish insensitivity to Holden's problems in several ways. Worse, Ward Stradlater, who is "madly in love with himself," borrows a sports jacket from Holden and then asks him to write his English composition (English is the one subject Holden is not flunking). Holden agrees, and his composition describes the baseball glove of his dead brother, Allie (from whose death, it soon becomes clear, Holden has still not recovered), but Stradlater blows up when he sees the theme: "'You don't do *one damn thing* the way you're supposed to'" (41). Holden is upset to learn that Stradlater has been out that night with Jane Gallagher, a girl Holden likes and thinks of as defenseless against such an "unscrupulous bastard" as his roommate. (When they played checkers, Jane "wouldn't take her kings out of the back row" [78].) Holden wildly attacks Stradlater, but the larger boy overpowers him and bloodies his nose. "Lonesome," unable to stop thinking about Jane, and "sort of crying," Holden flees Pencey.

On the train to New York, Holden meets the mother of a schoolmate, and another pattern begins: Holden takes on an alias (here "Rudolf Schmidt," the name of the dorm janitor) and is nice to the woman, telling her how modest and popular her son is (two lies). In New York, Holden gets a room at the Edmont Hotel, where he plans to stay until he can return to his family's apartment later in the week. And here Holden Caulfield's urban odyssey really begins. While the incidents and encounters in New York may seem unconnected or pointless at first, they ultimately reveal the two levels of Holden's journey to adulthood: on the one hand, the novel is a social tour of the "phony" world of postwar 1940s America; on the other—as the absence of time coordinates tells us—it details Holden's wanderings in a symbolic and psychological underworld.

Holden dances with three girls in the Lavendar Room of the hotel and then takes a cab to Ernie's nightclub in Greenwich Village (asking the cab driver if he knows where the ducks go in winter), but he is depressed by all the "jerks" there and walks back to the Edmont. The elevator operator asks Holden if he would like to have "a good time," but when Sunny, the prostitute, gets to his room, Holden feels "more depressed than sexy" (he admits to us that he is a virgin) and sends her away. Maurice, the pimp, returns to extort more money and punches Holden in the stomach when he refuses to pay. The next morning, Sunday, Holden checks out of the hotel, meets two nuns in a coffee shop in Grand Central Station, and forces money on them (and accidentally blows smoke in their faces). He starts to feel better when he buys a record for Phoebe and hears a kid singing, "'If a body catch a body coming through the rye'" (115). He takes Sally Hayes to the matinee of a play and then ice skating, confesses how unhappy he is, and asks her to run away with him. When Sally says they must wait, Holden tells her she gives him "'a royal pain in the ass'" and then has to apologize "like a madman" (133-4). He leaves Sally, thinks about calling Jane (a thought he has often in the novel and never acts on), and ends up going to the Christmas show at Radio City Music Hall (which he had earlier criticized the three girls in the Lavendar Room for doing). He meets an older friend, Luce, for a drink and confesses how "lonesome" and depressed he is, but Luce is no help: "'When in *hell* are you going to grow up?'" (146). Holden gets drunk, cries again, breaks Phoebe's record, and wanders around Central Park vainly looking for the ducks. Throughout most of this odyssey, Holden thinks often of Phoebe and of Jane and feels "depressed and lonesome."

Clearly, he is heading for a crack-up. In the crucial closing scenes of the novel, this crisis begins to be resolved.

Holden sneaks into his family's apartment late that night, wakes up his sister, and has a long talk with her. It is soon clear how much they love each other (although neither says it); Phoebe hits Holden when she finds out that he has been expelled from still another school and accuses him of not liking "'anything.'" Holden can only think of the two nuns, James Castle (a schoolmate at Elkton Hills who jumped out of a window and killed himself rather than give in to school bullies), and Allie. "'Allie's *dead*'" (171), Phoebe reminds her brother, and the same could be said (at least symbolically) for the others on his short list. It is obvious that Holden can only love the *dead* (Allie, James Castle) and the *innocent* (Jane, Phoebe, the two nuns). "'You know what I'd like to be?'" he asks Phoebe; "'I'd just be the catcher in the rye'" and protect children in play from falling off "'some crazy cliff'" (172–3). Holden and Phoebe dance, he cries when she gives him her Christmas money, and then he leaves.

Holden has invited himself to the apartment of Mr. and Mrs. Antolini to stay for the rest of the night. Mr. Antolini was teaching at Elkton Hills when Holden attended it earlier; it was he who carried the dead James Castle to the infirmary. He tells Holden, in response to a long story of Richard Kinsella and his "digressions" in a Pencey speech class, that we all need structure and rules. Mr. Antolini clearly likes Holden (he has recently had lunch with Holden's father to talk about the boy, and he earlier advised D. B. not to go to Hollywood), and now he is worried that Holden is headed for a fall, "'a special kind of fall, a horrible kind'" (187). When Holden wakes up later that night on the Antolini's couch, Mr. Antolini is "sitting on the floor right next to the couch, in the dark and all, and he was sort of petting me or patting me on the goddam head" (192). Fearing this apparently homosexual advance, Holden flees the apartment and spends what remains of the night in Grand Central Station. He wakes up to the realization that he has nowhere to go and that maybe he was "wrong" about Mr. Antolini. "And I think I was more depressed than I ever was in my whole life" (194).

By now it is the Monday before Christmas, and as Holden crosses streets, "I had this feeling that I'd never get to the other side" (197), and he starts praying to his brother: "'Allie, don't let me disappear. Allie, don't let me disappear'" (198). Now he decides to run away to the West, where he can pretend to be a deaf-mute, and he walks to Phoebe's school to leave her a message to meet him to say goodbye. He finds "Fuck you" scribbled on the wall of a school stairway and erases it, but he soon finds another and realizes that it is hopeless: "If you had a million years, you couldn't rub out even *half* the 'Fuck you' signs in the world" (202). A little later, waiting for Phoebe at the Museum of Natural History, Holden goes down to the tomb to visit the mummies and finds still another "Fuck you" scribbled on the wall. He realizes that there is no place "nice and peaceful" (262), no sanctuary from the obscenities of this world. In the museum bathroom he passes out and falls to the floor, and he comes out of the museum to find Phoebe dragging a large suitcase—"'I'm going with you. Can I? Okay?'" (206). They argue, and Holden agrees not to run away, takes his sister to the carrousel in Central Park, and sits happily on a bench in the rain while she rides.

> I felt so damn happy all of a sudden, the way old Phoebe kept going around and around. I was damn near bawling, I felt so damn happy, if you want to know the truth. I don't know why. It was just that she looked so damn *nice*, the way she kept going around and around, in her blue coat and all. God, I wish you could've been there. (213)

It is a closing image of peace and acceptance. Holden is not through with all of his problems (he will soon suffer some kind of collapse and be sent to an institution to recover), but he has successfully navigated the first rapids of adolescence: he has left childhood, at least symbolically, and entered adulthood.

Characters

Holden Caulfield is one of the most original and complex characters in modern American fiction, and millions of readers over the years have identified with his problems and shared his complaints about our society. He is also the only character in the novel whom we see in any depth and detail.

Part of our difficulty in understanding the novel, of course, is that Holden is the narrator of his own story, and, as with the young narrator of another classic American initiation novel—Huck Finn—we believe him more than perhaps we should. For Holden exaggerates the faults in others at the same time that he lies or is silent about himself. Certainly his peers (Ackley, Stradlater, Sally Hayes) are neither sensitive nor helpful to Holden, but they are also typically adolescent: selfish, concerned with status and security, trying to impress others. And Holden himself is guilty of many of the same faults. He is extremely class-conscious and judges others by their social standing, their money, their clothes—even their suitcases. His difference from someone like Mr. Haas—the headmaster at Elkton Hills who would snub poor or "funny-looking" parents—is that Holden *likes* those who are different (the nuns, James Castle). Part of

Holden's problem, in fact, is that he wants to be different himself (wearing his red hunting cap) and at the same time to fit in (he calls Sally Hayes to apologize again). And it is revealing to list all the people to whom Holden is "nice" (Mr. Spencer, Ackley, Mrs. Morrow, etc.), for he does not brag about this quality. Holden Caulfield, in short, has an embryonic and sometimes contradictory value system.

His peers may not help him much—but Holden never lets them know (or does not know himself) the trouble he is in. Clearly, there is more going on beneath the surface of Holden's life than he admits, as his sudden bouts of crying indicate, but all Holden can tell us is that he feels "sad" and "lonesome." Part of Holden's problem, then, is his inability to communicate the depths of his own despair. The novel itself is Holden's therapy on his road to health, but in it he is unable to express or explain everything; instead, the novel describes how he "acted out"—which, all in all, makes for a rather normal teenager.

Psychologically, Holden is a case of arrested development. In some way that he does not understand, Holden has been stopped in his own emotional growth by the death of his brother Allie. The night Allie died, "I broke all the windows in the garage . . . with my fist" (39), and he still carries Allie's baseball mitt with him. (He has only told one other person, Jane, about the glove; Ward Stradlater, of course, failed to grasp its significance for Holden.) To grow up would somehow be to betray the memory of Allie, the child who will always remain one, frozen in death (like the mummies or, possibly, the ducks) as an eternal innocent. As his hair (half gray) reveals, Holden is half boy/half man, stalled in his own development between the two stages and leaning back toward the first. Like Jane Gallagher, who leaves her kings on the back row, Holden comes to the world as a child lacking all the right weapons (he even left the fencing team's foils on the subway in New York). Among other indications of his childlike nature, he has had no sexual experience.

Other characters help or retard Holden's progress in the novel. Certainly a whole crew of people, from Maurice and Sunny to Luce to various unfriendly cab drivers, show what kind of adult world Holden is headed for: cold, self-centered, filled with status seeking, materialism, instrumental relationships, and so forth. It is no wonder that Holden tries to hold on to the innocence and security of childhood.

But there is a second set of characters who definitely help Holden: the precious and precocious Phoebe, who loves Holden and would do anything for him; Mr. Antolini, who also cares for Holden and whose wistful, drunken gesture at the end of the novel is so misread by the anxious boy; and other characters who never actually appear but whose goodness Holden draws upon (Allie, Jane Gallagher, James Castle).

Holden is surrounded by good people, or by their spirits, and at the end of the novel we feel that he will continue growing and become one of them. In spite of all the "phonies" in his way. In fact, Holden has become a model in American literature of someone who stands up for the young and innocent (as one himself) and points out the insincere and inauthentic in all corners of American life. His wavering integrity, his acuity, his sensitivity, his self-effacing humor—these and other qualities make him a hero in a landscape without many others. Generations have by now wandered New York City feeling like Holden Caulfield—and feeling better for the identification.

Themes

More than in most modern novels, the themes in *The Catcher in the Rye* are unified by the idea of initiation. The story of the novel is Holden Caulfield's journey, albeit a reluctant one, from boyhood to adulthood, and the stages of this growth are subtle and symbolic.

Clearly, Holden is trying "like crazy" *not* to grow up. Like the ducks he often wonders about in Central Park, he is frozen into childhood and unable to push himself into adulthood. He is certainly fixated on the innocence of childhood, for all those he loves are either physically children (Allie, Phoebe) or act like them (Jane, the nuns). As in several of his best short stories ("A Perfect Day for Bananafish" and "For Esmé—with Love and Squalor"), only children in Salinger's writing are capable of unconditional love, and the phoniness Holden always complains of is simply the absence of such love.

Holden wants to become a "catcher in the rye," he tells Phoebe, and he misquotes the line from the Robert Burns poem: Holden substitutes "catch" the body for "meet," and a relationship between equals becomes, in Holden's version (which he actually got from another kid [115]), one between protector and protected. He wants to keep children from falling over the "cliff" (like keeping Jane from Stradlater), to protect them from the "horrible" fall that Mr. Antolini warns Holden he is headed for himself. But Mr. Antolini was not able to break the "fall" of James Castle—he could only pick up his broken body after it—and even Allie, a "catcher" in the outfield, was not able to catch himself. And neither can Holden break his own final fall from innocence to experience: his collapse in the museum bathroom symbolizes his movement into adulthood and his acceptance of the way things are in the world—the "Fuck you's" that are everywhere. It is immediately after this fall that Holden watches Phoebe on the carrousel and decides that he cannot protect children any more. "The thing with kids is, if they want to grab for the gold ring, you have to let them do it, and not say anything. If they fall off, they fall off, but it's bad if you say anything to them" (211). Holden is obviously talking about himself as well.

But Holden is fixated not only on images of innocence but also on images of death, and the two are interwoven into this story of his initiation into adulthood. In the end, Holden twice enacts his own symbolic death: his fall in the bathroom and his "disappearance" crossing the street. In the latter incident he is saved by his prayers to the dead-innocent Allie: "'Allie, don't let me disappear'" (198). Throughout the novel, Holden wonders what happens in winter to the ducks in Central Park. Are they frozen into the lagoon like the fish, or do they somehow escape? When he finally goes to look for them, he cannot find them; they have apparently avoided death and moved on—just as Holden himself will eventually escape his entombment in a static adolescence.

The dominant motif (a recurring idea or incident) in this theme is the Museum of Natural History. "The best thing . . . in that Museum was that everything always stayed right where it was. Nobody'd move. . . . The only thing that would be different would be *you*" (121)—but that is exactly the passage to maturity that Holden is trying to avoid. When Sally Hayes argues that they should wait to go off together, Holden yells at her that they'll be *different* then, that is, grown up. "Certain things they should stay the way they are" (122), he says on his first visit to the museum—and then tries to balance two kids on a seesaw, to be a catcher again. But when Holden finally returns to the museum and descends to the tomb of the mummies, he finds that it, too, has been desecrated. In some symbolic way, the ugliness and obscenity of the adult world have permeated even this temple of the dead and unchanged, and Holden unconsciously realizes that he cannot hold onto childhood and innocence (or death and stasis) any longer: he passes out in the bathroom and then "passes out" into adulthood. He has fulfilled his own rite of passage. He has solved his own "riddle of the mummies": the child must grow up.

There are, of course, subsidiary themes in this novel, but they are largely tied into the initiation story. The idea of appearance/reality, for instance, is caught in the ad for Pencey Prep, which claims to be "molding boys into splendid, clear-thinking young men" (2)—clearly not working in Holden's case—but is described by our hero as a "terrible school" of thieves and "morons."

One of the appeals of *Catcher* for readers is how perfectly its sardonic protagonist captures the selfishness and hypocrisy of adult society. In a number of ways, the novel is one of the best critiques of American culture to come out of the post–World War II years, when people pursued possessions in the new prosperity and human love seemed solely

the province of the innocent. Holden impales this world on his wit—and
it is a world that still surrounds us. Adults, like old Spencer and
Mr. Antolini, keep telling Holden that he must play by the rules, but
Holden identifies with the misfits and outcasts (Richard Kinsella, James
Castle) who violate the rules or refuse to play the game. Some of the
funniest scenes in the book (as when Edgar Marsalla disrupts a pompous
alumnus speech) revolve around this conflict between generations and
between the rule-makers and the rule-breakers. Holden worries about
those people he likes (Mr. Antolini, D. B.) who may have sold out to this
commercial, conformist society, and his commentary throughout provides a biting critique on this society.

Style and Language

It is remarkable in how many different ways *The Catcher in the Rye*
resembles *The Adventures of Huckleberry Finn*. Not only are their
themes and humor similar, but so, too, are their structures and their
styles. Like Huck Finn's journey down the Mississippi, Holden's odyssey
is *picaresque* in structure: the hero wanders through a series of adventures without any apparent narrative direction. (Early novels—*Don
Quixote* in 1605, for example, or *Tom Jones* in 1749—were often picaresque or episodic in structure.) And like its nineteenth-century predeces-
sor, *The Catcher in the Rye* is a first-person narration in which the reader
is directly addressed. ("God, I wish you could've been there" [213].) Yet,
as in *Huckleberry Finn*, readers must be careful: first-person narratives
tend to fool us, for our tendency is to nod in agreement at what the
narrator is telling us. What soon becomes clear in *Catcher*, however, as in
its parent novel, is that Holden, like Huck, lies and is not always correct
in his interpretation of events or appraisal of people. (Holden is probably
wrong about Mr. Antolini, for example.) Put another way: the novel is
being narrated—as we are told in the first and last "frame" chapters—
from an institution where Holden Caulfield is recovering from his breakdown, where he is now 17 years old and looking back on these two
troubled days, and where he now actually *misses* Ackley and Stradlater
and even "that goddam Maurice"—proof of his recovery and a hint that
he may have exaggerated their failings earlier. Holden Caulfield is not, by
any standard, the most reliable of narrators, which means, as it does in
Twain, that readers must read the novel with more care than it first seems
to demand—and with a skeptical ear.

What contributes to *Catcher*'s uniqueness in modern fiction—and,
again, it is the same contribution we get from *Huck Finn*—is its use of
language. One of the major reasons for its continued popularity, espe-

cially among younger readers, is that the novel has captured the American male adolescent voice, with all its anxiety, humor, and exaggeration. Salinger has translated a particular moment in human sexual development into a unique, vernacular, literary voice. (It is also, of course, a particularly 1950s vernacular.) If there are few characters like Holden Caulfield in modern fiction, there are even fewer voices that ring as true. Salinger captured the language of a generation and put it into fiction, from which it has continued to influence later generations of readers and writers alike.

At once slangy and idiomatic, this voice is also deceptively literary. On the one hand, the novel is full of verbal irony: no one, for example, could be further from being "a real prince" than Ackley. But this language can also be highly metaphorical: James *Castle* and Jane Gallagher (who kept her *kings* in the back row) share the royal language of chess— but both are truly defenseless.

It is this very language, of course, that has also caused the continuous censorship problems for *The Catcher in the Rye*. The use of obscenities in the novel has by now offended an untold number of authorities, which is ironic, given the fact that few novels are so moral: there is no sex in the book, and Holden wants to *erase* "Fuck you" from the walls and thus to protect the innocent from such language.

TEACHING THE NOVEL

Teaching Suggestions

Teachers may want to begin *The Catcher in the Rye* by considering one of its greatest strengths: *point of view*. Students are usually captured by Holden Caulfield's colloquial adolescent voice, but they need to "read between the lines" and recognize that Holden is not telling us everything. Consider, for example, Holden's statement, "I was sort of crying" (52). What does that line mean? How can someone "sort of" cry? (The "sort of" probably diverts our attention from the "crying.") More important, *why* is Holden crying? (He does not tell us.) If students can be skeptical and look for this gap between Holden's words and his actions, they may come to understand his situation more quickly and also realize that more is going on beneath the surface than Holden tells us (or understands). It is fairly easy to come up with other examples of this discrepancy between what Holden says and what he does. For instance, notice how nice he is to people he says he does not like—Mr. Spencer, Ackley, Mrs. Morrow. What is the point? Similarly, why does he miss everyone at the end?

Another way into the novel is through discussion of Holden's embry-onic value system. As students read and think about the novel, they should look for the various attitudes and ideals that Holden embodies and those that he is in rebellion against. Students may want to keep a Reading Log entry on these developing values. What does he admire in other characters? Criticize? What do these qualities tell us about Holden himself?

Aside from point of view, the literary element that may be most important in this novel is its *symbolism*. *The Catcher in the Rye* is full of detail, most of which means something or should become part of the reader's interpretation of the novel. For example, Holden's recognition at the end of the novel that you have to let the kids on the carrousel reach for the gold ring, even though they might fall off in doing so, seems to stand for peace and acceptance. How do we get students to recognize how incidents in a novel relate to other actions and also have significance beyond themselves? One way is to have them see the symbolic nature of items in everyday life; for example, a car equals freedom, a road equals a journey. It is this symbolic quality to the events and characters of the novel that may get readers most easily inside its meaning. Why is Holden so curious about the ducks in the lagoon and the mummies in the museum, for example? What do they have in common? What do they symbolize? Or, as another example, Holden likes the two nuns, James Castle, Phoebe, Allie, and Jane Gallagher. What do these people have in common? What human qualities do they share that explain Holden's attraction to them, and what do they have to do with his growth? What, in other words, do they *stand for*? Innocence, idealism, otherworldliness?

Discussion and Writing Ideas

The writing topics suggested here should help students understand Holden; getting them to write about their own experiences first can be a way of making Holden's feelings and behavior concrete.

1. Write a list of your own most important values. Compare it to the list of Holden's values you have compiled in your Reading Log. How do you differ from Holden? Describe three of his ideals or attitudes that you do not share.
2. Describe an experience in which you felt an "outsider" like Holden. Why did you feel outside? What finally changed your situation? What did you learn from the experience, if anything?
3. Describe a situation in which you were not completely truthful to yourself. What was the reason? What was the outcome? Do you find

any parallels to how Holden omits or changes the truth in his narration?

4. The novel takes place in the late 1940s. How and where could it be taking place today? How would the story be different in a contemporary setting?

5. Find a paragraph in the novel in which Holden writes about "phonies" or about absurd events or adults. Comment on it, drawing on your own experiences. What are "phonies" today? In your own language, describe this behavior that Holden constantly complains of. Are we all "phonies" sometimes? How?

6. Find a paragraph you like in the novel and translate it into today's slang.

7. *The Catcher in the Rye* has been described as a typical *quest* novel (a romance in which the hero experiences trials and tests but is ultimately successful in his search). Describe a quest you have had, including the test and the final outcome.

8. Where is Holden today? What is he doing?

9. Write Holden a letter in the hospital as though you were D. B. or Phoebe.

10. You are Holden's psychiatrist: write a final report releasing him from the hospital and giving a prognosis for his future.

11. How would you characterize the adults in the novel? Why do they keep telling Holden about rules? (Notice that Holden admires people—Jane Gallagher, Richard Kinsella—who violate the rules.)

12. What is the significance of the novel's title? How does it describe Holden's relations with children throughout the novel?

Bridging to Other Novels

POPULAR ADULT AND CLASSIC AMERICAN NOVELS

Mark Twain, *The Adventures of Huckleberry Finn* (1884); see Chapter 2. Compare themes, points of view, character, structure, humor, and language in the two novels. How do Huck and Holden have similar relationships to their respective societies? In what ways are Huck and Holden both heroes?

F. Scott Fitzgerald, *The Great Gatsby* (1925); see Chapter 6. Refer to Holden's comments on this novel (141) and then compare Gatsby and Holden and the themes in the two novels (innocence/experience, appearance/reality, materialism, and so forth).

John Knowles, *A Separate Peace* (1960). Note the parallels in setting (a boys' school) and characters.

Sylvia Plath, *The Bell Jar* (1963); see Chapter 5. How do Esther Greenwood's experiences parallel those of Holden?

Judith Guest, *Ordinary People* (1976); see Chapter 4. Compare Holden
Caulfield and Conrad Jarrett on questions of family, love, loss, and
so forth.

Brett Easton Ellis, *Less than Zero* (1985). How does Holden Caulfield
look next to the narrator of this contemporary novel about adolescents?

OTHER NOVELS WITH YOUNG PROTAGONISTS

Robert Cormier, *The Chocolate War* (YA, 1974); see Chapter 3. Note the
similarities of character and setting. Who would make a better
friend, Holden or Jerry? Why?

Terry Davis, *Vision Quest* (YA, 1979). Loudon Swain, the protagonist in
this novel, resembles Holden in several crucial ways.

Danny Santiago, *Famous All Over Town* (1983). This contemporary
Chicano coming-of-age novel has some of the same feelings as
Catcher in the Rye.

Sue Townsend, *The Adrian Mole Diaries: A Novel* (1986). Adrian Mole
shares much of Holden's tone and humor in this popular British first-
person novel.

2 "All right, then, I'll *go* to hell"

ADVENTURES OF HUCKLEBERRY FINN

Author: Mark Twain (Samuel L. Clemens, 1835–1910)
Genre: romantic realism
Time of novel: about 1840 ("forty to fifty years ago")
Locale: the Mississippi Valley, from St. Petersburg (Hannibal) in northern Missouri down to the Arkansas-Louisiana border
Point of view: first person
First published: 1884
Edition used: University of California Press paperback (The Mark Twain Library, 1985); 362 pp.
Grade level: 9–12
Principal characters:
   Huck Finn, a sensitive but unsophisticated 13/14-year-old boy living in St. Petersburg, Missouri
   Pap, his father, the town drunkard, who has been missing for more than a year when the novel opens
   Tom Sawyer, Huck's best friend, an imaginative and romantic schemer
   Jim, a slave owned by Miss Watson
   Miss Watson, the spinster sister of the Widow Douglas
   the Widow Douglas, a kind woman with whom Huck is living at the opening of the novel
   Silas and Sally Phelps, relatives of Tom Sawyer in southern Arkansas with whom Huck and Tom stay in the last chapters of the novel

ANALYSIS OF THE NOVEL

Story and Setting

Adventures of Huckleberry Finn is an episodic (or "picaresque") novel that takes Huck and Jim from St. Petersburg, Missouri, through a series of adventures down to southern Arkansas. The spine of the book, the structural design that holds all their adventures together, is the great Mississippi River; the setting is the rural South in its last peaceful moments before the Civil War, when slavery is in force and industrialization is still some years away.

The novel is truly unique in American literature; it is a book that readers can enjoy all of their lives, for as they grow older, they uncover its layers of meaning. For the younger reader, the humor and adventure of the novel are probably most prominent, but the more mature reader soon sees the serious themes beneath the surface of the river of the book— ideas such as freedom and tolerance that are at the heart of American democracy. *Huckleberry Finn* is, in a number of ways, an American classic.

The novel started as a sequel to Twain's popular *Tom Sawyer*; Twain began the second volume soon after completing his boys' story in 1876, actually subtitling it *Tom Sawyer's Comrade.* "You don't know about me, without you have read a book by the name of 'The Adventures of Tom Sawyer,'" Huck Finn begins his own novel with his colorful and ungrammatical voice (including a triple negative!), "but that ain't no matter" (1). *Huckleberry Finn* picks up most of the characters and the story of the earlier book, but only briefly. Huck's $6,000 share of the loot he and Tom found in the robber's cave in *Tom Sawyer* has been turned over to Judge Thatcher, and Huck, whose drunken father has not been seen for a year, has been informally adopted by the Widow Douglas, a sweet, well-meaning woman who tries to teach Huck the Bible and manners. Huck has been in school for some months and is getting used to the comforts of home—even to the lectures of Miss Watson, the Widow Douglas's spinster sister. Huck joins "Tom Sawyer's Gang" for some make-believe adventures (a reminder of *Tom Sawyer* and an anticipation of the closing chapters of this novel)—and then Pap reappears. Failing to get Huck's money, Pap kidnaps the boy and takes him to an isolated cabin a few miles up the river from St. Petersburg—and to real adventure. Huck soon falls back into his "old ways" of smoking, loafing, and fishing. But resenting Pap's beatings and feeling "dreadful lonesome" much of the time, he decides to get away and to "fix up some way to keep pap and the widow from following me" (39). Huck devises an elaborate escape plan that makes it look as if he has been killed and flees in a canoe to Jackson's Island, a few miles below St. Petersburg.

Huck feels comfortable but "lonesome" on the island until he stumbles onto Jim, a slave who has run away from Miss Watson because she was going to sell him down the river for $800. "I warn't lonesome now" (51), Huck tells us. Huck and Jim find a dead man in a house floating down the flooded river (Jim recognizes Pap but does not tell Huck), the first of 13 corpses Huck will see in the novel. And then, as a joke, Huck puts a dead rattlesnake in Jim's blanket, only to have Jim bitten by the snake's mate. (Huck does not admit to Jim that he was responsible.) In his first foray onto shore—disguised, as Huck usually travels back to society—Huck finds out that local men are about to search the island for Jim. "'They're after us!'" (75) Huck warns Jim, and they pile all their possessions onto a raft and head down the river. The pronoun *us* is incorrect, of course, for the men are only searching for the runaway Jim, but the word signals the fusion of the fates of these two fugitives, in Huck's mind as in ours.

The sequel to *Tom Sawyer* has now been abandoned, and *Huckleberry Finn* has really started, with its twin concerns: the developing relationship between Huck and Jim in their quest for freedom (their plan is to take the raft down the Mississippi to Cairo, Illinois, and at that river junction take a steamboat up the Ohio to a "free" state) and the relationship of this pair to the society they visit along the river. Their life on the raft is almost idyllic—"Take it all around, we lived pretty high" (80)—but their encounters with the shore reveal the cruelty and violence of Southern society.

In their first adventure, Huck and Jim are stuck on a wrecked steamboat, the "Walter Scott," with a band of murderers, but Huck saves the pair by stealing a boat and telling a ferryboat watchman a story that will make him get the authorities to search the wreck themselves. (Typically, Huck feels sorry for the murderers.) In a bad fog a few nights later, Jim and Huck are separated and apparently miss Cairo and the confluence of the Ohio. Equally important, at least in the developing relationship between the two runaways, Huck pulls another trick on Jim by trying to get him to believe he dreamt the fog; but Jim responds by saying, "'trash is what people is dat puts dirt on de head er dey fren's en makes 'em ashamed.'"

> It was fifteen minutes before I could work myself up to go and humble myself to a nigger—but I done it, and I warn't ever sorry for it afterwards, neither. I didn't do him no more mean tricks. (105)

Chapter 16 begins with the long "raftsmen's passage," which Twain for reasons of economy cut from the first edition of the novel—it was originally published in Twain's 1883 *Life on the Mississippi*—but which has been restored in some later editions. The deleted passage is really a long, separate short story in which Huck swims to a large raft to get information about where they are on the river but instead overhears a humorous/scary tall tale of Dick Allbright and the "ha'nted bar'l." The center of the chapter has Huck wrestling for the first time with the problem of helping a runaway slave to freedom—an act that goes against everything he has been taught. Huck sets out to turn Jim in, Jim calls Huck "'the on'y white genlman dat ever kep' his promise to ole Jim'" (125), and Huck changes his mind. When challenged by two white bounty hunters, Huck cleverly makes up a story to keep them away from the raft (and which gets them $40 instead!) and lies about Jim—"'He's white'" (125–126). Huck resolves his conflict by deciding pragmatically to "after this always do whichever come handiest at the time" (128).

On the heels of this adventure, the raft is hit one night by a steamboat and Huck and Jim are separated, but Huck swims to the safety of the Tennessee shore—and right into the middle of a violent feud. Huck identifies himself now as "George Jackson" (an orphan from Jackson's Island, presumably) and thinks that the Grangerfords who take him in are aristocrats and that their house has "much style." But as Huck cannot recognize the shallowness of these people, likewise he cannot fully comprehend the absurdity of their feud with the Shepherdsons, a feud that has been going on for so long that no one can recall its origin. Both families attend church with all their weapons—to hear a sermon, as Huck reports, "all about brotherly love, and such-like tiresomeness" (147). All Huck comes to realize, after the feud erupts into a bloody massacre in which his young friend Buck Grangerford is killed, is that "I wished I hadn't ever come ashore that night, to see such things" (153). He sees the violence, but he fails to grasp its full significance.

Back with the recovered Jim, "We said there warn't no home like a raft, after all" (155). The contrast between this idyllic life on the raft and the hatred and cruelty of the shore is unmistakable.

> Sometimes we'd have that whole river all to ourselves for the longest time.
> . . . It's lovely to live on a raft. We had the sky, up there, all speckled with stars, and we used to lay on our backs and look up at them, and discuss about whether they was made, or only just happened. (158)

Now the "lonesomeness" is only "of the river," for Huck and Jim have established a brotherly sanctuary on their raft.

But their idyll is interrupted when two other fugitives join Huck and Jim and take over the raft. A sign of Huck's perceptiveness is that he recognizes the "Duke" and "King" for the "low-down humbugs and frauds" that they are. The two con men begin practicing their trade in small towns along the Mississippi shore, working camp meetings and doing poor Shakespeare imitations. In one town, Huck witnesses two separate incidents of some significance. An aristocratic Colonel Sherburn warns a local drunk named Boggs, who is harmlessly threatening him; when the drunk persists, Sherburn shoots him down in cold blood, then tells the mob that comes with ideas of lynching him that he knows them. "'Your mistake is, that you didn't bring a man with you; that's one mistake, and the other is that you didn't come in the dark, and fetch your masks'" (190). Later, at a circus, Huck sees a horseback rider pretending to be a drunk thrill the crowd. "It warn't funny to me, though; I was all of a tremble to see his danger" (193). In typical doubling technique, Twain has juxtaposed two scenes that highlight each other and point up the violence and hypocrisy of Southern society.

In the next adventure, the Duke and the King advertise themselves as actors in "The Royal Nonesuch"—"Ladies and Children Not Admitted"—and of course draw a great crowd for their show, but they are nearly caught by their victims. In their flight further into Arkansas, the two pull their greatest deception, pretending to be the long-lost English brothers of a Peter Wilks who has just died and left a small inheritance. Huck, feeling sorry that the Wilks daughters (especially the lovely Mary Jane) will be cheated out of their fortune by the two impersonators, hides the bag of money in the coffin of their father. When the two frauds sell the Wilks slaves, Huck also devises a way to get them back—by pretending that they stole the money. The story reaches a climax when the *real* English brothers show up and Huck and the two con men narrowly escape back to Jim and the raft before the mob catches them.

At their next stop, "a little bit of a shabby village, named Pikesville" (266) in southern Arkansas, the Duke and King sell Jim for $40. Huck sets out to free him, but not before a long and agonizing struggle with his conscience, which tells him that he will be condemned to everlasting perdition if he helps a runaway slave to escape. Huck's conclusion, and the moral center of the novel: "'All right, then, I'll *go* to hell'" (271).

Jim is being held at a small farm, and when Huck arrives he is shocked to be greeted as . . . Tom Sawyer! In a plot reversal that does not completely work—which is one reason this last section of the novel is referred to as "the evasion chapters"—Twain has Huck come to the Phelps farm, where Silas and Sally are momentarily awaiting the arrival of a nephew Sally has never met, Tom Sawyer. Huck heads Tom off and, after convincing him that he is not dead (Tom, like other St. Petersburg friends, was fooled by Huck's escape from Pap), tells Tom what has happened since he left home. Huck takes on Tom's identity, and Tom pretends to be his brother, Sid Sawyer; Tom also agrees to help Huck rescue Jim. Huck can hardly believe it: "Tom Sawyer a *nigger stealer!*" (284). The reason, of course, is that Tom knows that Jim was freed by Miss Watson on her deathbed, a fact that he does not share with Huck.

Before their rescue adventure begins, however, Huck and Tom find out that the Duke and King have been caught trying to work their Royal Nonesuch show again and see them tarred and feathered. Typically, Huck feels bad about the pair:

> Well, it made me sick to see it; and I was sorry for them poor pitiful rascals, it seemed like I couldn't ever feel any hardness against them any more in the world. It was a dreadful thing to see. Human beings *can* be awful cruel to one another. (290)

Huck would go in and rescue Jim directly from the shack where he is being held, but Tom argues that this plan is "'too blame' simple'" (292) and lacks the "style" that Tom would add to it. Huck gives in to Tom's leadership, and Tom makes the rescue into an elaborate—and for readers, highly comic—game, à la Sir Walter Scott or Alexandre Dumas, complete with secret inscriptions, anonymous letters, a coat of arms, and other conventions of this literary rescue genre. Huck and Jim go along with Tom's plans, but both lose something of their humanity in the process and cause both themselves and the Phelpses enormous pain and hardship. When Jim is finally rescued by the boys one night, Tom is shot and wounded in the escape and Huck must go for a doctor while Jim tends Tom. Tom recovers, Aunt Polly (Sally's sister) arrives and confirms Tom's story of Jim's having been freed—so Huck finally understands how Tom "*could* help a body set a nigger free, with his bringing up" (358)—and Jim is legally freed. In "Chapter the Last," the loose ends are tied up, and Huck exits with the comment that

> if I'd a knowed what a trouble it was to make a book I wouldn't a tackled it. . . . But I reckon I got to light out for the Territory ahead of the rest, because aunt Sally she's going to adopt me and sivilize me and I can't stand it. I been there before. (362)

Characters

Unlike most classic American novels, *Adventures of Huckleberry Finn* depends to a large degree on flat secondary characters. Put another way, the novel only occasionally rises in characterization above its origins in *Tom Sawyer* and other romantic adventure literature. Certainly a number of stock characters, both villains (Pap) and heroes and heroines (the doctor, Mary Jane Wilks), people the novel, and many characters depend for their identities on story and action rather than having clear, definable self-motivations. The novel, in short, is not strong on characterization.

Certainly Tom Sawyer exemplifies this deficiency. The leader of the St. Petersburg gang of boys, and the character who takes over the novel in its last quarter, Tom is a dreamer and schemer who lacks Huck's sensitivity and heart. Because of Tom, a great number of people are hurt and put to a good deal of trouble—all to satisfy his addiction to romantic adventure. What was childish play in his own novel appears in this more serious work to be a real character defect. Viewed thematically, Tom represents the genteel society from which Huck and Jim have escaped, with its shallow dependence on rules and conventions.

Even Jim suffers at the hands of his creator. He is clearly meant as a character of real human feeling, and at certain moments he achieves it—especially in those stretches alone with Huck on the raft (including the scene when Huck catches him "moaning and mourning" about his wife and children [201]) and when he is helping Huck. It is through his relationship with Jim that Huck will gain his own humanity. But for much of the novel Jim is dressed up, tied up, and in other ways humiliated by whites, including Huck, whether intentionally or not. His necessarily subservient role detracts from his fullness as a literary character.

The fullest character, of course, the one who achieves the most depth in the novel, is the title character, Huckleberry Finn himself. Part of his fullness comes from the novel's point of view: not only is Huck the narrator of his own story, but Twain has cleverly constructed the novel so that Huck does not always know what is going on (both Jim and Tom know more at different times) or see the full significance of what he is narrating (the shallowness of the Grangerfords, for instance). This tension between what is actually happening and Huck's understanding of it means that we view Huck with a kind of depth perception that results from the combination of two perspectives—what Huck tells us intentionally, and what he reports without being aware of its significance.

Furthermore, Huck grows during the course of the novel, and his moral development is at its center. At the start of the novel, Huck is almost a shadow of Tom Sawyer, but when he escapes to Jackson's Island and teams up with Jim, then the real Huck begins to emerge: clever, pragmatic, spontaneous, and resourceful. And in his internal debate with his "conscience" about Jim, the authentic, human Huck emerges. He starts by thinking he can turn Jim in, discovers in a crisis that he cannot, and ends up believing that he will go to hell for helping the runaway slave—but going ahead and doing it anyway. His moral progress in the novel is remarkable, for his struggle is real. His conscience incorporates the morality represented by Miss Watson, the Widow Douglas, and other authority figures in his world, but he goes against their values and responds to the demands of his own heart, his commitment to Jim.

There is other growth as well. Huck recognizes the Duke and King as frauds, for example, and in the Wilks incident acts to save the daughters from the two con men. Part of our disappointment in the evasion chapters is exactly this: that a character we have watched grow morally and act heroically has allowed himself to become a mere player in the comic but destructive games of Tom Sawyer—a character, as we have seen, who has little of Huck's sensitivity and nothing of his heart.

Themes

There are three major themes in *Adventures of Huckleberry Finn*, as Henry Nash Smith summarized them more than a quarter of a century ago. The first is "the flight toward freedom"; the second, the "social satire of the towns along the river"; and the third, "the developing characterization of Huck" (84).

When Twain began the novel, the first theme was clearly the major one, and it sustained him through at least 16 chapters, which he originally wrote in one burst of energy in 1876, soon after completing *The Adventures of Tom Sawyer*. It is this element that provides the adventure line to the novel, but it is important to recognize how this story is dropped from time to time in favor of the second theme, the social satire of shore life. For long periods—during both the middle sections of the novel and the last evasion chapters—Jim is hardly a character at all, and the story of his quest for freedom has been shelved. In fact, when Tom reveals in the penultimate chapter that Jim has actually been free for some time, Twain's first theme is badly undercut, for much of the flight now seems to have been unnecessary.

Twain's structural failure notwithstanding, the question of Jim's freedom forces the serious reader to confront the whole issue of slavery, which in turn provides entrée into the second thematic element of the novel, Twain's social satire and criticism, especially of Southern society and the Southern mentality. Huck and Jim create an Eden aboard their raft, a sanctuary from civilization, but whenever they touch shore, they encounter the deceit, greed, and cruelty of rural Southern America. Actually, this element is present from the very beginning of the novel. Miss Watson is extremely religious—and cannot miss the opportunity to sell Jim down the river for $800. (Her deathbed change of heart hardly cancels her original greed.) Such indictments of this society run throughout the novel. The Phelpses are loveable, kind-hearted people—and they lock Jim up like some animal. Even at the end, when the doctor says what a help Jim was in saving Tom, the Pikesville residents respond in character, and Twain (through Huck) satirically reports:

> Then they all agreed that Jim had acted very well, and was deserving to have some notice took of it, and reward. So every one of them promised, right out and hearty, that they wouldn't cuss him no more.
> Then they come out and locked him up. (354)

Other examples of social satire and criticism abound. The Grangerford/Shepherdson feud is perhaps the prime instance, for it is the first separate, extended section of the novel, ending in the tragic, pointless death of young Buck. Here is Southern society at what Huck, at least, considers its best—and the two families slaughter each other for some outmoded concept of honor. The chapters with the Duke and King also contain this element, although the burlesque and buffoonery of their antics often mask it. In order to be successful as con men, the Duke and King must have a gullible audience, and they find it without much trouble in the small towns they strike along the river. Most of the people in the novel, in fact, are busy duping each other, usually for profit, and the Duke and the King are merely the champion con men here. (Well, not quite: Huck is probably better at fooling people, with pseudonyms and disguises, but he generally acts for self-protection or to save Jim.)

It is easy to analyze most of the incidents in the novel to prove how they reveal the greed and hypocrisy of this society. The Boggs/Sherburn incident shows the mob mentality that masks the real cowardice of people. The Wilks chapters spotlight small-town morality, where everyone is concerned with everyone else's business. Whenever Huck and Jim leave the raft, in fact, they must put on disguises and assumed names, because they are moving into a foreign country—at least foreign to the values they have established on the raft, such as honesty, sharing, and tolerance. On the raft, the two learn to depend on each other; on the shore, they discover that few people can be trusted.

Huck's major problem is that he *accepts* the values of the shore that Twain is satirizing, and this tension produces the most important theme of the novel, which is Huck's developing character. It is also the third theme that ties together the other two, for it is through the quest for freedom that Huck finally comes to stand up against the shore values that Twain is satirizing and to assert his own character. It is the final victory of Huck's heart over his "conscience."

When Huck first comes upon Jim on Jackson's Island, he promises the runaway slave that he will not tell on him. "People would call me a low down Abolitionist and despise me for keeping mum—but that don't make no difference. I ain't agoing to tell" (52–53). The real conflict for Huck occurs in Chapter 16, when his "conscience" tells him that he must turn Jim in; but when the opportunity comes, Huck lies to the two slave hunters and says about Jim, "'He's white.'" After that he decides to be pragmatic, but the conflict does not disappear, for Huck's morality, or conscience, is a product of his society, just as much as Jim is, and Huck will continue to wrestle with the problem. Huck needs to keep lying to people about Jim (as to the Duke and King, that Jim is his own slave), but, at the same time, Jim's humanity continues to work on Huck (both his friendship with the young boy and his clear love for his own family: "I do believe he cared just as much for his people as white folks does for theirn," Huck says before Jim's touching story of his deaf and dumb daughter [201]). Huck comes to care about "my old Jim" (149) as a brother, and even when Jim is away, Huck acts for his good: in the Wilks episode, Huck tells Mary Jane that they must be careful how they expose the Duke and King, for, if they fail, "'there'd be another person that you don't know about who'd be in big trouble'" (240).

The climax to this theme comes in Chapter 31, after the King and Duke have sold Jim to the Phelpses and Huck must decide whether to rescue the runaway slave himself. His "conscience" pulls him one way, and he pens a letter to Miss Watson telling her where Jim is; but his heart pulls him another, and he remembers what friends they have been to each other. Huck finally accepts the moral condemnation of his society—"'All right, then, I'll *go* to hell'" (271)—and tears up the letter. It is one of the moments of moral triumph in the American novel, for Huck has opted for humanity over the conventions and traditions of society—and Twain wants us to applaud his effort.

Huck's development is neither straightforward nor complete, how-ever. When he first arrives at the Phelps farm, he tells Aunt Sally that there was an accident on his steamboat, and to her question of whether anyone was hurt, he responds, "'No'm. Killed a nigger'" (279). Thus Huck's commitment to Jim is an individual case; he as yet fails to understand the larger racial implications of his relationship. When Tom agrees to help Huck free Jim, Huck is struck dumb; he cannot believe that a boy as "well brung up" as Tom "was actuly going to help to steal that nigger out of slavery" (292). Huck sees himself as an outcast and as someone who has already condemned himself to hell; he cannot under-stand the motivation of someone with "character" such as Tom.

Thus Huck's transformation is limited. When, in the last paragraph, he tells us that he is going to have to "light out for the Territory," we understand the pressures he is under. He has seen, if not always recognized, the brutality and hypocrisy and greed of his society—in fact, he has been both a victim of and a participant in them—but he has also helped another human being to gain his freedom and his humanity. The conflict will always be there for Huck in this society, which is why he must leave it. His only hope for his own continued development is to get away to some place new and open, where freedom still lives because "civilization" has not yet arrived.

Style and Language

Ernest Hemingway, certainly one of the most important writers of the twentieth century, was also one of the first to recognize *Huck Finn*'s importance for American literature—as well as the failure of the last chapters:

> All modern American literature comes from one book by Mark Twain called *Huckleberry Finn.* If you read it you must stop where the Nigger Jim is stolen from the boys. That is the real end. The rest is just cheating. But it's the best book we've had. All American writing comes from that. There was nothing before. There has been nothing as good since. (*Green Hills of Africa* 22)

Hemingway was recognizing not only the importance of Twain's ideas but also the influence of his realistic *style*, for it was Twain who showed American writers how to use language as it occurs in speech. American literature before Twain was dominated by the literary language of English literature (e.g., Sir Walter Scott) or that of its East Coast heirs (Longfellow and the other Boston Brahmins), but Twain proved that a writer could make a literary language out of natural speech. Huck's narration is a triumph of literary expression, a vernacular style that expresses the young boy, in all his faulty grammar and homely vocabulary, as well as his author's humor and serious ideas. The language of the novel is clear and colloquial, but its simplicity is deceptive. In one of his most famous aphorisms, Twain once remarked that "the difference between the *almost right word* and the *right* word" is the difference between lightning and the lightning bug ("The Art of Composition" 228), and that concern for linguistic exactness is here. In his "Explanatory" note before the novel opens, Twain jokes about using seven different dialects in the novel, but contemporary scholars have shown how accurate that description is: Twain actually *did* capture those seven different voices in various characters. Twentieth-century literature would be unthinkable without this literary language that renders American speech in such varied and natural expressions.

The *structure* of the novel is both a strength and a weakness. As noted before, the Mississippi River acts as the spine of the book, as Huck and Jim travel down that wide and protean stream, stopping for various adventures in homes and villages along the way. But Hemingway warned readers to put the book down before the Phelps farm scenes, for the ending violates not only the spirit but also the structure of the book. While the evasion chapters seem to return to the pastoral mood of the first chapters in St. Petersburg, they really undercut the serious themes that Twain has been developing. It is a tacked-on ending that Twain, for whatever reasons, felt he must use. The excuses are numerous, but the most plausible is that Twain himself was not strong enough to sustain the rebellion against society that his protagonist threatened. His own growing skepticism kept him from imagining Huck heroic enough to free Jim at the end. Moral tragedy becomes farce.

The triumph of the novel is its humor, which has a number of purposes and processes. Some of the humor in the novel comes out of set pieces, like the Dick Allbright story in Chapter 16, while some of it is particularly literary, like the Emmeline Grangerford poetry in Chapter 17 or the burlesque of Shakespeare in Chapter 21. Similarly, much of it is social satire (the King working the camp meeting as a reformed pirate), while some of it is linguistic humor, which is much more subtle and ironic. The most important generalization about the humor in *Adventures of Huckleberry Finn* is its particularly *American* origins, for much of it is frontier humor that Twain had found in his travels in the Southwest: tall tales (like those of Pecos Bill, Paul Bunyan) and other oral literary materials that Twain showed could be used in literary novels. He was one of the first to use such American materials in serious American fiction.

TEACHING THE NOVEL

Teaching Suggestions

The *language* of *Adventures of Huckleberry Finn* is both a trap and a triumph, and teachers must consider both possibilities. Black readers, among others, may rightfully resent the word *nigger*, which today is a painful racial epithet but which was, as the notes at the end of this edition point out, an "everyday term for black people in the South during the period of Huck's adventures" (376). Students should be apprised of the difference before beginning the novel. Once launched, readers will probably recognize how much of their own identification with Huck Finn comes from his natural and authentic voice. Students should note how individual and colloquial Huck's language is—how it differs from other dialects (Jim's, for example) in the novel—and should jot down any expressions that they do not understand. (The edition used here has a helpful glossary of words and phrases—*dead beat, fox-fire, mud-cat, texas,* etc.—that may challenge readers.)

Certainly the language of the novel is responsible for much of its *humor,* and an easy entry into *Huck Finn* is a discussion of what readers find funny in the novel. Such a discussion can lead naturally to an analysis of the different kinds of humor in the book, both situational (Tom's gang of robbers attacking a Sunday-school picnic) and verbal (irony, literary parodies, etc.).

One goal of any study of the novel should be the *character* of Huckleberry Finn and, specifically, how he grows in the course of the novel. Students should be encouraged to look for examples of Huck's moral development, for his dawning awareness of Jim's humanity, and for other signs of his evolution (his actions at the Wilkses', for example).

Huck Finn deals with an issue that has been perhaps the major social conflict in American history: the prejudice and cruelty inflicted by the dominant white majority on the country's ethnic minorities, from the first treatment of Native Americans to the present tensions concerning Hispanic and Asian immigrants. *Huck Finn* was one of the first novels to explore this theme, after *Uncle Tom's Cabin* in 1852. But while Stowe's novel is about slavery, Twain's is really about the bigotry and cruelty that are the legacy of that horrible institution. Twain's answer to the problem—the wisdom of the human heart over the training of society—can still be ours. Because these ideas in Twain's novel continue to be so important in American life (which is why the novel has become a classic—and why it is still periodically banned), it is essential that any treatment of the novel, at whatever level, explore these *themes*: not only Huck's moral development but also the ideas of freedom (the escape from slavery) and social satire (ridiculing aspects of American society) that are interwoven into that central story.

Any discussion of the novel can lead to its themes simply by pursuing the implications of Huck's narrative and by thinking through the consequences of his actions. Here are questions keyed to such a thematic analysis of the Grangerford/Shepherdson feud in Chapters 17 and 18:

1. What kind of story does Huck make up about himself when he stumbles upon the Grangerford house? (*Notice that he is always an orphan in his elaborate lies.*)

2. Why does Huck call himself "George Jackson," and what does that name remind us of? (*Jackson's Island*) What is its significance? (*Huck is now a child of Jackson's Island, where his new, free life with Jim really started.*)
3. What is Buck like? (*A perfectly normal kid*) How does his character make what is about to happen much worse? (*These are adults killing not only one another but also children.*)
4. How does Huck show his resourcefulness the next morning? (*Asking Buck to spell his name—"G-o-r-g-e J-a-x-o-n"—when he cannot recall the alias he is using.*)
5. What does Huck think of the Grangerford house? (*He thinks it has "style."*) What is the evidence that Twain wants us to see it differently? (*Gaudy decorations, chipped artificial fruit that "showed the white chalk . . . underneath," etc.*)
6. What does Twain think of Emmeline Grangerford's paintings and poetry? (*Twain is clearly burlesquing Emmeline's exaggerated romantic art.*)
7. What is the significance of the scene in church? (*Irony/hypocrisy: the feuding families bring their guns to hear a sermon "all about brotherly love, and such-like tiresomeness"—and then go out and slaughter each other.*)
8. What is the point about the love affair between Sophia Grangerford and Harley Shepherdson? (*This romantic story contrasts sharply with the hatred and violence that follow it.*)
9. What is the import of this entire Grangerford/Shepherdson episode? (*Here are what Huck considers the finest Southern people, and they are involved in this senseless, violent feud, the origins of which they have even forgotten. Huck witnesses the violence—"I wished I hadn't ever come ashore that night"—but cannot yet understand the larger consequences; he even blames himself for the bloodshed. Life on the raft looks better after this incident; Twain is clearly establishing a contrast between raft and shore values here.*)

Discussion and Writing Ideas

1. Huck helps Jim to escape to freedom. What would you have done in a similar situation? Why? How?
2. Huck feels "lonesome" for much of the early part of the novel, or until he finds Jim. Write about (a) a time when you were lonesome or (b) a friendship that saved you from such lonesomeness.
3. Describe an experience in which you had to choose between a rule of

society and your own moral sense. What were the consequences?
What did you learn from the experience?

4. Huck often lies in the novel to protect himself and/or Jim. Describe
an experience in which you had to lie in order to protect yourself or
someone close to you. What happened? What did you learn?

5. Huck Finn is constantly dressing up and disguising himself in order
to survive. Describe a situation in which you disguised yourself (by
changing your name or your clothes). What was the reason? The
outcome?

6. Summarize what the novel tells us about one of the following subjects:

freedom	superstitions
religion	honesty and truth
friendship	morality (or "conscience")
violence	

7. What are the differences between Huck Finn and Tom Sawyer? Who
is the better person? Why?

8. Analyze one of the humorous stories or incidents in the novel (Chapter 14, for example). What is funny or comic about the scene?

9. *Adventures of Huckleberry Finn* is a *Bildungsroman*, or "novel of
education." What does Huck learn, and what is the significance of his
lessons?

10. *Huck Finn* poses a contrast between "river" values (in other words,
the values that Huck and Jim establish on their raft) and "shore"
values (or the values that people in the towns live by). What is the
difference between these two sets of values? Which set is better?
Why?

Bridging to Other Novels

POPULAR ADULT AND CLASSIC AMERICAN NOVELS

F. Scott Fitzgerald, *The Great Gatsby* (1925); see Chapter 6. Many of the
things that Nick Carraway learns about his world and Jay Gatsby
echo discoveries in *Huck Finn*.

John Steinbeck, *Of Mice and Men* (1937). A modern novel about two
outcasts trying to sustain each other in a difficult world.

J. D. Salinger, *The Catcher in the Rye* (1951); see Chapter 1. Holden
Caulfield is often called a twentieth-century Huck Finn, and in many
ways his wanderings in New York City and his struggles both within
himself and against his society parallel those of Twain's hero.

Ernest Hemingway, *The Old Man and the Sea* (1952). This novella, too, concerns courage, survival, and friendship.

Ken Kesey, *One Flew over the Cuckoo's Nest* (1962). This work treats such similar themes as freedom and the individual against society.

OTHER NOVELS WITH YOUNG PROTAGONISTS

William Golding, *Lord of the Flies* (1955). This English novel is about youth and evil, courage, and so forth.

Harper Lee, *To Kill a Mockingbird* (1960); see Chapter 8. This is another child's-eye view of the failures and foibles of Southern society, less than a hundred years after Huck.

Charles Portis, *True Grit* (1968). Another novel with a young protagonist, this Western has much of the humor and charm of Twain.

William Armstrong, *Sounder* (YA, 1969). This novella about a young black in the South at the turn of the century has a number of reminders of *Huck Finn* in subject and story.

Robert Newton Peck, *A Day No Pigs Would Die* (YA, 1972); see Chapter 11. This novel has parallels of character and theme with *Huck Finn*.

Robert Cormier, *The Chocolate War* (YA, 1974); see Chapter 3. Different as their worlds are, Jerry Renault must learn many of the same lessons as Huck Finn about the nature of evil, the hypocrisy of society, and so forth.

3 "Do I dare disturb the universe?"

THE CHOCOLATE WAR

Author: Robert Cormier (b. 1925)
Genre: psychological realism (YA)
Time of novel: early 1970s
Locale: a Catholic boys' school in Boston
Point of view: third-person omniscient
First published: 1974
Edition used: Dell Laurel-Leaf paperback (1985); 191 pp.
Grade level: 7–10
Principal characters:
  Jerry Renault, a 14-year-old freshman at Trinity
  James Renault, his father, a pharmacist
  Archie Costello, a senior at Trinity and the leader of The Vigils, a
    secret but powerful school society
  Brother Leon, a teacher and the acting headmaster at Trinity
  Roland ("Goober") Goubert, Jerry's best friend at Trinity
  Obie, the secretary of The Vigils
  Carter, the president of The Vigils
  Emile Janza, a school bully trying to get into The Vigils
  Brian Cochran, a student Brother Leon assigns to tally figures in the
    annual Trinity chocolate sale

ANALYSIS OF THE NOVEL

Story and Setting

The Chocolate War is an unrelentingly bleak and brutal account of life in a Catholic boys' school, from its opening line—"They murdered him" (7)—to the closing defeat of its young protagonist and the reascendancy of the school's evil forces. Yet the novel is also an important example of the realistic quality of much of today's young adult (YA) fiction. Set in Boston, the novel could take place in any urban academic setting—at least in any school where the dual pressures of grades and repressed sexuality create such an unhealthy and competitive atmosphere. Trinity is a school where privacy "was virtually non-existent" (140), where teachers intimidate students and students brutalize one another. Cormier's view of Trinity is singularly gloomy, but few readers would argue that it is totally unrealistic.

The story in this short (191 pp.), fast-paced novel is neither complex nor difficult. Jerry Renault is in his first year at Trinity and trying to become a quarterback on the football team. He needs this success badly—which is one of the reasons he takes the daily physical punishment—because his mother has died the previous spring, after a painful battle with cancer, and now Jerry is living in a new apartment with his father, who sleepwalks through his days. Jerry wants desperately to fit in, but a contrary impulse also motivates him. In his school locker, Jerry has a poster that

> showed a wide expanse of beach, a sweep of sky with a lone star glittering far away. A man walked on the beach, a small solitary figure in all that immensity. At the bottom of the poster, these words appeared—*Do I dare disturb the universe?* By Eliot, who wrote the Waste Land thing they were studying in English. Jerry wasn't sure of the poster's meaning. But it had moved him mysteriously. (97)

In the course of the novel, Jerry is going to discover the full import of the poster's message.

Like many Catholic schools these days, Trinity has financial problems, and, further, the headmaster is sick and Brother Leon is running the school in his place. In an apparent effort to strengthen his position at Trinity, Leon has doubled the order for the annual chocolate drive—to 20,000 boxes, which means that every student will have to sell 50 boxes—and overextended himself in paying for them. A sign of Leon's insecurity is that he has to enlist the help of The Vigils in the chocolate drive, through Archie, their "Assigner" and true leader. "Officially, The Vigils did not exist" (25), but much of the activity of the school revolves around this powerful secret society, and most students want to join—even Jerry, who accepts an "assignment" (a school stunt or prank) from The Vigils to refuse to sell the chocolates for ten days. Every day Brother Leon reads the class roll, and every day Jerry says "'No.'" But when his ten days are up, Jerry continues his rebellion, in protest now against Brother Leon's authoritarian tactics, the impersonality of the school, and his own isolation there. Soon other students start to respond to Jerry's actions, and chocolate sales drop. Brother Leon warns Archie that The Vigils "'will go down the drain'" if the "'rebel'" Jerry is not stopped, and the pressure on Jerry is increased. In addition to the daily physical punishment on the football field, Jerry is intentionally made to look bad when his teammates start to drop passes; in school he is ignored, nearly shoved down the stairs, and has his locker trashed; he and his father are harassed day and night by crank phone calls. But the intimidation only hardens Jerry in his resolve, and he gains a new identity through his rebellion: "'I'm Jerry Renault and I'm not going to sell the chocolates'" (149), he declares to Brother Leon and the other students in his homeroom. Meanwhile, The Vigils whip up school support for the chocolate sale and ensure that everyone has sold his 50 boxes—everyone except Jerry. Emile Janza, a school bully who wants badly to get into The Vigils (and also get back a compromising picture of himself he thinks Archie holds), enlists a gang of younger kids to beat Jerry up. Jerry does not want to fight Janza "for the same reason he wasn't selling chocolates—he wanted to make his own decisions, do his own thing, like they said" (153). But when Archie arranges a boxing match in front of the entire student body between Jerry and Janza, Jerry accepts.

> What could he say? After the phone calls and the beating. After the desecration of his locker. The silent treatment. Pushed downstairs. . . . What guys like Archie and Janza did to the school. What they would do to the world when they left Trinity.
>   Jerry tightened his body in determination. At least this was his chance to strike back, to hit out. (1972)

But the fight has been arranged so that Jerry cannot win, and, in fact, the young hero loses the very individuality he had earlier gained in his protest.

> A new sickness invaded Jerry, the sickness of knowing what he had become, another animal, another beast, another violent person in a violent world, inflicting damage, not disturbing the universe but damaging it. He had allowed Archie to do this to him. (183)

In the end, Jerry is being treated for a possible broken jaw and internal injuries, he is advising his friend Goober, "Don't disturb the universe," and The Vigils and Brother Leon are even more firmly in control of Trinity.

Characters

The Chocolate War is a powerful psychological novel, and its characterization is realistic, if unremittingly grim. Villains tend in general to be more two-dimensional than heroes, and that rule certainly holds true here, where there are more evil characters than in most YA novels. But even the secondary characters ring true, in part because Cormier's omniscient point of view allows us to see many of them from the inside. Brian Cochran lives in fear of both Brother Leon and The Vigils, but he gains status as treasurer for the chocolate sale. Goober is "one of those kids who always wanted to please everybody" (29), but he quits the football team and stops selling chocolates in order to support Jerry and to protest the "evil" that Trinity is inflicting on both Jerry and himself. Obie is Archie's flunky, but he hates the Assigner and unsuccessfully plots his downfall.

The novel centers on three major characters, the "trinity" of Jerry, Archie, and Brother Leon. If there is a question of who is more evil, Archie or Leon, then the nod must go to Leon. Archie, after all, is still a teenager and has a chance (admittedly, not a good one) of changing. But Leon is an adult, a member of a religious order, and his malignant character is permanently formed. In scene after scene, we watch Leon run his classroom and the school through fear, intimidation, and brutality. In a typical action, Leon blackmails a student (through fear of failing) into revealing Jerry's reason for not selling the chocolates. The student walks away from his grilling convinced "that life was rotten, that there were no heroes, really, and that you couldn't trust anybody, not even yourself" (87). Leon's evil character permeates the school.

Archie Costello's personality may be slightly more complex. A cynic at 16, Archie believes that "'Life is shit'" (17). "The world was made up of two kinds of people—those who were victims and those who victimized" (80), and "'we're all bastards'" (175). In one sense, Archie is a mirror image of Leon, a malign force operating on a slightly different plane in the Trinity world, but one with similar morals and methods. Obie recognizes "how awesome Archie's power really was" (13), but, as with most despots, Archie's hold on The Vigils is really tenuous—which makes him even more malicious and dangerous.

The protagonist in the novel, the counter to these two evil forces, is Jerry, who is as simple and complex as any young teenager. On the one hand, he is a lonely boy who misses his mother, does not want to become as numb as his father, wonders about girls ("Would a girl ever love him?" [18]), and has an ambivalent attitude toward violence. Yet Jerry is also someone who *is* different, or wants to be. He ponders the meaning of his poster for the whole novel, but he *does* disturb the universe and discovers the consequences of such acts of courage: "Jerry suddenly understood the poster—the solitary man on the beach standing upright and unafraid, poised at the moment of making himself heard and known in the world, the universe" (143). In the last scene, lying broken and defeated on the boxing stage, Jerry tries to tell Goober the lessons he has learned.

> He had to tell Goober to play ball, to play football, to run, to make the team, to sell the chocolates, to sell whatever they wanted you to sell, to do whatever they wanted you to do. . . . They tell you to do your thing but they don't mean it. They don't want you to do your thing, not unless it happens to be their thing, too. It's a laugh, Goober, a fake. Don't disturb the universe, Goober, no matter what the posters say. (187)

It is a tragic defeat, for someone who had the courage to stand up to peer pressure and teacher intimidation has been beaten down. On the other hand, readers will long retain the image of Jerry standing alone, with the strength to "disturb the universe."

Themes

The meaning of *The Chocolate War* is complex and, for many readers, depressing, but it is an important novel for young people, if one that needs to be read carefully and discussed clearly. As with any novel of this complexity, there are a number of subthemes: loss, for example; violence, in its many forms; and power, how it is maintained in human society and the hatred and brutality that its misuse breeds. *The Chocolate War* is a novel of initiation in which the young protagonist, like the reader, learns a number of crucial lessons about the adult world—most of them negative.

The major theme of the novel is, generally, the relation of the individual to society. More specifically, the novel is about the price one pays for *conformity* and—the other side of this theme—the greater price one must pay to achieve one's *individuality*. Early in the novel, a young "hippy" calls Jerry "square boy" and tells him, "'You're missing a lot of things in the world'" (20)—ironic, given the fact that Jerry is about to launch his own rebellion against the school and The Vigils. Jerry starts his action as a Vigil stunt, but the prank soon gains its own momentum, and Jerry uses it to protest the unfair bullying by both Brother Leon and The Vigils, their tactics of intimidation and coercion. As Goober says to Jerry, "'There's something rotten in that school.' . . . 'It's what they do to us, Jerry'" (116). Jerry's protest is not an easy decision. "It had all been going so beautifully. Football, school, a girl who had smiled at him at the bus stop" (124). Soon after his rebellion begins, he has "the sense that his bridges were burning behind him and for once in his life he didn't care" (129). But Jerry gains a new identity from his act of protest. "'My name is Jerry Renault and I'm not going to sell the chocolates,' he said to the empty apartment. The words and his voice sounded strong and noble" (129).

This protest develops into the concept of being true to oneself and standing up to the evil that one perceives in the world. Brother Leon hits and bullies a student and then praises him and condemns the class for not coming to his defense: "'you were true to yourself,'" he says to the crying Bailey (39). The lesson is an ironic one, of course, because most of the time Leon is trying to force the students into rigid molds of school conformity. "School spirit" is what Leon calls it, but mind control is more like it. The only character who *is* true to himself is Jerry—but at what a terrible price. Goober tries to emulate Jerry—he quits the football team and stops selling the chocolates—but, in a crucial test, he caves in: when The Vigils make sure a "50" is posted after his name in the auditorium, Goober does not have the courage to challenge it and tell the truth. He knows he is a "traitor" to Jerry. The subject raises all kinds of questions, in the novel as in society: Which is more important, loyalty to oneself or to the group? Which takes more courage? What are the real consequences of conformity? How *can* evil be stopped except by individual human action?

The lesson of Jerry's life is not a simple and clear-cut one, and readers may have some difficulty in interpreting the book. Certainly Jerry has been defeated at the end, and his last thoughts are, "Don't disturb the universe, Goober, no matter what the posters say" (187). Archie and Leon are in even firmer control by the end of the novel: "Beautiful," Archie thinks in the penultimate chapter, "Leon and The Vigils and Archie. What a great year it was going to be" (189). The evil trinity has triumphed.

On the other hand, Jerry *did* disturb the universe: he stood up against peer pressure and teacher intimidation to protest the evil he recognized in the world, and his example is a model of courage in the face of cowardice and conformity. He is, in the true sense of the word, a martyr, and if he gives in at the end, that action only makes the novel more realistic and his earlier courage even greater. The evil at Trinity can only be defeated if more people like Jerry stand up. The power of *The Chocolate War* is this social and psychological realism: the novel shows what happens to someone who stands up for his rights in a totalitarian system. But Cormier sides clearly with Thoreau, Twain, and other American writers in his belief in the power of the individual to effect social change, and he applauds the young hero's attempt to fight the system and change it—at the same time that he is realistic about the outcome. As with the hero (Randall McMurphy) of Ken Kesey's *One Flew over the Cuckoo's Nest*, the example of Jerry's rebellion is much more important than the image of his ultimate defeat. He will be back, and, meanwhile, we have a model we can remember and emulate. For students raised on the easy solutions of television, the novel's most important legacy may be its grim realism.

Style and Language

There are several stylistic elements that distinguish *The Chocolate War* from most YA novels. For one thing, the point of view is much more complex than in most adolescent novels. Cormier uses no one central intelligence through which we witness the events of the novel; rather, the story is narrated from the perspective of half a dozen characters (significantly, no adults—not even Brother Leon), allowing us to witness action and character from a number of different vantage points. Younger readers may find this shifting perspective troublesome at first (especially when they come across several points of view in one chapter), but the device certainly quickens the pace of the novel and helps to build its momentum at the end. Most readers are "hooked" into the novel by the third or fourth chapter. The brisk dialogue in the novel also helps this pace.

The language in the book is not terribly difficult, but the honesty and maturity with which its subjects are treated may cause problems for some readers. The students here act like real teenagers, for they swear and think about sex a great deal. (They joke about masturbation, Jerry does it, and Archie is blackmailing Emile Janza because of a photograph Archie supposedly has of Janza doing it.) Such sexual obsessiveness is not unusual in this environment, and most readers should be able to recognize this fact.

The novel is also unique for its subtle use of language. *Irony* plays a large part here, and readers should be aware of the double meanings that pepper *The Chocolate War*. It is ironic, for example, that Brother Leon should praise Bailey for being "true to yourself" when Leon is doing everything in his manipulative power to make sure that the students at Trinity are *not* true to themselves. It is more than ironic that Jerry should become an animal like the rest of the student body at the very moment when he is trying to be better than they are; by accepting Archie's challenge for the boxing match with Janza, Jerry actually *loses* his individuality. In this instance, we also see how subtly the irony of the novel shades off into symbolism. The boxing match, as just one example, is symbolic of the way that all the people at Trinity are manipulated by others: the kids calling the punches in the fight are like The Vigils and Leon controlling the actions of all the students. Likewise, the names here are revealing: Archie (from *arch*, meaning cunning), The Vigils (vigilantes? vigil lights?).

There is also a rich religious symbolism in the novel. Early in *The Chocolate War*, we see the "network of crosses, empty crucifixes" (17) that the goal posts make on the football field, and religious echoes like that run throughout the story. On one level, Jerry is a Christ figure (not unlike Randall McMurphy in *Cuckoo's Nest*) who tries to change things in this world but who is metaphorically crucified in the attempt. The first line of the novel—"They murdered him"—introduces this notion. And in that first chapter, the football coach bellows, "'For Christ's sake'" (8), and then spits on Jerry—another clear allusion to the Christ story. Likewise, the crowd at the boxing match shouts, "*kill him, kill him,*" and Jerry realizes that "they wanted him killed, for Christ's sake" (184). "Jesus, the pain," Jerry thinks when the fight is over—and then renounces his role as rebel (186). In the first chapter of the novel, Jerry calls himself a Peter ("he had been a Peter a thousand times and a thousand cocks had crowed in his lifetime" [8]) for not standing up and telling the truth to the coach about how much he hurts; but it is Goober who later fulfills that role, in not challenging The Vigils. Trinity is a religious school, but evil predominates over any kind of Christian love or spirit. And the religious symbolism in the novel underscores the themes that Cormier is raising: Must someone else be crucified before the evil here is banished? What will it take to change Trinity?

TEACHING THE NOVEL

Teaching Suggestions

When *The Chocolate War* was first published in 1974, the American Library Association's *Booklist* gave the novel a black-bordered review, "suggesting an obituary for youthful optimism" (Gottlieb, 24). Prior to this work, even the most realistic young adult novel left its protagonists on an upbeat note. After Cormier, the YA novel was capable of tragedy.

The most striking feature of *The Chocolate War* is its grim and unrelieved *realism*, and readers may complain that the story is too depressing. One way to counter this objection is to argue that all litera-

ture demands "a willing suspension of disbelief" during the period of its
reading, as Coleridge phrased it, and this YA novel is no different.
Students can certainly see that the events of the novel are *probable*, that
they could have happened.* But what readers may complain about is that
too many adverse events are piled upon each other here, that there is little
relief from the bleak and gloomy portrait of human behavior. But
Hamlet and other great works of literature could have the same charge
brought against them. The question is not whether a work is depressing
but whether it is realistic, true to human nature and human interaction,
and here Cormier must be recognized as a master of psychological
realism.

The most important literary element in this psychologically realistic
novel is *character*, and any approach to *The Chocolate War* should stress
those aspects of the novel that help to develop its characterization,
particularly *point of view*. One way of beginning the novel is to assign
different groups of students to different characters (Archie, Obie,
Goober, etc.) as they read the novel. Later, the groups can select
members to represent their characters in mock debates on such questions
as loyalty to Trinity, friendship, self-image, and so forth. Students should
recognize through this activity not only how well they have gotten to
know the different characters by learning about them from the inside—
through a narrative technique that gets into characters' heads—but how
these multiple perspectives have really deepened their understanding of
character.

Because the novel is so strong on characterization, it is a perfect place
to study both *motivation* and *conflict*. Character in novels, as in drama,
motivates action; without actors, there is no story. Students should look
for the motivation behind the actions of the novel: Why does this character act in this way? Why, for example, does Brother Leon take on twice as
many chocolates for this year's sale? Why does Jerry defy The Vigils and
refuse to sell the chocolates? Conversely, why is it so important to him to
make the football team? The answers to these and hundreds of similar
questions reveal the motivation in character that produces action and
thus furthers the plot of the novel.

The plot of a novel is often simply the story of different characters in
conflict—within themselves, with each other, or with society. Certainly

---

*For those who doubt it, consider the following recent news item: "Lisa Ortiz, the drum
majorette at Northview High School in Covina, Calif., was relegated to the sidelines last
month because she didn't sell enough candy. . . . Her failure to sell more candy reflected a
'poor attitude,' says band director Rick England. 'Lisa was intending to sell none until I
required her to take one box'" (Bleifuss, 5).

we have three kinds of conflict here: Jerry is battling himself (whether to conform or not), Archie and Emile, and the evil world of Trinity. To learn the importance of conflict, students can select two characters and then study how their conflict moves the action forward (e.g., Obie and Archie, Carter and Archie, Leon and Archie, Goober and Jerry). Through such a focus on motivation and conflict in character, the other major elements of the novel—plot and themes—will naturally emerge in discussion.

Discussion and Writing Ideas

1. How did you feel when you finished reading *The Chocolate War*? Why?
2. Write another short chapter: What will Jerry do now? Then read Cormier's sequel, *Beyond the Chocolate War*.
3. What would Jerry be like if he were at your school? Is there some activity or rule he might rebel against? What do you think would happen in the struggle?
4. Describe an incident you know of in which someone went against the rules of a school or other institution. What were the consequences? (Recently, a girl in California sued her school for its couples-only prom rule. She won, went to the dance, and had a good time.)
5. What principles does Jerry represent or stand up for? Are they important? Could he somehow modify his idealism a little?
6. Describe a personal experience in which you went against the wishes of the group. What were the consequences of your action? How did you feel?
7. How important is *setting* in this novel? Could *The Chocolate War* have been set in any other environment and been as effective? Where?
8. What is the relationship of Jerry to Goober? (Consider Chapter 23 in particular.) Is Jerry a good friend to Goober? Why or why not?
9. What is the meaning of Jerry's poster?
10. Is Jerry a hero? Make a case for or against this notion.
11. You are brought in as the new headmaster at Trinity: What changes would you begin in order to make it a school where students would not feel such fear and intimidation?

Bridging to Other Works

The Chocolate War would fit neatly into a thematic unit on "The Individual and Society." Below are other literary works that blend well with this novel in such a unit. (For further suggestions on thematic units, see Appendix A.)

SHORT STORIES

Shirley Jackson, "The Lottery." Compare the black boxes, the rituals, the violence, and the conformity.
Herman Melville, "Bartleby the Scrivener." Compare the protests in the two works.
John Updike, "A & P." Compare heroes and initiations.

POEMS

T. S. Eliot, "The Love Song of J. Alfred Prufrock." Discuss the poem in terms of Jerry's poster and the actions of the novel.
Robert Frost, "The Road Not Taken," "Stopping by Woods on a Snowy Evening." These are poems about personal choices.
Claude McKay, "If We Must Die." Compare ideas of courage and heroism.

ESSAYS

Henry David Thoreau, *Walden* and "Civil Disobedience." Compare the ideas of a different drummer and a majority of one.

DRAMA

Henrik Ibsen, *A Doll's House.*
Jerome Lawrence and Robert E. Lee, *The Night Thoreau Spent in Jail.*
Arthur Miller, *The Crucible.*

NOVELS

Robert Cormier, *Beyond the Chocolate War* (YA, 1985). Note what happens to Cormier's characters in this sequel.
Terry Davis, *Vision Quest* (YA, 1979). Compare violence, sexuality, and initiations.
William Golding, *Lord of the Flies* (1955). Compare violence, gangs, and rituals.
Judith Guest, *Ordinary People* (1976); see Chapter 4. Compare the two protagonists and the ideas of death, friendship, and emergent sexuality.
S. E. Hinton, *The Outsiders* (YA, 1967). Note the violence in the two novels, the gangs, the ideas of loyalty, and the issue of conformity.

Ken Kesey, *One Flew over the Cuckoo's Nest* (1962). Compare in terms of the heroes and the theme of fighting the bureaucracy.

John Knowles, *A Separate Peace* (1960). Compare setting, character, and themes.

J. D. Salinger, *The Catcher in the Rye* (1951); see Chapter 1. Compare the struggles of these two protagonists against their respective societies.

Mark Twain, *Adventures of Huckleberry Finn* (1884); see Chapter 2. Compare the two heroes, the conflict between principles and social rules, and, again, the issue of conformity.

FILMS

My Bodyguard. Compare the violence and the notions of friendship and courage.

Breakfast Club.

4 "Growing up is a serious business"

ORDINARY PEOPLE

Author: Judith Guest (b. 1936)
Genre: psychological realism
Time of novel: early 1970s
Locale: suburban Chicago: Lake Forest, Evanston, Illinois
Point of view: third-person limited omniscient
First published: 1976
Edition used: Ballantine paperback (1980); 245 pp.
Grade level: 10–12
Principal characters:

Conrad Jarrett, a 17-year-old high school student who attempted suicide after the death of his brother

Jordan (Buck) Jarrett, Conrad's brother, who drowned in a boating accident with Conrad on Lake Michigan

Calvin Jarrett, Conrad's father, a 41-year-old tax attorney

Beth Jarrett, his wife and Conrad's mother

Dr. T. C. Berger, the Evanston psychiatrist who helps Conrad work out his problems

Jeannine Pratt, a girl Conrad falls in love with at school

Joe Lazenby, once Conrad's best friend

Kevin Stillman, another former friend from the swim team

Howard and Ellen, Conrad's maternal grandparents

Karen Aldrich, a friend of Conrad's from the hospital, who later kills herself

ANALYSIS OF THE NOVEL

Story and Setting

Ordinary People is a touching story of male initiation, of a young man who is growing into adulthood against incredible psychological odds. The locale is the Midwest and the time is the early 1970s, but the novel could be happening anywhere and at any time, which is one of the reasons students respond to it so easily. Conrad Jarrett could be any of us in adolescence: full of awful secrets, trying to gain control of his own world, worried about how others view him, wishing just to become "ordinary."

Conrad's secret is, as his psychiatrist Dr. Berger might say, "a tough nut." He and Buck, his older brother by 14 months, were in a sailboat one August afternoon when a sudden storm capsized them. Conrad saved himself, but Buck drowned. As the novel opens, Conrad is still trying to deal with his guilt about the accident and its aftermath. The year before, his junior year in high school and the year following the accident, Conrad had a nervous breakdown and slit his wrists. He was hospitalized for some months, but now he is back in school (a junior again, while his former friends are all seniors), trying to get through each day. Life is a continuing struggle: "He escaped this time, but even the smallest, most insignificant encounter is alive with complication and danger" (20).

The novel covers several months in Conrad's life, during which time he turns 18. Estranged from his friends, a stranger in his own house—where his mother is very cold to him—Conrad wants to learn "control," as he early tells Dr. Berger; Berger tries to get Conrad to give up control and, instead, to let his emotional self out of the closet where he keeps it confined. (This is the same thing, of course, that Beth needs to learn to do; Conrad is very much like his mother.) With Dr. Berger's help, Conrad begins to work out his brother's death, his guilt about his suicide attempt, and his problems with his mother, managing to gain some measure of emotional stability by novel's end. Through a series of interactions in his world—which comprise the plot of *Ordinary People*—he becomes whole. To cite but two examples: Conrad quits the swim team (where we sense he was always competing with the spirit of Buck) and then fights one of his old swim-team friends who belittles him and Buck; both actions are ultimately healthy. He also starts dating Jeannine Pratt; through his deepening sexual and emotional relationship with her, he finds a positive way to reach out and establish a relationship with the world. But his progress is not without reverses. Just when he feels strongest with Jeannine, he must confront the suicide of Karen, a friend from the hospital where they were both recovering earlier. Again with the help of Berger, Conrad uses the crisis to break through his last barriers and finally deal with his self-punishment over the death of Buck.

At the same time that Conrad is finding out about himself, his father, Calvin, is engaging in a similar journey into self. His story is in some ways a mirror of Conrad's, for he is making similar discoveries—about himself, about relationships, and about dependency. The novel's chapters alternate between Conrad and Calvin as centers of consciousness (until the crises at the end, when several chapters in a row concern one or the other of these two main characters). And while the more important chapters concern Conrad, his crises and resolutions, half the novel centers on Calvin, his worries about Conrad (he knows he missed the danger signals when Conrad attempted suicide), and his deteriorating relationship with Beth (he feels "beneath them a fault, imperceptibly widening, threatening" [132]). Soon after urging Conrad to see Dr. Berger, Calvin begins to see the psychiatrist himself to work out his own problems. Thus the novel has two centers, and readers come to see that Calvin and Conrad have similar problems. As Calvin muses early in the novel, "Nobody's role is simple, these days. Not even a kid's" (8)—and certainly not an adult's.

On a golfing vacation in Dallas late in the novel, the tensions between husband and wife break through to the surface, and the fragile thread that has been holding them together since the death of Buck finally snaps. After they return to Chicago, Beth goes on to Europe, and father and son are left to deal with their grief and to work out their own relationship. "'It's nobody's fault,'" Calvin tells Conrad. "'I love you, man,'" Conrad says to his father in the last scene; "'I love you too,'" Calvin answers (239–40). In the brief epilogue, Calvin and Conrad have moved from the large Lake Forest house to an apartment in Evanston and Conrad is reaching out to make friends with Joe Lazenby again; Conrad is also realizing that he and his mother will one day be able to reconnect, for she "knows just as he does that it is love, imperfect and unordered, that keeps them apart, even as it holds them somehow together" (245).

Characters

One of the real strengths of *Ordinary People* is the psychological realism of its characters, and Conrad Jarrett is the fullest of all. Recently released from a mental hospital, feeling estranged from schoolmates, friends, and family both because of what has happened to him (Buck's death) and what he has done to himself (his suicide attempt), Conrad enters the novel with a great deal of "anxiety" and "despair." But Dr. Berger helps these "real problems" with "real solutions," although, as Conrad's friend Karen says, in the final analysis, "'the only one who can help you is you'" (51).

In psychological terms, Conrad is an onion, with layers of meaning that must be peeled slowly down to the core. His progress combines analysis, healthy human interaction, and growing self-esteem; all are interdependent. It is after Conrad first expresses his feelings to Berger ("'Trust that guy in the closet, will you?'" the psychiatrist argues) and goes out with Jeannine that he allows himself a positive memory of Buck. Earlier, his grief and his sickness had demanded most of Conrad's energy. But even after his release from the hospital, his guilt about Buck's death keeps him from letting go of his grief, which in turn prevents him from letting people get close—"He has pushed everyone away who tries to help" (107). But Berger ultimately helps him break out of this unhealthy cycle. After that first good memory of skiing with Buck, "At peace with himself, he walks home through the falling snow" (96).

For every step forward, there is a smaller step back. At Christmas, still harboring anger and bitterness at his mother for her clear inability to love him, Conrad explodes at her and then tells his father, "'She hates me. There's nothing I can do about it'" (105). In his session with Berger after this outburst, he breaks through himself: he figures out "'Who it is who can't forgive who.'" It is not just his mother, who somehow has never been able to forgive Conrad for living while her first-born and best-loved (Buck) died; Conrad himself must come to understand and forgive his mother—as Berger says, "'She's not perfect. Recognize her limitations'" (110). Berger knows that "'there's somebody else you gotta forgive'" (111): Conrad must also forgive himself, but he is not yet ready for this, and Berger lets it go.

First Conrad must find out that he is worth loving, and this he discovers through his developing relationship with Jeannine. She casually forgives him for his suicide attempt ("'People do worse things than that,'" she says [141]), and then they go on to have a normal date. A later crisis at Jeannine's house (she wants her divorced parents to reconcile) shows Conrad just how "ordinary" others are, and he is able to comfort Jeannine: "He has never felt so strong, so needed" (185). After a swim meet he fights Stillman, and in the fight "a sweet rush of mindless ecstasy washes out everything in perfect release and makes him whole again" (166). Calvin recognizes that Conrad has finally turned his anger outward and is no longer aiming it solely at himself. But there is always that step backward: Conrad tells his old friend Joe Lazenby, who is trying to reconnect with him after the fight, "'It hurts too much to be around you'" (168); it is clear that he wants to hold onto his grief for Buck and not let anyone else share it. But these two incidents, the fight with Stillman and his support of Jeannine, start to give Conrad back pieces of himself— even though he holds onto remnants of his grief and his self-punishment.

It is a process; "He is becoming, Berger says" (194). But at this moment, Karen kills herself and Conrad starts a downward spiral; yet in the end he uses this crisis to break through the final walls. Walking the

streets, he is stopped by policemen who warn him about all the "'nuts in
the world'" who might be wandering around late at night; Conrad feels a
great sense of relief in these warnings—"Meaning you aren't one of them.
. . . *You're all right kid. Ordinary*" (199). Karen's death somehow frees
him to reexperience the trauma of the boating accident, when Buck
drowned. He turns to Berger, who helps him explain the causes for his
self-punishment. "'You hung on, kiddo. That's it. That's your guilt'"
(207). But self-punishment "'doesn't do a damn thing for the guilt, does
it?'" (210). The depression he has been experiencing has been "'plain and
simple *reduction of feeling*'" (208), Berger tells Conrad. Now Conrad is
feeling again, in part because of the tragic death of Karen. Berger
explains:

> "Listen, what happened this morning was that you let yourself feel some
> pain. Feeling is not selective, I keep telling you that. You can't feel pain, you
> aren't going to feel anything else, either. And the world is full of pain. Also
> joy. Evil. Goodness. Horror and love. You name it, it's there. Sealing
> yourself off is just going through the motions, get it?" (209)

Like its epigraph from Edna St. Vincent Millay ("But what a shining
animal is man"), the novel is about getting through the pain to the joy
that exists simultaneously on another plane. Conrad lets his grief out
and, a short time later, makes love with Jeannine for the first time. His
passage to health is marked by his simultaneous initiation into the joy
and mystery of sex. Conrad feels "the sense of calm, of peace slowly
gathering, spreading itself within him. He is in touch for good, with hope,
with himself, no matter what. Berger is right, the body never lies"
(232–3).

Dr. Berger is a complex character—a messy, insightful "slightly un-
dersize gorilla" (37)—and hardly the stereotype of the psychiatrist, but
Conrad comes to trust him as a friend and to learn from him. He
becomes the "significant other" in Conrad's life. Conrad's relationship
with his father is equally strong, and by the end of the novel, they are
working together as two adults. Calvin Jarrett is clearly someone who
does not know himself: "*I'm the kind of man who—hasn't the least idea
what kind of man I am*" (47), as he admits early in the novel. An orphan
who has attached himself to a strong but emotionally closed woman, he
also comes to see something of himself and of his relationships by the end
of the novel; it is a novel of Calvin's initiation as well.

The most problematic character in the novel is Beth Jarrett, in part
because we do not see her in the same depth and detail as we see her two
men. We view their interactions with her—Conrad's polite and careful

dance, Calvin's needy attempts at communication about what matters—and hear her words, but we do not get inside her head; and that is a problem, because clearly she is the antagonist in the piece. She is a perfectionist who has always had a hard time with any lack of organization; she is, in Calvin's view, "all elegance and self-possession" (24). Arnold Bacon, Calvin's first mentor, warns him that Beth "'is not a sharer'" (161). Calvin knows the coda to that description: "And she does not forgive" (162). Beth's most constant worry is how she and her family appear to others; she explodes at Conrad at Christmas because she has found out from someone else that he quit the swim team. Calvin admits "he never knows how to read her, and she offers him no clues," for, as his sister-in-law tells him, "'emotion is her enemy'" (188). Through his analysis, as well as through his interactions with Beth, Calvin comes to recognize that "her outer life is deceiving; that she gives the appearance of orderliness . . . but inside, what he had glimpsed is not order, but chaos" (235).

Beth Jarrett makes emotional sense, but a weakness of the novel is that we can only view her from the outside. We never know, for example, exactly how much of her character was the same before Buck's death. She leaves, at the end of the novel, when she is threatened by the changes she sees in the men around her; she has been unable to break through her own defenses to love someone else, especially Conrad, and can only flee. But her own needs have not been met either. The novel is her tragedy as well, but we never get to see it from her own perspective.

Themes

One of the major subjects of *Ordinary People* is family relationships. "Happy families are all alike," Tolstoy wrote in *Anna Karenina*; "every unhappy family is unhappy in its own way." And the Jarretts are clearly not happy. Rich and successful, they own many secrets and too few vehicles of caring and communication. They are "ordinary" only in their sadness and their inability to talk to one another about truly important subjects. Certainly they have endured a tragedy that few other families face, but their response to it makes them like so many others. Calvin and Conrad have a superficially good relationship and can joke with each other from the beginning, but what the novel shows is how much is going on beneath this apparently calm surface, the pains and problems in their heads and lives that they can barely communicate. Half the novel, at least in terms of numbers of chapters, is Calvin's, and we learn a great deal about his failed marriage: its unhealthy dependency, the lack of communication, the different goals and strategies, the withholding. *Ordinary*

People has a happy ending, but it shows a great deal of the unhappiness of family life before it gets there. The novel is also incredibly realistic, down to the smallest details of family holidays and squabbles, visits with the grandparents, and so forth.

The main theme of the novel is Conrad's successful initiation into adulthood. On his 18th birthday, his parents give him a new car, but, in the psychological symbolism of the novel, he is not yet ready to drive it. His suicide attempt was a clear message of his inability to keep growing in the face of his tragedy; through the course of the novel, he begins to achieve that maturity. He deals with the death of Karen, works out his guilt about his brother, makes peace (at least in his mind) with his mother, and enters into adult relationships with Jeannine and his father.

The novel actually follows a classic pattern of initiation, at least as it is portrayed in American culture, in inducting the young male protagonist into adulthood through both violence and sex. The two acts make sense in the psychological terms of the novel—Conrad needs to work his anger out against someone other than himself, and his relationship with Jeannine is a natural part of his growing recognition of his own self-worth—but they also reflect a reality of American culture. In a society lacking clear demarcations between childhood and adulthood, maturity is often symbolically associated with some physical act that *means* more to the participants than the act itself may warrant. Both sex and violence have this ritualistic role in American culture (which is why recent adolescent films are so full of both of them—*The Breakfast Club*, for instance, or *River's Edge*).

Proof of Conrad's maturity rests on his last act: he calls on his old friend Joe Lazenby and asks him if he wants to play golf. Joe was the only friend who wrote to Conrad when he was in the hospital—"'I miss you, man'" (89) was his simple message; but Conrad had to push Joe and other friends away after his hospital experience—"'It hurts too much to be around you'" (168). This explanation, however, is obviously incomplete: Conrad cannot let Joe and others share his grief because to do so would mean he would also have to let go of some of his self-criticism and start feeling good again. And thus the significance of the novel's closing act: when Conrad *does* let go of his self-punishment, he can start to reconnect with old friends.

Style and Language

Ordinary People is a realistic contemporary novel, and there are few difficulties in reading and comprehending its meanings. The language is straightforward and clear, if adult (especially, perhaps, in some of its psychological terminology), and the only thing that may confuse younger readers is the point of view, which shifts in alternate chapters between Conrad and Calvin. Guest can go into the heads of any of her characters but chooses to enter only those of Calvin and Conrad. Much of the novel's power comes from its realistic transcription of thoughts and feelings: Conrad and Calvin think and feel like men their ages might, and readers can only nod in agreement. (One of the weaknesses of the novel, again, is that because we do not get into the head of the third important character in this triangle, Beth, we never fully understand her motivation or needs.) There is nothing particularly poetic about the language; Guest uses it to convey thought and conversation as realistically as possible. She italicizes thoughts and dreams to highlight them, but it is not particularly difficult to figure out who is doing the dreaming or holding the brief interior monologues.

The sex in the novel may cause problems for younger readers, but it is actually handled with care and sensitivity. When Conrad masturbates (although the act is not described), he feels brief relief from the pressures in his world and, later, guilt. When he and Jeannine make love, it is a tender and caring act, described with the broadest of brush strokes. If there is any novel that is excellent for introducing teenagers to the pleasures and responsibilities of adult sexuality, *Ordinary People* must be it, for the sexual language never calls attention to itself.

TEACHING THE NOVEL

Teaching Suggestions

One reason for teaching *Ordinary People* is its insights into human development and its lessons about guilt, self-punishment, and self-esteem. Most teenage readers are intrigued with the psychological realism of the novel's depiction of the problems and progress of Conrad Jarrett. This special strength of *Ordinary People*, however, can also be a handicap to readers not familiar with its psychological language or the stages of emotional development; some students may need to be "prepped" in order to deal with its terminology and to appreciate its insights.

Ordinary People is less about friends and friendship than it is about their opposite: the feeling of being an outsider. One reason for the book's popularity, especially among younger readers, is that it describes a condition that many adolescents experience occasionally and some feel is an

almost permanent part of their teenage years: a sense of estrangement or
alienation from others—family, friends, even self. Conrad is a textbook
"outsider"; as he himself describes his condition:

> At school it is the same. Everywhere he looks, there is competence and good
> health. Only he, Conrad Jarrett, outcast, quitter, *fuck-up*, stands outside the
> circle of safety, separated from everyone by this aching void of loneliness;
> but no matter, he deserves it. (107)

Conrad's estrangement is, of course, both self-imposed (he refrains from
calling Joe Lazenby because his relationship with Joe reminds him of
Buck and would force him to share his grief) and imposed from outside
(Stillman calls Conrad a "flake," and other students probably look at him
as different because of his suicide attempt and hospitalization). Students
reading *Ordinary People* can identify with Conrad, for most of them
have felt, at one time or another, an outsider themselves: adolescence is,
among other things, that difficult time when we leave what is for many of
us the security and comfort of home and enter a "real world" in which
disappointment and rejection lurk around every corner. Conrad's passage through this world makes all of us feel a little better, but his journey
from isolation and estrangement to "connections"—with Jeannine, Joe
Lazenby, others—can also be a real focus of learning, and getting students to talk or write about their identification with Conrad Jarrett is one
easy access to the novel.

The best way to get at the ideas in *Ordinary People*, as in any novel,
is to ask questions that stimulate thought about the work, and these
move most effectively from what *happens* in the novel to what such
incidents or actions *mean*. Here are a few questions designed to open the
novel to this kind of examination:

> How does the epigraph connect to the novel?
> Why does Conrad feel as he does at the beginning?
> What are Conrad's relations with his parents like?
> How does Conrad resemble his mother?
> What specific worries does Calvin have about Conrad?
> Why has Conrad pushed away Lazenby and other friends?
>
> Why does Conrad quit the swim team?
> Why does he blow up when his mother confronts him about it?
> Why does he fight Stillman?
> In what ways are all three acts positive?

In what specific ways does Dr. Berger help Conrad?

Why does Conrad want "control"?

What does Berger mean when he says "'Trust that guy in the closet'"?

Who cannot forgive whom here? For what?

What is significant about the woman at the library staring at Conrad and calling him "good-looking"?

How is Jeannine's house like everyone else's?

What do the "'stupid'" things she did in the past say about her?

How does Conrad's relationship with Jeannine show his growth into maturity and health?

What is Christmas like in the Jarrett house?

What is Conrad's relationship with his grandparents like? How is it different from his relationship with his parents?

What is Conrad's response to Karen's suicide? How does this crisis lead to a breakthrough for Conrad?

How do the policemen help Conrad the night he is wandering the streets?

How does Berger help Conrad? What does he know that Conrad must do about his feelings and his guilt?

What does Conrad learn about the death of Buck?

What happens to Beth and Calvin in Dallas?

Why does Beth leave home?

What is going to happen to Conrad and Calvin now?

What does Conrad believe will happen in his relationship with Beth in the future?

What does Conrad's visit to Joe Lazenby at the end show?

What has Conrad learned about himself in the novel?

What values would Conrad and Dr. Berger now agree are necessary for a healthy and happy life?

Discussion and Writing Ideas

1. Describe Conrad ten years later.
2. Have you ever had a crisis in which you felt you could not cope? What did you do? What helped?
3. Jeannine says to Conrad, "'You certainly don't have a very clear idea of what you do well.'" What does she mean? Is she right? Discuss.

4. Describe Conrad's changing relationship with Calvin, Beth, or Dr. Berger. What are the main elements of the relationship? What does Conrad get/learn from it?

5. What does Conrad learn in the novel about *survival*? What strategies does he learn to use to cope with daily life and grow stronger? What works?

6. What does the novel say about family life in America? (Cite other examples besides the Jarretts.)

7. What does *Ordinary People* say about the importance of friendship? (Cite at least three instances from the novel.)

8. What does the novel say about feelings and the importance of expressing them? (Cite examples.)

9. Compare the novel to the film version of *Ordinary People*. Is Conrad more or less sympathetic in the film? Calvin? Beth? What ideas in the novel are dropped in the film? What is added? How is the film finally different from the novel?

10. Miss Mellon, Conrad's English teacher, asks him about the title character of Thomas Hardy's *Jude the Obscure*: "'Do you think he was powerless in the grip of circumstances, or could he have helped himself?'" (17). The question, of course, applies to Conrad as well. Discuss.

11. Conrad learns a number of important lessons from Dr. Berger—for example, that although feelings can be painful as well as joyful, the absence of emotion ("reduction of feeling") that depression leads to is worse; or that it is necessary to recognize people's limitations, including our own. Find another value in the novel (about feelings, caring, guilt, and so forth) and write a paper showing its source in the novel and its importance in your own life.

Bridging to Other Novels

J. D. Salinger, *The Catcher in the Rye* (1951); see Chapter 1. Holden Caulfield is headed for a breakdown and hospitalization himself.

John Knowles, *A Separate Peace* (1960). This novel, set in an eastern boarding school, also deals wtih male bonding and competition.

Sylvia Plath, *The Bell Jar* (1963); see Chapter 5. This intense novel deals with a young woman's breakdown, hospitalization, and recovery.

Hannah Green, *I Never Promised You a Rose Garden* (1964). This novel tells of a young woman's hospitalization and eventual recovery from this mental breakdown.

Paul Zindel, *The Pigman* (YA, 1968). Two young people learn about the responsibilities of caring for someone else.

John Neufeld, *Lisa, Bright and Dark* (1969). The novel deals with adolescents in psychological crisis.

Robert Cormier, *The Chocolate War* (YA, 1974); see Chapter 3. Compare the situations of Conrad and Jerry Renault.

Judy Blume, *Forever* (YA, 1975). This is the best young adult novel available on the subject of sex.

Terry Davis, *Vision Quest* (YA, 1979). Another high school student deals with sex, sports, and so forth.

Judith Guest, *Second Heaven* (1982). Guest's next novel, this is also about the problems of both adolescents and adults.

5 "There ought . . . to be a ritual for being born twice"

THE BELL JAR

Author: Sylvia Plath (1932–1963)

Genre: psychological realism

Time of novel: summer through winter of 1953

Locale: New York City, suburban Boston

Point of view: first person

First published: 1963 (England); 1971 (United States)

Edition used: Bantam paperback (1979); 200 pp.; with "A Biographical Note" by Lois Ames

Grade level: 11–12

Principal characters:

Esther Greenwood, a bright college student undergoing a mental breakdown

Mrs. Greenwood, her widowed mother, a teacher of business English at a Boston city college

Buddy Willard, a medical student Esther has been dating for several years

Dr. Nolan, a psychiatrist who helps Esther recover

Doreen, one of the 12 girls working in New York as college editors of a leading women's magazine, and an attractive friend of Esther's for that month

Jay Cee, the *Ladies' Day* editor Esther works under

Lenny Shepherd, a New York disc jockey who dates Doreen

Constantin, a simultaneous interpreter at the U.N. who takes Esther out in New York

Marco, a "woman-hater" Esther goes to a dance with

Dr. Gordon, an obtuse psychiatrist who first treats Esther back home in Boston

Philomena Guinea, a romance novelist and Esther's patron at college

Joan Gilley, a college friend hospitalized with Esther, who later kills herself

Irwin, a math teacher Esther picks up to complete her sexual initiation

ANALYSIS OF THE NOVEL

Story and Setting

The Bell Jar describes a young woman's descent into a private psychological hell and the first faltering steps of her recovery. Like Esther Greenwood, its protagonist, the novel itself is broken into several uneven parts. In the first and longest section, Esther describes her frantic summer month in New York City as one of 12 student editors for a special college issue of *Ladies' Day*. (Like Sylvia Plath herself, Esther has earned this honor by three years of hard work at a leading women's college.) Echoing J. D. Salinger's *The Catcher in the Rye* (1951), this first part of *The Bell Jar* has a particular 1950s humor, pathos, and naiveté. Like Holden Caulfield, Esther Greenwood is slowly coming apart in Manhattan, as she is rushed through a frenetic round of lunches, meetings, and dances.

"It was a queer, sultry summer, the summer they electrocuted the Rosenbergs, and I didn't know what I was doing in New York" (1), Esther begins. In the first episode, on the way to a magazine party, Esther and her attractive friend Doreen are picked up by Lenny Shepherd, a New York City disc jockey, and the three end up back at his apartment, where Lenny and Doreen ignore Esther as they sexually attack each other. Esther walks alone back to the Amazon Hotel, where the women are staying, takes a bath to purge herself, and subsequently feels "pure and sweet as a new baby" (17). The next day, Esther and the other girls are poisoned at a magazine luncheon and end up in their hotel beds being nursed by Doreen (who skipped the luncheon to spend the day with Lenny).

But each forward narrative move in this first part of the novel—like Esther's own mental progress—usually means several steps backward: here a flashback to a meeting with her boss, Jay Cee, that morning (during which she realizes that she does not know what she wants to do with her life) reminds Esther of how she cleverly avoided college chemistry. Esther recovers from the food poisoning the next morning to a call from Constantin, a simultaneous interpreter at the U.N. (who has gotten her number from the mother of Esther's boyfriend, Buddy Willard), but this forward narrative flow only leads to several further eddies: to a recap of her romance with Buddy, a description of a visit she made to his medical school, where she first saw cadavers and "bottles full of babies," and her discovery of an affair the "hypocrite" Buddy had with a waitress. ("When I was nineteen, pureness was the great issue" [66].) She decides to end her own virginity by seducing Constantin, but they both fall asleep before anything happens (and he hardly seems interested). On her last night in Manhattan, she attends a dance with Doreen and is matched with Marco, a "women-hater" who savagely attacks her. At the end of this nightmare, Esther stands on the roof of the Amazon Hotel, calmly feeding her new "wardrobe to the night wind" (91). She is slowly coming unglued, and her experiences in New York City have only quickened the pace of her decline, for she is now thinking of suicide: "The thought that I might kill myself formed in my mind coolly as a tree or a flower" (79).

At this point in the novel, where Holden ended *The Catcher in the Rye*, Esther begins her frightening descent into the nightmare world of mental illness. In the second third of the novel, Esther returns home to Boston—still marked by the blood from her struggle with Marco—to discover that she has been rejected for a summer writing course she had counted on. She considers writing a novel, then tries to work on her senior thesis on James Joyce, and finally contemplates switching colleges, only to discover that she has few of the necessary credits. Obsessed by her own inadequacies, she wanders through Boston seeking some sign of her identity and contemplating suicide. (When she picks up a sailor on the Boston Common, she calls herself "Elly Higgenbottom," "an orphan.") Still wearing the borrowed outfit she returned from New York in, she complains that she cannot sleep and that her handwriting looks like a child's. Her mother and the family doctor ignore Esther's pleas of distress but do send her to Dr. Gordon, an unsympathetic psychiatrist who gives her painful shock treatment. Her thoughts of suicide increase, but she is unable to complete the act. (On a blind date to the beach, Esther swims out and tries to drown herself, but "each time popped up like a cork" [131].) Her mother had not allowed her to attend her father's funeral, but now Esther finds his grave and "laid my face to the smooth face of the marble and howled my loss into the cold salt rain" (137). She is hospitalized after crawling into a hole in her cellar and swallowing a bottle of pills.

What is Esther's problem? In part, it is the difficulty of being a bright and self-conscious young woman in the restricted 1950s, and not a little of the novel's power, like that of *The Catcher in the Rye*, lies in its ability to suggest the limitations to human possibility in this Eisenhower world. Yet at a deeper level, the problem is Esther's sexual identity, or lack of it. As Esther says, "pureness" is a big issue in the 1950s, and it is an even bigger issue for a sheltered young woman whose father died when she was nine and whose mother seems to spend her whole life working to survive. Esther has never been able to figure out her own sexual identity in her partial family in this parochial 1950s world. Whenever she thinks about sex, she thinks about babies, and especially about the fetuses in bottles that she saw with Buddy Willard the year before. Esther herself is like a baby in a bottle—or bell jar—stopped or arrested in her own psychological development and unable to move into adult heterosexuality. Her suicide attempt is an effort to escape from this prison.

In the last third of the novel, Esther begins the slow and painful process of recovery. After bad experiences at two hospitals, her college patron, the romance novelist Philomena Guinea, has her transferred to a private hospital, where she comes under the sensitive and understanding care of Dr. Nolan. Esther considers her first shock treatment here a "treachery" by Dr. Nolan, but the psychiatrist treats her with trust and love, Esther grows stronger, and the "bell jar" under which she feels she has been trapped finally begins to lift.

Her recovery is marked by two significant events. First, on passes from the hospital, she has herself fitted for a diaphragm ("I am climbing to freedom," she says [182]), and then she meets and seduces Irwin, a young Boston math professor. But Esther hemorrhages badly after this first sexual experience and must get a friend, Joan Gilling, who was in the last institution with Esther, to take her to a local hospital, where the doctor tells her, "'It's one in a million it happens to like this'" (190). It should be, for, in the psychological symbolism of the novel, Esther is giving birth to herself, to her first adult sexual identity. There ought to be "a ritual for being born twice" (199), she says. Later, Joan hangs herself, but, as Dr. Nolan tells her, Esther cannot be responsible for the death of another, only for herself. "'Nobody did it. *She* did it'" (196). Esther survives both these events—a birth and a death—and, in the last scene, walks alone into her final interview with the hospital board before her release. She will recover. In fact, as clues at the beginning of the novel tell readers, she is married with a baby as she is narrating the novel and is "all right again" (3).

Characters

The central character in this novel of initiation is, of course, Esther Greenwood, but other characters play important roles in her passage into adulthood. In certain ways, characterization in *The Bell Jar* resembles a fictional Rorschach test in which Esther is being forced to choose among various 1950s roles. As she describes it early in the novel, her life is like the fig tree in a story she read, for from

> the tip of every branch, like a fat purple fig, a wonderful future beckoned and winked. One fig was a husband and a happy home and children, and another fig was a famous poet and another fig was a brilliant professor, and another fig was Ee Gee, the amazing editor. (62)

Sadly, Esther can only imagine herself sitting "in the crotch of this fig tree, starving to death, just because I couldn't make up my mind which of the figs I would choose" (63).

Part of Esther's problem is that each role she observes is restrictive and exclusive. Esther's mother works so hard to support Esther and her brother that she has no life of her own. Buddy Willard's mother, in perhaps the best metaphor of all, braids rugs that her family immediately walks on, while Esther's neighbor Dodo Conway produces babies year by year. Each woman's family role is thus a box, a trap. Yet career women here are limited, too. Jay Cee, Esther's editor at *Ladies' Day*, is hard and aggressive, and Esther cannot imagine her married life. Esther's patron at college is the popular women's novelist Philomena Guinea, who will not help Esther in the hospital if there is "a boy in the case" (151). Other choices are more sexual, but just as limited, from the promiscuous Doreen in New York City to the apparently bisexual Joan in Boston. Esther believes that she must choose among these social and sexual roles for her own future, but by the end of the novel—and with the help of the only *whole* person here, Dr. Nolan—Esther has discovered and is choosing herself instead.

The roles for men in this world are hardly wider. Buddy Willard is an uptight and repressed young man whose sexual awkwardness almost matches Esther's. A medical student who is recuperating from TB in an Adirondacks sanitorium, Buddy proposes to Esther, but she rejects the rigid future life with him would hold. In New York City, Esther meets Lenny, Doreen's hypersexual boyfriend; Marco, the women-hater; and Constantin, a simultaneous interpreter at the United Nations who is apparently asexual (or at least so with Esther). In Boston, she encounters Dr. Gordon, the successful family man who is insensitive to his patients' real needs, and Irwin, precocious but sexually immature. The men in the novel, in short, are as limited as the women. In spite of the fact that some of these characters are types, Plath's rich poetic style breathes life into them, fleshes them out beyond the caricatures that they might have been in another author's hands.

Esther suffers from faults of her own. Like other first-person narrators in the American novel—Holden Caulfield, Huck Finn—Esther is not always able to see the full significance of her own story or to describe her own character very accurately. Certainly she is a young woman from several sheltered worlds (home, college) who is undergoing severe psychological problems (probably manic depression, although it is not named). She accuses Buddy of deceit for his affair, for instance, but fails to recognize the hypocrisy of her happiness when Buddy gets TB and is hospitalized. She is someone with little self-knowledge (until the end of her story), someone who can recognize the flaws in others but who is too obsessed with her own problems to recognize her own shortcomings.

Themes

The Bell Jar has multiple layers of meaning. On one level, it is an initiation novel, a book about growing up female in America, with all the role restrictions and psychological hurdles that a woman may face in her struggle to define herself. In this regard, it is a novel about the dead ends of the 1950s, when anti-Communist hysteria contrasted so sharply with the blandness of American cultural life. A symbolic echo of that period is the execution of the Rosenbergs, which Esther personalizes in her first paragraph and which recurs, metaphorically at least, in her own shock treatments in two hospitals. A number of Esther's comments—on diets, for example, and dating, and marriage—point up the limitations of this world.

At its deepest level, *The Bell Jar* describes the world of mental illness from the inside, and Sylvia Plath's poetic style renders this complex psychological story realistically and with terrible immediacy. Images of babies and bell jars, of fetuses and figs, of electroshock and drowning— all help carry the reader through Esther's descent, hospitalization, and beginning recovery. In the end, these two major themes of the novel are inextricably intertwined: the psychosexual story of Esther's faltering attempts, in spite of her illness, to gain her own identity—to deal with the death of her father and find her own sexual self—and the social journey (again, like *The Catcher in the Rye*) through the 1950s world of conformity and hypocrisy (e.g., the limited sex-role models). Few first novels have the thematic depth or the rich poetic language of *The Bell Jar*.

In many ways, Sylvia Plath created the critical framework within which the book is today read and discussed. Perhaps because its history has paralleled the growth of the women's movement in the United States, *The Bell Jar* has become a feminist touchstone. Certainly there were psychological novels about women before *The Bell Jar*, such as Mary Jane Ward's *The Snake Pit*, but Sylvia Plath wrote an initiation novel that coincided with the emergence of contemporary feminist literary consciousness in the United States; since its publication here in 1971, the novel has stood at the top of a long and growing list of works by women writing about themselves in this society. Whenever the feminist initiation novel is discussed—from Hannah Green's *I Never Promised You a Rose Garden* and Margaret Atwood's *Surfacing*, through Lisa Alther's *Kinflicks* and Marilyn French's *The Women's Room*, to a slew of contemporary novels—*The Bell Jar* is cited as a beginning. In a number of ways, the novel captures the experience of growing up female in America—the limited roles and choices, "being under a man's thumb," and numerous other issues. For the feminist critic, furthermore, the novel has become a weapon in the fight to bring the discussion of literature back into the context of the lives out of which it has grown. The emotional power of *The Bell Jar*, such critics argue, cannot finally be separated from the life and death of Sylvia Plath.

On a broader canvas, *The Bell Jar* is representative of a number of novels to come out of the changing sociopolitical energy of the 1960s, from Joseph Heller's *Catch-22* and Ken Kesey's *One Flew over the Cuckoo's Nest* through Jerzy Kosinski's *The Painted Bird* to Kurt Vonnegut's *Slaughterhouse-Five*. In these and other essentially 1960s works, the focus is on the relationship between the individual and society; war and madness become metaphors for the human condition, and hospitals (or the army) become both microcosms of and escapes from the insanity of society. Like a number of novels that followed it, *The Bell Jar* focuses our concern on the individual lost in a society that can no longer respond to individual needs and whose institutions no longer work. Like the earlier *Catcher in the Rye*, *Bell Jar* becomes an indictment of a society that does not respond to the needs of its individual citizens.

Style and Language

The Bell Jar is often discussed in the context of Sylvia Plath's important work as a poet, particularly the collections *The Colossus* (1960) and *Ariel* (1965), which bracket her only novel. Certainly it is a poet's novel, and any analysis must acknowledge its figurative language. Her writing is full of poetic images: in a bar with Doreen and Lenny, for example, "I felt myself melting into the shadows like the negative of a person I'd never seen before in my life" (8). Later, she imagines her future years "spaced along a road in the form of telephone poles, threaded together by wires" (101) and her future days "stretching ahead like a series of bright, white boxes, and separating one box from another was sleep, like a black shade" (104).

The title is a perfect image of Esther's dilemma, trapped as she is in a airless chamber and cut off from the world—and perfect also because it is an academic image (from a physics lab), and Esther draws on that college experience for her only successes. But images in Plath are hardly ever static, and they usually carry some symbolic weight. Esther first uses the story of the fig tree, for example, as a symbol of her sexual fear (of eggs and babies) and then as a symbol of the range of human possibilities— which Esther feels cut off from as well. Images of babies proliferate in the novel; even the face of President Eisenhower appears to Esther "bald and blank as the face of a fetus in a bottle" (72). She first sees "big glass bottles full of babies that had died before they were born" (51) on the visit to Buddy's medical school; then "In the afternoon we went to see a baby born" (52). In some ways Esther is herself the baby in a bottle: arrested in her own psychological and sexual growth, as in a bell jar, and afraid to break through to the next stage because of her fear of both sex (her own identity) and pregnancy (the baby being born). When she first recovers, she gets fat from her medication, as if she were pregnant; after her encounter with Irwin, she symbolically gives birth to herself and begins a new pattern of growth, no longer having "'a baby hanging over my head like a big stick, to keep me in line'" (181). Images flow into metaphor and then into symbol, as so often happens in poetic language. Finally, few novels are as colorful; any one paragraph often contains a rainbow of hues. Of other twentieth-century American novels, only *The Great Gatsby* carries as many colorful and poetic descriptions.

The structure of *The Bell Jar* is somewhat more problematic. The novel is broken into three uneven parts, and the moods are never really reconciled. The comedy and pathos of the first part, for example, conflict with the intense psychological drama and trauma of the second and third. Further, the novel is narrated (particularly in its first third) in a series of associative flashbacks that have the jumpy connections and distortions of Esther's own mind. What helps hold the novel together is the humor: drinking out of the finger bowl at her first lunch with Philomena Guinea, for example, or telling the dense Buddy Willard that she has a date with "'Peter the Hermit and Walter the Penniless,'" two medieval crusaders she convinces Buddy are Dartmouth undergraduates. In many ways the humor resembles that of *The Catcher in the Rye*; even Esther's language and syntax sometimes recall Holden Caulfield's false bravado—"I felt wise and cynical as all hell" (6), Esther begins her story. But the humor is necessary here, for without the relief it provides the novel would be exceedingly bare and cold in both subject and tone—and still is for some readers.

TEACHING THE NOVEL

Teaching Suggestions

The first problem raised in most discussions of *The Bell Jar* is the biographical one. The novel was published in January 1963 in England, where Sylvia Plath was then living, under the pseudonym Victoria Lucas.

Less than a month later, Plath took her own life. The novel was first published in the United States eight years later, under Plath's own name, and has known both popular and critical acclaim ever since that second publication. Readers usually know that its story closely parallels the author's own, and they often confuse Esther Greenwood and Sylvia Plath. Such a confusion is natural, but it may do little for our understanding and appreciation of the novel itself. The ending of the novel, for example, is positive: Esther *does* recover and gains her "freedom" from both mental illness and her psychosexual stasis: "I was my own woman" (182), she says at the close; "I am, I am I am" (199).

As the "Biographical Note" included in this edition reveals, Sylvia Plath was not as fortunate: "'I've tried to picture my world and the people in it as seen through the distorting lens of a bell jar,'" she wrote to her mother in 1962. "'My second book will show that same world as seen through the eyes of health'" (214). But, as Esther Greenwood says toward the end of the novel, "To the person in the bell jar, blank and stopped as a dead baby, the world itself is the bad dream" (193). From that dream, Plath herself never awoke, and, ever since the publication of the novel, readers have not been able to discuss *The Bell Jar* without thoughts of the tragic early death of its author. Teachers need to present this biographical information, but then they need to confront the novel as they would any piece of literature: as a fabric of language and meaning that needs to be examined on its own terms. The biographical history, in short, should not be allowed to confuse the imaginative truth of Plath's novel.

Esther Greenwood is a young woman who, through the first half of the novel, is getting increasingly sicker and then, in the second half, healthier. Students can benefit from a detailed analysis of the stages of Esther's sickness and recovery, perhaps, but they can find all the details of her journey through careful reading themselves. (For example, what are the symptoms or signals of sickness that her mother and others miss?) Much of the novel's psychological meaning is carried in Plath's rich metaphorical language, and students should also be encouraged to look for key examples of Plath's colorful prose: for example, images of death (cadavers), twins (Esther/Elly), and sex (babies). *The Bell Jar* is a sophisticated novel, but it is also accessible to readers who pay attention to its poetic language and think about its actions.

One way into the novel is to have students brainstorm personal goals for themselves, share them in groups, and put them in some kind of rough order—*before* they begin *The Bell Jar*. Then read Plath's story of the fig tree from the novel (pp. 45, 62–63). The story can lead to a discussion of what happens to goals in real life, such as how we choose them and the obstacles to their achievement. This discussion then becomes a theme that a teacher can return to throughout the novel. A similar kind of discussion-to-novel could be done for other subjects in the novel—sex, for example. Students are often interested in the sexual incidents in the novel, and particularly its descriptions of homosexuality. Esther's rejection of Joan, like her earlier rejection of Buddy, is part of her own sexual self-definition. (When Esther asks Dr. Nolan, "'What does a woman see in a woman that she can't see in a man?'" the reply is, "'Tenderness'" [179]. In the face of male sexual behavior in the novel—consider Lenny and Marco—the answer is significant.) Students can discuss the sexual options available today compared to the limited choices Esther sees for herself. The point is to preview the novel by connecting it to something from the students' own lives, and then to use that connection to highlight the novel.

Such a discussion leads naturally to the novel's major themes, sketched earlier. In many ways, *The Bell Jar* is a manifesto *against* the limitations of social and sexual roles, for men as well as for women. A discussion of the limited models for Esther in the novel (Doreen, Jay Cee, et al.) moves easily to a consideration of those roles in our own world. The novel, in short, should stimulate questions about who we are, what our society says we should be doing, and what kinds of models and roles are provided for us, as both men and women. (Who are the popular heroes today, in entertainment and sports, for example? How broad or limited are these models for us?) Such a discussion could lead to numerous writing activities (see below) and to a deeper appreciation of the novel itself.

Discussion and Writing Ideas

1. Write about a time when you *needed others*. How did you reach out? What was the response of other people? Was the response what you expected?
2. Imagine that you are a friend of Esther's when she returns home to Boston. What do you notice about her (her clothes, handwriting, etc.)? What could you do to help her? What would you tell her?
3. Write a report on Esther, as Dr. Nolan might, for the hospital committee. (Be as specific as possible.) Do you think she is ready to go home? What is your prognosis for her future?
4. Write a description of Esther ten years after the novel ends. What is she doing, and what is she like? When she thinks back on these months in New York and Boston, what will she say she has learned?

What would she say now about her relationship with her mother, with Buddy, with Dr. Nolan?

5. Discuss Esther's work as a hospital volunteer. What is the point in this scene (132–34)?

6. What is the import of Esther breaking her leg while skiing with Buddy (77–80)?

7. Analyze the roles of *women* in *The Bell Jar*; what are the limitations and restrictions of their roles? What can they do, and what can they *not* do? What do each of the following women represent: Doreen, Jay Cee, Dodo Conway? Which role, if any, do you prefer?

8. Analyze the roles of *men* in *The Bell Jar*; what are the restrictions and limitations to their roles? What are their relations with women like? What does each of the following men seem to represent: Buddy, Constantin, Lenny, Marco? Is there any pattern to Esther's relations with and attitudes toward men? Explain.

9. Compare *The Bell Jar* to *Catcher in the Rye*. How are Esther and Holden similar, how are they different?

10. Analyze the *figurative language* in *The Bell Jar*. What characterizes Plath's use of images and symbols (the bell jar, babies, fig tree, etc.)?

11. Analyze the humor in *The Bell Jar*. What is it like, and how does it work? Find one short scene and write about what makes it funny (the magazine luncheon, for example).

Bridging to Other Novels

Carson McCullers, *The Heart Is a Lonely Hunter* (1940) and *Member of the Wedding* (1946); see Chapter 9. Both novels contain female protagonists in search of identity.

J. D. Salinger, *The Catcher in the Rye* (1951); see Chapter 1. A number of parallels exist between these two novels, particularly in their New York scenes and their 1950s vocabulary and atmosphere.

Ken Kesey, *One Flew over the Cuckoo's Nest* (1962). Chief Broom's narration of this novel echoes Esther's hospital experiences.

Hannah Green, *I Never Promised You a Rose Garden* (1964). This is another story of a young woman who recovers from her hospitalization.

Jerzy Kosinski, *The Painted Bird* (1965). A young boy witnesses the brutality of World War II and slowly becomes mute in response to its horror.

Judith Guest, *Ordinary People* (1976); see Chapter 4. Compare the interior monologues of Esther Greenwood and Conrad Jarrett, as they both view their worlds through distorted lenses.

William Wharton, *Birdy* (1979). This popular contemporary novel concerns a young man, hospitalized after war, whose recollections of adolescence help in his recovery.

Robert Cormier, *The Bumblebee Flies Anyway* (YA, 1983). A young man tries to figure out why he has been hospitalized with young people who are terminally ill.

6 "You're worth the whole damn bunch put together"

THE GREAT GATSBY

Author: F. Scott Fitzgerald (1896–1940)
Genre: romantic realism
Time of novel: summer of 1922
Locale: Long Island estates, New York City
Point of view: first person
First published: 1925
Edition used: Collier paperback (Scribner Classic, 1980); 182 pp.; with an introduction by Charles Scribner III.
Grade level: 10–12
Principal characters:

Nick Carraway, a 30-year-old bond salesman living in West Egg, Long Island, and working in New York City

Jay Gatsby (James Gatz), a wealthy bootlegger, living in West Egg and in love with

Daisy Buchanan, a distant cousin of Nick's, living across the bay in East Egg, with her husband

Tom Buchanan, a brutal man of great wealth but no particular occupation

Myrtle Wilson, Tom's mistress and the wife of George Wilson

George Wilson, a nondescript and "spiritless" garage owner

Jordan Baker, a professional golfer and friend of Daisy's, with whom Nick has a brief affair

ANALYSIS OF THE NOVEL

Story and Setting

The story Nick Carraway tells in *The Great Gatsby* is essentially a mystery: Who *is* Jay Gatsby? Where did he come from? What kind of *work* does he do? Which of the many stories about him are *true*? Over the pages it takes to tell the story, Nick slowly unravels the full history of

Gatsby, until the novel's violent ending closes the case. But, like so many other important American novels (Ishmael's story of Ahab in *Moby Dick*, for example), *The Great Gatsby* is not only about the central character but also about the *effect* of this character on the narrator. Nick learns—through the actions of and reactions to Gatsby—what life in contemporary America is all about, and by the end of this story he has been initiated into adulthood and into a more mature, if cynical, view of modern life.

Nick is back in the Midwest when he tells the story (all the major characters are, in fact, from the Midwest), and it is two years after the events of that tragic summer on Long Island. Nick had graduated from Yale in 1915, served in Europe in World War I, and returned to the Midwest; but after the excitement of the War, he became restless, "so I decided to go East and learn the bond business" (3). He got a job in New York City and a little house next to the mansion of a man named Gatsby in West Egg, Long Island. (West Egg is one of two egg-shaped peninsulas that jut into Long Island Sound; the second, East Egg, where Daisy and Tom Buchanan live, is the more "fashionable" of the two.)

The story proper begins one summer night when Nick drives over to East Egg to have dinner with the Buchanans, a couple he has known distantly before but whom he will now get to know intimately. Daisy is beautiful but shallow, and her "hard," "hulking" husband Tom Buchanan is a bully repeating "stale" racist ideas. Jordan Baker, a friend of Daisy's and a professional golfer, is also there, and, like the Buchanans, is bored and restless. It is such portraits of the rich in the 1920s for which Fitzgerald is most famous, and his descriptions of them are vivid and often poetic: Nick, on first hearing Daisy that night, muses that "It was the kind of voice that the ear follows up and down, as if each speech is an arrangement of notes that will never be played again" (9). It is at this dinner that the complications begin: Nick learns that there is some mystery surrounding Gatsby (at the same time that Daisy first learns that Gatsby is living nearby) and that "'Tom's got some woman in New York'" (15). When Nick gets home later that night, he sees Gatsby on his lawn and is about to call to him but stops himself when he sees Gatsby stretching out his arms at the "single green light" across the bay in East Egg (at the end of the Buchanans' dock, as we later learn).

The novel is built like this, in a series of brilliant and colorful scenes. In the next chapter, Tom takes Nick into New York City, but they get off the train near a "desolate area of land"—a "valley of ashes" (23), as Nick describes it—so that Nick can meet Tom's "girl," Myrtle Wilson, the wife of a garage owner and a crude, not very pretty woman in her 30s. Tom and Nick arrange to meet Myrtle in the city, and at the apartment that

Tom maintains for her they hold a small party at which Nick gets drunk
with a group of rather strange characters, a party that ends with Tom
breaking Myrtle's nose for repeating Daisy's name.

In contrast to this surreal party, the next chapter depicts the lavish,
extravagant parties thrown by Gatsby, who regularly opens his mansion
to hundreds of people, most of whom he does not know. At this first
party, Nick meets Jordan Baker again; and then Gatsby takes her into his
library to tell her "'the most amazing thing,'" as Jordan later informs
Nick. In the next scene, Gatsby drives Nick into New York for lunch,
where Nick meets Meyer Wolfsheim, a "'friend'" and business associate
of Gatsby's (and also the gambler who fixed the 1919 World Series, as
Gatsby tells Nick when Wolfsheim leaves). It is also at this lunch that
Gatsby tells Nick part of his own history ("'I didn't want you to think I
was just some nobody'" [67]), obviously part of a ploy to set Nick up to
do something for him. What it is we do not learn until Jordan Baker,
later that afternoon, tells Nick more of the story that she has gotten from
Gatsby (and verified from her own childhood acquaintance with Daisy):
that Gatsby, while in officer training in the South in 1917, fell in love with
the beautiful young Daisy Fay of Louisville, Kentucky. He was shipped
overseas, and she later married Tom Buchanan (although not before
receiving a letter from Gatsby the day before her wedding that caused her
to get drunk for the first time). Tom and Daisy began their wedding
journey, which turned into a series of stops at various vacation spas of
the rich (where Tom apparently got involved with other women). Daisy
had a baby, the couple spent time in Europe, settled back in Chicago,
then moved to Long Island (complete with Tom's string of polo po-
nies)—and then Daisy heard Gatsby's name again.

> "It was a strange coincidence," I said.
> "But it wasn't a coincidence at all."
> "Why not?"
> "Gatsby bought that house so that Daisy would be just across the
> bay." (79)

We still have not learned Gatsby's full story, but he has told Jordan
enough of it to relay to Nick—and with a purpose: Gatsby wants to know
"'if you'll invite Daisy to your house some afternoon and then let him
come over'" (80). Thus Nick is to be a go-between in this rekindled
romance. The afternoon is planned, and Gatsby meets Daisy again and
then takes Nick and Daisy on a tour of his huge mansion; when Gatsby
throws his dozens of custom-made shirts before them, Daisy breaks
down and cries. For years, Gatsby has worked toward this moment, to

recapture Daisy for himself. "There must have been moments even that afternoon when Daisy tumbled short of his dreams—not through her own fault, but because of the colossal vitality of his illusion" (97).

In the next chapter we get still another piece of the puzzle of Jay Gatsby, another part of the story of this self-made man. And "self-made" is the best label for him, for Jay Gatsby had started out as James Gatz, who, at the age of 17, just happened to be at the right spot on the beach of Lake Superior when he saw that a yacht offshore would soon be pushed onto a sandbar. He rowed out to the *Tuolomee* to tell the owner, Dan Cody, and was taken in by the millionaire, eventually becoming his assistant. He should have inherited some of Cody's money, but was cheated out of it by the opportunist Ella Kaye. Still, he had had a taste of wealth. Gatsby went into the army, met and lost Daisy, fought in World War I as an officer, and spent some time after the war at Oxford University. Back in the United States, without money or means, he went to work for Meyer Wolfsheim and apparently made his fortune through bootlegging and other illegal activities. Finally, when he had climbed nearly all the way up the economic ladder, he bought an estate across the bay from Daisy. His climb, in short, had been with the "single dream" of recapturing Daisy.

> He wanted nothing less of Daisy than that she should go to Tom and say: "I never loved you." After she had obliterated four years with that sentence they could decide upon the more practical measures to be taken. . . .
>
> He talked a lot about the past, and I gathered that he wanted to recover something, some idea of himself perhaps, that had gone into loving Daisy. His life had been confused and disordered since then but if he could once return to a certain starting place and go over it slowly, he could find out what that thing was. (111–12)

"'I wouldn't ask too much of her,'" Nick warns Gatsby. "'You can't repeat the past.'. . . 'Can't repeat the past?' he cried incredulously. 'Why of course you can!'" (111) Gatsby is a hopeless romantic, a man of "appalling sentimentality" (112) caught up in a quest to recapture his own past.

Gatsby invites Tom and Daisy to one of his lavish parties, then fires his house staff and hires an entire new crew when Daisy starts to visit him regularly in the afternoon. Rumors about Gatsby have circulated constantly—that "'he's a nephew or a cousin of Kaiser Wilhelm's'" (33), that "'he killed a man once'" (44), that he is the "'underground pipe-line to Canada'"—for curiosity about Gatsby, Nick tells us at this point, was at its highest, and "Gatsby's notoriety" (98) and mystery only deepen.

Now the novel moves quickly toward its climax. All five major characters meet at the Buchanans for lunch on a "broiling" hot afternoon; when the tension and boredom become too much, they decide to drive into the city. Daisy and Gatsby take the Buchanans' car, while Tom drives Gatsby's yellow roadster with Nick and Jordan as passengers. Tom realizes now that his wife is in love with Gatsby, and when he stops for gas at Wilson's garage, Wilson tells him that he is leaving town with Myrtle: he had made "a parallel discovery less than an hour before" (124); that is, that *his* wife is cheating on him. The impact on Tom is catastrophic, for in less than an hour he has lost both his wife and his mistress. He speeds into town—but not before Myrtle, locked in an upstairs bedroom by Wilson, looks out the window and sees Tom in the big yellow car with Jordan next to him (mistaking Jordan for Daisy, as she will soon confuse the two cars).

The five reconvene in a suite at the Plaza Hotel, and Tom, in his last-ditch effort to keep Daisy, attacks Gatsby. Gatsby tells Tom that his wife does not love him, but when he tries to get Daisy to tell Tom that she *never* loved him, she refuses. "'Oh, you want too much. . . . I did love him once—but I loved you too'" (133). Gatsby has pressed too far, and when Tom starts exposing his background and the illegal means by which he has gained his vast wealth, Daisy slips out of his reach. Tom tells them all to drive home, so confident of his power that he lets Daisy and Gatsby drive together in Gatsby's car while he follows with Nick and Jordan in his own. At the "valley of ashes," Myrtle Wilson sees the speeding yellow car approaching and, thinking that it is Tom, breaks free from Wilson and runs into its path. But it is Daisy driving, and she runs over Myrtle without stopping. When Tom and the others arrive at the garage a few minutes later, Myrtle is dead—and Tom thinks that Gatsby has killed her. Back at the Buchanans', Nick finds Gatsby hiding in the bushes, waiting to make sure that Daisy is all right; but when Nick looks into a pantry window, he sees Daisy and Tom "sitting opposite each other at the kitchen table" with "an unmistakable air of natural intimacy" (146). Tom is talking to Daisy (and undoubtedly telling her that their marriage will be better in the future, when he will stop cheating on her), and Daisy . . . is saying nothing. Tom will always believe that Gatsby killed his mistress.

Nick realizes that Gatsby has "broken up like glass against Tom's hard malice" (148), and now, back at Gatsby's mansion, he hears the story of how Gatsby fell in love with Daisy and lost her, how he "had committed himself to the following of a grail" (149). When he leaves Gatsby early the next morning, it is with his greatest praise.

"They're a rotten crowd," I shouted across the lawn. "You're worth the whole damn bunch put together."

> I've always been glad I said that. It was the only compliment I ever gave
> him, because I disapproved of him from beginning to end. (154)

It is also the last time that Nick will see Gatsby alive. The crazed Wilson
goes to the Buchanans' house to find the car that killed his wife—a car
that he assumes belongs to Tom—but Tom tells him that it is Gatsby's
and lets the armed Wilson leave with that information. As Gatsby is
waiting by his pool for a call from Daisy that will never come—"I have an
idea that Gatsby himself didn't believe it would come, and perhaps he no
longer cared" (162)—Wilson shoots Gatsby and then himself.

Nick tries to make arrangements for a funeral, but most of the people
he is able to contact, including Wolfsheim and various guests from
Gatsby's parties, want nothing to do with Gatsby now. Gatsby's father,
Henry C. Gatz, arrives and is impressed that his son has become so
successful, but the funeral procession has only three mourners: Nick,
Gatsby's father, and "Owl-eyes," a drunk Nick met at one of the lavish
parties. Gatsby has died to silence. "'The poor son-of-a-bitch,'" Owl-eyes
says (176), and it is a fitting, if ironic, epithet for Gatsby.

After the funeral, Nick decides to leave the East, which now "was
haunted for me" (178), and go back to the Midwest. But first he ties up a
few loose ends. For one last time, he meets Jordan Baker, who tells him
he has not been "'an honest, straightforward person'" (179), and then
Tom, who tells Nick how hard Myrtle's death was on him and how
Gatsby deserved his death:

> "He threw dust into your eyes just like he did in Daisy's, but he was a tough
> one. He ran over Myrtle like you'd run over a dog and never even stopped his
> car."
>   There was nothing I could say, except the one unutterable fact that it
> wasn't true. (180)

He lets Tom walk away without telling him the truth: that his own wife
killed his mistress. "I couldn't forgive him or like him, but I saw that what
he had done was, to him, entirely justified. It was all very careless and
confused." (180)

Nick pays one last visit to Gatsby's empty house before he leaves—
and finds an obscene word "scrawled by some boy with a piece of brick"
(181); and, like Holden Caulfield in Salinger's *The Catcher in the Rye*, he
erases it, thus preserving some image of Gatsby he still has in his head.
Sprawled on Gatsby's beach, Nick is reminded of how Long Island must
have appeared to the first Dutch sailors—the "dream" that America

represented to its early explorers—and he thinks of the parallel "wonder" when Gatsby

> picked out the green light at the end of Daisy's dock. He had come a long way to this blue lawn, and his dream must have seemed so close that he could hardly fail to grasp it. He did not know that it was already behind him, somewhere back in that vast obscurity beyond the city, where the dark fields of the republic rolled on under the night.

Gatsby, standing in West Egg and looking east to Daisy's dock, failed to understand that the American Dream, which first lured sailors to this new land, has already moved behind him, that is, to somewhere out in the West (or the Midwest), where people are still somehow motivated by such ideals. Gatsby was the last romantic.

> Gatsby believed in the green light, the orglastic future that year by year recedes before us. It eluded us then, but that's no matter—tomorrow we will run faster, stretch out our arms farther. . . . And one fine morning——
> So we beat on, boats against the current, borne back ceaselessly into the past. (182; ellipses in original)

Characters

The title character in *The Great Gatsby* is also the central figure in this mystery novel. It is Jay Gatsby's Horatio Alger, rags-to-riches story that is the focus for readers, as for Nick. Born James Gatz in North Dakota, Gatsby is truly a self-made man, not only financially but because he "sprang from his Platonic conception of himself" (99), as Nick Carraway says in the middle of telling of how Gatsby met Dan Cody:

> He was a son of God—a phrase which, if it means anything, means just that—and he must be about His Father's business, the service of a vast, vulgar, and meretricious beauty. So he invented just the sort of Jay Gatsby that a seventeen-year-old boy would be likely to invent, and to this conception he was faithful to the end. (99)

There is "something gorgeous about him," as Nick tells us, "some heightened sensitivity to the promises of life," and this "responsiveness," this "romantic readiness" (2), is Gatsby's very strength.

But where did Jay Gatsby get this ideal, this "conception of himself" to which he must be true? From American history and myth, Fitzgerald intimates. When Gatsby's father appears for the funeral, he shows Nick Carraway "a ragged old copy of a book called *Hopalong Cassidy*" (174)

which Gatsby had read as a boy, and in which he had kept a daily
schedule and a list of resolutions. "'Jimmy was bound to get ahead,'" his
father tells Nick proudly, for he always "'had some resolves like this . . .
about improving his mind'" (175). But the schedule and list are echoes of
Benjamin Franklin's *Autobiography* of a century before, the popular
work wherein the notion of the self-made man was first articulated: that
anyone—with industry, perseverance, thrift, and so forth—could become
successful. Gatsby is living proof of Franklin's wisdom—except that now
he is dead proof.

Where did he go wrong? Part of the problem can be traced back to
Franklin and to the notion that, by following some mechanical prescrip-
tion for self-help, one will automatically advance. (The same idea is
behind all of today's best-sellers that guarantee success in health, wealth,
diet, and so forth through following some simple formula.) The larger
failure here is the perversion of ends by means. Gatsby's goal is success,
and that success will be gauged by his possession of *things*, most notably
of Daisy. On his climb up, Gatsby met Daisy, and her beauty and social
position came to represent to him true success in American terms. Now
he showers her with shirts, shows off his house and cars in his effort to
win her back. But these are only possessions, and, like Daisy and his very
profession, they will betray him. He is a bootlegger, an associate of the
gambler Wolfsheim, and he is now selling bonds illegally (it is never made
exactly clear what he is doing, but it is obviously outside the law). When
Tom finds out about some of his shady dealings, he is able to confront
Gatsby with them and thus to scare Daisy. So while Gatsby's dream or
goal may be noble, his methods defeat him in the end.

Gatsby is also defeated by his own dream, or, perhaps more accurately,
by the rigidity with which he holds on to it. If only he would not have tried
to force Daisy to deny her love for Tom completely, he could have her, we
sense. But Gatsby is the self-made man, and he therefore holds onto his
dreams even more violently than others; there is, in short, an almost
adolescent fixation in Gatsby that gives his dreams a rigid, inflexible
quality. Like the innocent, pure Galahad who sought the Holy Grail,
Gatsby's very strengths are his limitations—at least in this corrupt world of
the very rich of "the valley of ashes"—and his quest is bound to fail.
Gatsby's "incorruptible dream" (155) becomes "the dead dream" (135), for
Gatsby "paid a high price for living too long with a single dream" (162). It is
not his gauche manners or rough edges—his "gorgeous pink rag of a suit"
(154), as Nick once describes Gatsby's dress—that finally defeat him, but
his own character limitations in a world that is itself morally corrupt.

One could argue that Gatsby really commits suicide, that he knows
Daisy will not call and is only waiting for Wilson, the inevitable agent of

the fate Gatsby knows awaits him. He has climbed to the top of the social ladder and seen how empty and shallow the world of this decadent American aristocracy really is; he kills himself rather than let his dream die. An example of the moral bankruptcy of this world is that Gatsby is killed by his lover's husband's lover's husband. Put another way, Tom's lover's husband kills Tom's wife's lover. It is a world in which relationships, like personal character, are marked by moral confusion and corruption. Gatsby is both author and victim of this evil.

The Buchanans are the perfect representations of the corruption of this world, of what has happened to American life since the "New World" was discovered. Bored, restless, unhappy, the Buchanans represent the epitome of the American upper classes gone to seed. Tom Buchanan is a "harsh," "cruel" man whose mind, like his body, is in decline. "Something was making him nibble at the edge of stale ideas as if his sturdy physical egotism no longer nourished his peremptory heart" (21). He is, in Fitzgerald's first telling description of him, "one of those men who reach such an acute limited excellence at 21 that everything afterwards savors of anti-climax" (6). Certainly his ideas are "stale" and racist, as his actions and behavior are brutal and selfish.

His wife is little better. Daisy Buchanan possesses a certain fragile and ephemeral beauty, as well as a seductive attraction (both to Nick and to Gatsby) parallel to the physical and social power of her husband, but she proves her shallowness by the end, for she will not give up her security with Tom for the romantic possibilities with Gatsby. She is not worthy of Gatsby's love, which is part of what Nick means when he says to him, "'You're worth the whole damned bunch put together.'" Sophisticated but insincere and cynical, she tells Nick that she hopes her daughter will be a fool, for "'that's the best thing a girl can be in this world, a beautiful little fool'" (17). The description might fit Daisy as well, if one added *callous* and *inane*. She kills Myrtle, lets Gatsby die for it, and then runs away with Tom without any explanation to Nick. She and Tom will soon undoubtedly show up at another watering hole of the rich. They are people without values or purpose wandering in this postwar world— restless, listless, pointless.

As noted at the start of this analysis, Nick is the central character in the drama here in the sense that he learns the most from the story. (Gatsby learns something, but it is negative knowledge that he cannot act on, since he is murdered, or commits suicide, soon after his revelation.) Much of what Nick learns is elemental: that Tom has a mistress, for example (or, in larger terms, what contemporary marriage is like); that someone could actually 'fix' the World Series (or, again in larger terms, the depth of the corruption in this world). His experiences with Gatsby and the Buchanans help Nick mature: "After Gatsby's death the East was haunted for me like that, distorted beyond my eyes' power of correction" (178). Nick Carraway has grown up, moved from his midwestern naiveté to an (eastern) recognition of the corruption of the world, and in the end he retreats back to his roots. He turns 30 the day of the confrontation in the Plaza Hotel, and that birthday marks his entrance into a new maturity. The responsibility he takes for Gatsby's funeral is one example of that new strength. Nick, in fact, is the only character in the novel to demonstrate any moral growth. He feels an obligation to his dead friend Gatsby ("I was responsible," he says, and "I wanted to get somebody for him" [165]), and he acts on this commitment.

As with *Adventures of Huckleberry Finn*, *The Great Gatsby* works best because of its narrative point of view. The story of Gatsby would have little power told from his own perspective or from that of the Buchanans, but through Nick's eyes the story takes on new meaning. The novel is narrated through a prism: Nick filters the information through his own particular consciousness, and that consciousness has a certain bifurcated vision. Twice, for example, Nick tells us that he "disapproved" of Gatsby, that Gatsby "represented everything for which I have an unaffected scorn" (2, 154)—and yet Gatsby is also "'worth the whole damn bunch put together.'" How is that contradiction possible? It is because Nick has a peculiarly ambivalent relationship to the major characters in the story. He sees the Buchanans' moral emptiness, and yet he still looks up to them. They are in a class above him (as he makes clear in the early pages of the novel), and he admires their power and wealth. When he sees Tom the last time, he keeps the truth—that his wife killed his mistress—from him. Why? Nick says it is because they are like children, but it is also because he *treats* them like children, as well as with the respect that Americans tend to reserve for the very rich. Similarly, Nick disapproves of Gatsby—of his humble beginnings, his illegal wealth—and yet he also admires his resourcefulness and the dreams that take him from poverty to wealth. Nick, like the Buchanans, is a "snob" (1)—which is what generates his disapproval of Gatsby—but he is also a romantic, which explains his admiration for the title character. It is this split vision in Nick, this double perspective on the story and its characters, that creates the tension in the novel and gives it some of its depth. (One of the reasons the several filmed versions of *The Great Gatsby* come off as flat is because it is hard to capture that first-person ambivalence on film.)

There is, however, another point about how this story is told. Like *Huckleberry Finn*, the narrator here cannot be completely trusted. For example, Nick tells us on the first page of his story that "I'm inclined to reserve all judgments" (1) and, later, that "I am one of the few honest people that I have ever known" (60). But he makes judgments all the time, he does not tell Tom Buchanan the truth about Daisy, and at the end Jordan Baker accuses him of not being "'an honest, straightforward person'" (179); thus his honesty and tolerance have certain limits, and readers must listen to Nick with a skeptical ear.

The other characters here are merely players in this tragedy. Jordan Baker is someone who cheats at golf and is "careless" in her relationships with other people, as Nick tells her. Like the Buchanans, Jordan has no consideration for others. Myrtle Wilson is a crude, "coarse" woman who is apparently attractive to Tom because of the contrast with his wife—the fragile, ethereal beauty of Daisy is certainly in clear opposition to the "thickish figure" (25) of Myrtle. Her husband is a nonentity—insecure, pallid, "anaemic," almost a mirror of the "valley of ashes" that surrounds him—until the end.

Themes

The major theme in *The Great Gatsby* is the American Dream or what we can call here the *end* of that Dream. Fitzgerald may not have been the first writer to develop this idea (Theodore Dreiser in *Sister Carrie* and Sinclair Lewis in *Babbitt* both explored it earlier), but he has since become known as our best chronicler of it, particularly in its 1920s version: that the American Dream is bankrupt and that the ideals on which this country was founded have been corrputed by both the wealth and privilege of the few and the materialism of the many.

What makes Fitzgerald's version so telling is its fresh social criticism and satire. Few novels have the graphic, comic images and incidents of *The Great Gatsby*. In scene after scene, Fitzgerald portrays the moral degeneration and mounting materialism of American life, but with brushstrokes both subtle and sure. Gatsby's parties are probably the major example of this power of the novel, and Fitzgerald lets readers spend a great deal of time wandering the lawns of Gatsby's mansion, observing this lost world of partiers. Here is the Jazz Age, with all its "romantic possibilities" (110)—but also with a kind of decadent absurdity. At the first party Nick attends, the drunken Owl-eyes in the Gothic library tells Jordan and Nick an astonishing fact about the books: "'They're real. . . . Absolutely real—have pages and everything'" (45). He is surprised, in this make-believe world, that there is anything authentic. At the end of this party, a car loses a wheel in an accident and the drunk driver cannot understand why it will not go; symbolically, the society is not working, and yet its citizens ignore this fact. (Note also that a car loses its wheel in the accident when Tom is first caught in infidelity; the imagery of the novel is almost flawlessly interwoven.)

Cars and driving, in fact, provide the main metaphors for the social criticism here. *The Great Gatsby* may be the first American automobile novel, the first novel in which this symbol of American speed and mobility figures so prominently. On the one hand, cars are a primary symbol of the crass materialism of this world: characters here are always showing them off or trying to buy and sell them. People in this 1920s world are beginning to define each other by their possessions, particularly by their cars, and this is the very reason Myrtle and Gatsby are killed: people confuse the cars with their drivers. (Myrtle is run over because she thinks that it is Tom she is jumping in front of; Gatsby is murdered because Wilson thinks he was driving the car that killed his wife.) It is what Marxists call commodity fetishism: the objects have not only come to stand for their owners—they have actually become more important than people.

The other idea that comes out of this car/driver metaphor is the notion of carelessness. Jordan Baker is a "careless" driver, Nick Carraway says, and he warns her that she might one day meet another driver "'just as careless as yourself'" (59). In their final parting, Jordan says Nick was right: she met another careless driver—meaning Nick. A page later, when Nick meets Tom Buchanan for the last time, he uses the same word, and it sums up the world of the rich and irresponsible:

> They were careless people, Tom and Daisy—they smashed up things and creatures and then retreated back into their money or their vast carelessness, or whatever it was that kept them together, and let other people clean up the mess they had made. (180–81)

It was in the 1920s that consumer goods and commodities first became a major force in American social life, and Fitzgerald was the first writer to capture their fatal attraction for us. Writers who have followed Fitzgerald have only continued his themes, but none has surpassed his portrait of a culture undermined by its very love of *things*.

The chief metaphor for the social themes in the novel is the "valley of ashes" that Nick describes on his first trip into New York with Tom. Above this "waste land" is a billboard advertising an oculist, Doctor T. J. Eckleburg, but the face has been worn away, and only the eyes remain: "eyes, dimmed a little by many paintless days under sun and rain, brood on over the solemn dumping ground" (23). In the religious symbolism of the novel, Eckleburg comes to represent God, and this waste land, what America has become. (The image of the waste land was, of course, a common one in the 1920s, especially after T. S. Eliot's 1922 poem *The Waste Land*.) This is an apt symbol for the America Fitzgerald sees, a postwar world in which material acquisition has replaced any older system of values and ideals. When Wilson is staring out the window of his garage after Myrtle's death, he says, "'You may fool me, but you can't fool God!'"; and Michaelis, who runs the coffee shop next door and is watching over Wilson, "saw with a shock that he was looking at the eyes of Dr. T. J. Eckleburg. . . . 'God sees everything,' repeated Wilson" (160). The symbolism here is complex but clear. If God is Eckleburg—the faceless eyes that overlook the vast waste land that America has become, this "solemn dumping ground"—then His son is Jay Gatsby, "a son of God" (99) who came down to earth to save man, but was murdered instead. The world is finally too corrupt for any religious salvation. (The Arthurian "grail" image of Gatsby's quest conveys much the same idea.) If the green light at the end of Daisy's dock represents dreams, then the "valley of ashes" represents what those dreams have become in modern America.

Style and Language

As in most major works of literature, the formal elements in *The Great Gatsby* consistently reinforce the power of Fitzgerald's ideas. The analysis above reveals some of the ways that language, imagery, and symbolism in the novel emphasize its themes, and we have already discussed *point of view* and how important it is in this story. What we still need to note is the structure of the novel. Told in a number of flashbacks, the novel really unfolds in a series of episodic scenes, like a string of pearls, and each scene is almost an autonomous and discrete short story, with little exposition between individual stories. The novel works well because Fitzgerald is so clever at parceling out the story of Gatsby. We learn his story, in bits and pieces—both the real version and his made-up ones—at the same time as rumors and legends about him grow. Simultaneously, it becomes increasingly clear that a man who does business by phone at night to major cities (and who is also a business associate of Meyer Wolfsheim and knows the police commissioner) must be involved in something illegal.

Another noteworthy element in the novel is Fitzgerald's descriptive power. His language has a definite force, and again and again he constructs the perfectly telling phrase or image. When Nick first sees Daisy and Jordan in the Buchanan house, he describes "an enormous couch on which two young women were buoyed up as though upon an anchored balloon" (8). Gatsby later characterizes Daisy as having a voice that's "'full of money'" (120). Colors are also important in the novel (green and white especially), and even names have their significance: most are of plants (Daisy, Carraway) or of animals (Wolfsheim). (Study the epic list of names of those who attended Gatsby's parties that summer [61–63] and this idea will be borne out.) Few novels in American literature are as glamorous and as colorful—perhaps because Fitzgerald himself was half in love with the world he was describing, as his biography bears out.

Finally, readers should not miss the humor in the novel, as when Nick tells Daisy jokingly that Chicago so misses her that "'All the cars have the left rear wheel painted black as a mourning wreath, and there's a persistent wail along the north shore'" (10). (Notice again the car metaphor and, here, the anticipation of the funeral at the end of the novel.) But the humor also includes the ironic use of language and incident (the epic list of names, for instance, or the car's losing its wheel).

TEACHING THE NOVEL

Teaching Suggestions

The Great Gatsby is the quintessential twentieth-century novel on the American Dream. Less an adolescent work than others studied here, it is still a novel of initiation; in the course of the novel he narrates, Nick Carraway learns a great deal about the attitudes and values that motivate behavior in America and—as he and the readers learn together—kill people as well as dreams.

Students may be interested in seeing the original American Dream formula—or, at least, its first secular, self-help version—in Benjamin Franklin's *Autobiography* (148–57), with its mechanical list of 13 "virtues" (e.g., "Humility. Imitate Jesus and Socrates."), the weekly schedule for the regulation of each virtue (illustrated for "Temperance. Eat not to dullness; drink not to elevation."), and the daily calendar for "Order" that resembles so closely young James Gatz's schedule on the flyleaf of *Hopalong Cassidy*. Students should be asked to consider what is wrong with this formula for success (stress on means over ends), and how the mechanical pursuit of "moral perfection" (Franklin's avowed goal) is connected to the materialism that Fitzgerald claims is destroying the dream. More to the point, how is the American Dream different today: What do people want, and how do they go about getting it? (Students can discuss what possessions or status symbols are important today—cars, electronic equipment—and how these differ from those of the 1920s.)

An easy access to the major ideas in the novel can be gained through its *images*, both the material possessions (such as cars and shirts) that are so prominent and the more symbolic metaphors of the "valley of ashes" and the search for the grail that lie just beneath its surface. One indication of the novel's artistry is that few of its elements are unconnected to its central themes, and discussion of the one (cars, the valley of ashes) usually gets to the other (decadence, the end of the Dream). Another aspect of the novel's beauty is its organization: we recall *The Great Gatsby*, not as one continuous narration, but as a series of brilliant and colorful scenes—such as the first party in New York, the confrontation at the Plaza Hotel, Myrtle's murder, Gatsby's murder and funeral. Students can start the novel by dissecting one such scene (such as Gatsby's first party in Chapter 3) and looking for clues of restlessness, mystery, dissipation, and so forth.

What students should also recognize at some point is the importance of *point of view* in the novel, both the uniqueness of Nick's perspective and his unreliability. Have students try to tell the story from another point of view (Tom, Daisy, Gatsby himself) to see how different the novel would be and what would be lost. Also, consider the evidence that Nick is not the "honest" narrator "inclined to reserve all judgments" (1) he claims to be. Students can be collecting evidence of the contradictions in his testimony from the beginning of the novel.

Discussion and Writing Ideas

1. Did you ever pursue a goal with single-minded devotion? What happened? Would you have gained your end in any other way?
2. Brainstorm and then draft your own formula for success; exchange formulas with another student and discuss them. Then write up what you believe to be your formula.
3. You have just found out that your best friend did something illegal (shoplifted a valuable item) and is in jail. What would you do? Why?
4. Is Jay Gatsby a "hero"? Why or why not? Do a brief *character sketch* of this central character. Is he the victim or the author of his tragedy?
5. How do you explain the contradiction that Nick "disapproves" of Gatsby and yet says that he's "'worth the whole damn bunch put together'"? What are Nick's deepest sentiments about Jay Gatsby?
6. What does Nick Carraway learn in the course of the novel? (List specific values and lessons.) Why does he go back to the Midwest at its end? What kind of moral growth does he demonstrate?
7. Discuss the significance of one of the minor characters in the novel— Jordan Baker or George Wilson, for example.

8. *The Great Gatsby* is one of the tragic love stories of the twentieth century. What is the attraction of Daisy Buchanan for Jay Gatsby? Why does Daisy abandon Gatsby for Tom? Explain. (And where do we find such stories today—movies? soap operas?)
9. Analyze the use of colors in the novel. What is significant about their use here? What does the "green light" represent to Gatsby, for example? Why green?
10. Write a short biography of Scott and Zelda Fitzgerald, showing how their lives are connected to the novel.
11. Write a short report on the 1920s and the Jazz Age. What are the parallels to our own age?

Bridging to Other Works

The Autobiography of Benjamin Franklin (Yale paperback, 1964).

Mark Twain, *The Adventures of Huckleberry Finn* (1884); see Chapter 2. Compare what Huck and Nick observe in their respective societies about loyalty, human cruelty, and so forth.

Stephen Crane, *The Red Badge of Courage* (1895); see Chapter 7. What does Henry Fleming learn that parallels the lessons of *The Great Gatsby*?

F. Scott Fitzgerald, short stories. Many of Fitzgerald's stories ("The Diamond as Big as the Ritz," "The Rich Boy," "Babylon Revisited," "Winter Dreams") repeat the subjects, settings, and themes of *The Great Gatsby*.

Sherwood Anderson, *Winesburg, Ohio* (1919). These stories of life in a small midwestern town anticipate the subjects of Fitzgerald's novel.

Sinclair Lewis, *Babbitt* (1922). This is another novel of the 1920s that captures the growing materialism and loss of essential values in American life.

T. S. Eliot, *The Waste Land* (1922). This is a difficult poem, but students may find parallels to Fitzgerald's novel, particularly in the idea of spiritual decay.

Ernest Hemingway, *The Nick Adams Stories* (1972, many of them from *In Our Time*, 1925). This collection of short stories centers on a character (Nick Adams) who is learning about the same world as Nick Carraway.

———, *The Sun Also Rises* (1926). Hemingway and Fitzgerald are generally considered the two best writers of "the lost generation," and Hemingway's best novel explores some of the same themes— disillusionment, moral shallowness—that we find in *The Great Gatsby*.

Jack Schaefer, *Shane* (1949). This classic American Western concerns heroism and initiation.

Larry McMurtry, *Horseman, Pass By* (1961). This contemporary American initiation story is better known to many under the title of the film adapted from it, *Hud*.

Robert Cormier, *The Chocolate War* (YA, 1974); see Chapter 3. How is the world of Trinity similar to the world Nick views?

7 "I know how you are, Henry"

THE RED BADGE OF COURAGE

Author: Stephen Crane (1871–1900)
Genre: psychological realism, naturalism
Time of novel: Civil War (1861–1865)
Locale: some unspecified battle site (but probably Chancellorsville, Virginia)
Point of view: limited omniscient
First published: 1895
Edition used: Penguin paperback (1983); 212 pp.; with an introduction by Pascal Covici, Jr.
Grade level: 8–11
Principal characters:
  Henry Fleming, an untested Civil War recruit
  Jim Conklin ("the tall soldier"), a regimental comrade Henry has known "since childhood"
  Wilson ("the loud soldier"), another friend of Henry's in the regiment
  "The tattered man," a wounded soldier Henry meets wandering behind the lines
  A soldier with a "cheery voice" who leads Henry back to his own regiment

ANALYSIS OF THE NOVEL

Story and Setting

The Red Badge of Courage is one of the ultimate war experiences in fiction, even though its young author—Crane was 25 when he wrote the novel—had never been near a battlefield himself, had, in fact, not even been born when the Civil War ended. The location for the novel is never specified. (Modern scholars have determined that Crane based his account on the battle of Chancellorsville, which took place in northern Virginia on May 1–2, 1863, and was won by the Confederate commander, General Robert E. Lee.) But if the location is left purposely vague, the settings are not. Crane's scenes are both painful and colorful, because of the psychologically intense focus on the protagonist, Henry Fleming, and because of Crane's vivid painter's eye.

When the novel opens, Henry Fleming's untested 304th New York Regiment has been bivouacked for some weeks in what is starting to resemble "a sort of eternal camp" (44). "The tall soldier," Henry's tentmate Jim Conklin, hears a rumor—on which information in this novel is so often based—that the army is about to move, but, of course, the rumor proves to be false. Meanwhile, Henry, "a youthful private," has retreated to his tent "to be alone with some new thoughts that had lately come to him" (45). He realizes that he is "about to mingle in one of those great affairs of the earth" (46) and is uncertain about how he will react in battle. In the only regression in the forward narrative movement of the novel, Henry thinks back to leaving home for the army. His widowed mother had "discouraged him" from enlisting for some time and, when he finally did join, gave him no last patriotic words but warned him instead to "'Watch out, and be a good boy'" (49). His triumphant trip by train from home has been followed by "months of monotonous life in a camp" (50), and now he wonders, when they finally *do* fight, whether he will run from battle. No one else seems to be undergoing his internal struggle; he wishes he were back on his farm.

But suddenly they are marching west and, after several days, are close to battle. "He was about to be measured" (68), Henry realizes. "They were going to look at war, the red animal—war, the blood-swollen god" (71). Henry wants to cry out and warn his fellows of their imminent danger; instead, when the self-absorbed youth lags behind, his young lieutenant begins "heartily to beat him with a sword, calling out in a loud and insolent voice: 'Come, young man, get up into ranks there. No skulking 'll do here'" (72). Henry hates the "aimlessness" of their march, for he is impatient to test himself in battle.

> The youth had been taught that a man became another thing in a battle. He saw his salvation in such a change. Hence this waiting was an ordeal for him. . . . He wished to return to camp, knowing that this affair was a blue demonstration; or else to go into a battle and discover that he had been a fool in his doubts, and was, in truth, a man of traditional courage. (73)

When they finally reach the battle site, Henry's friend Wilson asks him to keep a small packet of letters "done up in a yellow envelope," for Wilson thinks it is "'my first and last battle,'" ending his request "in a quavering sob of pity for himself" (75-6). Other soldiers apparently have the same doubts and fears that besiege Henry.

Readied as reserves, the 304th watch the command in front of them dissolve and run. "The composite monster which had caused the other troops to flee had not then appeared. He resolved to get a view of it, and then, he thought he might very likely run better than the rest of them" (81). When the 304th is charged by Confederate forces, the general urges them on: "'You've got to hold 'em back!'" (83). They do, but Henry fights automatically.

He suddenly lost concern for himself, and forgot to look at a menacing fate. He became not a man but a member. He felt that something of which he was a part—a regiment, an army, a cause, or a country—was in a crisis. He was welded into a common personality which was dominated by a single desire. For some moments he could not flee no more than a little finger can commit a revolution from a hand. (84)

Henry feels "the subtle battle brotherhood . . . a mysterious fraternity born of the smoke and danger of death" (84). But he also feels "the acute exasperation of a pestered animal" and the "impotency . . . of a driven beast" (85). The lieutenant beats a man who leaves his position; soldiers are being killed around Henry, including his own captain. But at last "an exultant yell went along the quivering line" (87). They have repulsed the rebel charge. The youth naps and awakens to the realization: "So it was over at last! The supreme trial had been passed. The red, formidable difficulties of war had been vanquished" (90).

Henry's "ecstasy of self-satisfaction" is rudely broken as the rebel troops attack again, and, when a few of his comrades turn and flee, Henry does likewise. "Directly he began to speed toward the rear in great leaps. . . . On his face was all the horror of those things which he imagined" (93). The lieutenant tries to stop him with his sword, but the youth runs "like a blind man." He imagines that the regiment is fleeing behind him and is shocked when he overhears a general, surveying the battle scene, saying, "'They've held 'em, by heavens!'" (97). The youth feels betrayed that his comrades have fought while he has fled. "The youth cringed as if discovered in a crime" (98). He walks further into a quiet woods and comes across a corpse in a "chapel" made of arching boughs. "The youth gave a shriek as he confronted the thing. . . . The dead man and the living man exchanged a long look" (101). But Henry has gained some "assurance" in nature, for, when the silence of the chapel is next broken by the noises of war, he heads toward the battle. He knows that "it was an ironical thing for him to be running thus toward that which he had been at such pains to avoid" (103), but the battle "was like the grinding of an immense and terrible machine to him. Its complexities and powers, its grim processes, fascinated him. He must go close and see it produce corpses" (105).

After some time he comes to a road and finds "a blood-stained crowd streaming to the rear" (105), which he joins. "He wished that he, too, had a wound, a red badge of courage," for he imagines the wounded men are staring at "the letters of guilt he felt burned into his brow" (110). Henry travels with two of these soldiers. A "spectral soldier" who "had the grey seal of death already upon his face" (106) and "seemed always looking for a place, like one who goes to choose a grave" (111) turns out to be Jim Conklin, Henry's childhood friend. Henry promises to take care of him, but Jim wanders away, apparently looking for his "rendezvous," and, when he finds it, does a horrible death-dance, falls, and dies. The youth shakes his fist at the battlefield, in frustration at this death, but can only say, "'Hell—.'" Crane concludes this powerful scene: "The red sun was pasted in the sky like a wafer" (116).

Henry, still feeling as if he carries a great "crime concealed in his bosom," escapes "the tattered man" who has befriended him but whose questions seem aimed at uncovering the source of his guilt. "They were ever upraising the ghost of shame on the stick of their curiosity" (120). Henry envies the dead, for his flight has only increased his own self-doubts, and he feels separated from the other men he sees on the road. "He now conceded it to be impossible that he should ever become a hero. He was a craven loon" (126). Only a defeat of his army would produce a "moral vindication" and erase "the sore badge of his dishonor" (127).

Henry tries to question another fleeing soldier, who strikes him in the head with his rifle, and now the youth has his own real "wound." Wandering that evening, he is befriended by a "man of the cheery voice" who leads the youth back to his own regiment's camp. Dreading "ridicule" from his comrades, Henry instead finds comfort. Wilson is the sentry; after Henry tells him that he had "'an awful time. I got separated from th' reg'ment'" (139), Wilson promises, "'I'll take keer 'a yeh'" (140). Wilson bandages what he thinks is Henry's bullet wound, gives him his bedding, and puts him to sleep on the ground.

The next morning, Wilson continues to mother Henry, who now complains about his rough handling. But Henry notices the changes that have come over his friend, who "was no more a loud young soldier" (147). Henry, too, has changed, if only in his mind.

> He did not give a great deal of thought to these battles that lay directly before him. . . . He had been taught that many obligations of a life were easily avoided. The lessons of yesterday had been that retribution was a laggard and blind. . . . He could leave much to chance. Besides, a faith in

himself had secretly blossomed. There was a little flower of confidence growing within him. He was now a man of experience. (153)

Henry has learned a great deal, but he has not given up some of his heroic illusions about himself: "furthermore, how could they kill him who was the chosen of gods and doomed to greatness?" He now has "scorn" for the others who fled battle. "As for himself, he had fled with discretion and dignity" (153). He now "felt quite competent to return home and make the hearts of the people glow with stories of war" (154).

On this second day of battle, the youth's regiment is "marched to relieve a command that had lain long in some damp trenches" (155) and then retreats through the woods. Henry feels "rage and exasperation" at the relentless foe and at his own commanders. The enemy attacks, and Henry fights instinctively, "like a dog," and, in fact, at one point is fighting "almost alone," thus drawing the notice of the lieutenant. "He called out to the youth: 'By heavens, if I had ten thousand wild cats like you I could tear th' stomach outa this war in less'n a week!'" (166). His comrades look at him as "a war devil," while Henry sees himself as a "knight." "He had been a tremendous figure, no doubt" (166).

During a break in the fighting, Henry and Wilson go to find a stream to fill the canteens of their comrades, but instead they overhear a conversation between the general and another officer who has volunteered the 304th to help repulse an attack. "'I don't believe many of your mule drivers will get back,'" the general concludes. The effect of this conversation is to turn the youth "aged . . . to learn suddenly that he was very insignificant" (171). But the knowledge also makes the youth and his friend special, at least to themselves: "They were the only ones who possessed an inner knowledge" (173).

Henry's regiment charges the rebel lines, hesitates, and is ravaged by enemy fire. The lieutenant rouses them, and Wilson starts again, which incites the rest of the men. They move forward, stop again, and then Henry, Wilson, and the lieutenant together lead the regiment in a final charge. When the flag bearer is shot, the two youths wrest the flag away from his death-like grip, and Henry takes it from his friend; but by now the regiment is falling back. Henry's "mortification and rage" center on the officer who called them "mule drivers." The regiment is fired on by the advancing enemy, but, after a short skirmish, the enemy retreats, and Henry's comrades again feel vindicated.

The impetus of enthusiasm was theirs again. They gazed about them with looks of uplifted pride, feeling new trust in the grim, always confident weapons in their hands. And they were men. (187)

Although they must retreat to their earlier position, the youth feels "a considerable joy in musing upon his performance during the charge" (190). But the general rides up to tell the colonel of the regiment of the "'awful mess you made'" by stopping "'a hundred feet this side of a very pretty success. . . . If your men had gone a hundred feet farther you would have made a great charge, but as it is—what a lot of mud diggers you've got anyway!'" (190–91). In spite of the general's reproach, the lieutenant and his men feel they fought well. And when Henry and Wilson hear that they were praised by their officers for leading the charge, "They were very happy, and their hearts swelled with grateful affection for the colonel and the youthful lieutenant" (194).

The youth is now filled with "serene self-confidence" (195) and surveys the war from above the battle. The regiment again advances and again is halted by enemy fire, but it is roused by the colonel who orders that they charge. "At the yelled words of command the soldiers sprang forward in eager leaps" (201). They are now "in a state of frenzy," "wild with an enthusiasm of unselfishness" and "recklessness," including Henry, who "felt the daring spirit of a savage religion-mad. He was capable of profound sacrifices, a tremendous death" (202).

In this final charge, Henry, Wilson, and their comrades overrun a section of the enemy's lines, capture their colors, and take four prisoners. Wilson and Henry rest "side by side and congratulated each other" (206). But their victory is short-lived, for the regiment is ordered to retrace its steps. "They trampled slowly back over the field across which they had run in a mad scamper" (208) and back toward the river. The mind of the youth "was undergoing a subtle change" (208). He realizes that he has escaped death and that his public bravery has canceled his private shame. "He saw that he was good" (209). But he cannot escape "the somber phantom of the desertion in the fields" (210) and the memory of the tattered soldier. Still, among the braggings of his comrades, he is able to

> look back upon the brass and bombast of his earlier gospels and see them truly. He was gleeful when he discovered that he now despised them.
>
> With this conviction came a store of assurance. He felt a quiet manhood, nonassertive but a sturdy and strong blood. He knew that he would no more quail before his guides wherever they should point. He had been to touch the great death, and found that, after all, it was but the great death. He was a man. (211)

In spite of the rain and the mud, "the youth smiled, for he saw that the world was a world for him, though many discovered it to be made of oaths and walking sticks. He had rid himself of the red sickness of battle. The sultry nightmare was in the past" (211–12). He now can think of nature, home, the future—"an existence of soft and eternal peace." "Over the river," Crane concludes, "a golden ray of sun came through the hosts of leaden rain clouds" (212).

Characters

For a realistic novel, *The Red Badge of Courage* is notably lacking in distinctive characterization. None of the half-dozen or so major figures in the novel are given much of a physical description, and half of them do not even have names. The soldier who leads Henry back to his regiment at the end of the first day of fighting, to cite the easiest example, is neither named nor described, except as "the cheery man." In fact, when he leaves Henry, "it suddenly occurred to the youth that he had not once seen his face" (137). This faceless figure thus takes on something of an allegorical quality: he is more important for what he does (or stands for) than for how he looks—he is "the cheery man" who helps Henry. Likewise with the other secondary characters in the novel. The "tattered man" who befriends Henry behind the lines is never named. The nameless lieutenant is recognizable mainly for the oaths he utters, the sword he wields to keep his men in the fighting, and the hand wound he receives. Jim Conklin, who is referred to as "the tall soldier" and then, just before his death, as the "spectral soldier," has little identity other than these labels. The effect of this blurry characterization is to keep us focused on Henry Fleming; other characters exist as mirrors to his center of consciousness.

The character we see most, other than Fleming, is Wilson, who goes through a major transformation. This "loud soldier," who begins the novel willing to fight Jim Conklin over the reliability of the latter's rumor, is transformed by that first day of battle into a peacemaker.

> He was no more a loud young soldier. There was about him now a fine reliance. He showed a quiet belief in his purposes and his abilities. And this inward confidence evidently enabled him to be indifferent to little words of other men aimed at him. (147)

This "blatant child," who earlier possessed "an audacity grown from his inexperience, thoughtless, headstrong, jealous, and filled with a tinsel courage" (147–48), has apparently "now climbed a peak of wisdom from which he could perceive himself as a very wee thing" (148). He suffers "great shame" at having asked Henry to hold his packet of letters—at having been afraid for his own death. Now, after the first day of battle, he must humble himself to Henry and ask for those letters back. But he does, and he goes on to act heroically the next day, freed from both his fears and his false bravado.

Wilson is important because his own growth is in such contrast to Henry Fleming's. The reason all of the other characters, including Wilson, are so poorly rendered is because the focus of the novel is on Henry's internal struggle. In this sense, *The Red Badge of Courage* is less about war than about its psychological effects on those who participate in it—in particular, on the mind of Henry Fleming, as he wrestles with himself in this war situation. And if the other characters appear rather fuzzy in this impressionistic or psychological painting of battle, the character of Henry Fleming stands out in bold relief, a three-dimensional character who is undergoing a powerful life experience and whose thoughts and feelings about that experience are almost always before us.

Henry Fleming actually goes through a series of changes that can be charted through the novel: the fear and doubt of the opening pages, the "ecstasy of self-satisfaction" after the first brief skirmish, the anger and betrayal after his comrades have held, the myriad of emotions as he wanders away from his regiment, and his conflicting feelings on the last day of battle. Much of the critical discussion about *The Red Badge of Courage* in recent years has centered on the question of whether Henry Fleming *has* in fact changed by the end of the novel. Finally to settle the question of Henry's growth is difficult, and this difficulty is compounded by several factors, not least of which is Crane's *ironic tone*, with which he describes Henry's actions and thoughts throughout the novel from an amused distance.

Our focus should be on what Crane wants us to see—not the final development of this one character, but a recognition of how limited each person's growth can be. The novel is great in part because it allows us to enter the confused and constantly changing mind of its young central character, a mind that is continually fooling itself, or, better, rationalizing its own traumatic experiences. Henry Fleming does not end the novel merely a hero. He ends it as a man who has been through an incredible experience, who *has* touched "the great death," and who has survived to tell the tale—but nonetheless a man with a number of his illusions intact, who will undoubtedly go to his grave telling stories about his war experiences that simply are not true. Henry Fleming fails to understand the full import of what he has experienced. If he begins the novel as a youth who "knew nothing of himself" (52), he ends it as a man who only knows *something*. The transformation, Henry's initiation into adulthood, is, finally, incomplete.

Themes

If the central theme of *The Red Badge of Courage* is this limited initiation of Henry Fleming through battle, there are a number of subsidiary themes, mostly centering on the idea of war itself. Crane's novel has long been cited as one of the classic studies of war precisely because it raises so many of these issues.

One of the main themes in the novel is the gap between the protagonist's dreams of what war will be like, his expectations of battle, and its actuality. There are a number of examples of this gap, from the "singular absence of heroic poses" (86) in the regiment's first encounter with the enemy, to the recognition after the last battle that the distances the troops have moved "as compared with the brilliant measurings of his mind, were trivial and ridiculous" (189). If Henry has failed to give up all of his illusions about himself and war by the end of the novel, the reader must surely recognize them. War is hell in the novel: dirty, boring, bloody, violent, and rarely touched by grace or heroism.

Crane's treatment of this theme defines him as a naturalist. In the first officers' conversation that Henry overhears, the regimental colonel shouts, "'Don't forget that box of cigars!'" (59). And Henry "wondered what a box of cigars had to do with war" (59). The answer, of course, is "everything!" War is not filled with gallant, heroic acts, but with trivial, boring repetitions of marching, resting, marching—and with cigars and brooms. (When Henry and Wilson later overhear the general, "The officer spoke of the regiment as if he referred to a broom" [171].) In war we are all insignificant; the soldiers here are only part of what Henry calls "a vast blue demonstration" and "a moving box." His notion of war as romantic and heroic is actually the opposite of its reality.

The philosophical definition for this point of view is *naturalism*, and *The Red Badge of Courage* is one of the primary examples in American literature of this movement. If realism tries to paint the world as it is, naturalism has a philosophical perspective on that experience. Crane wants us to see what war is really like—and what pawns we are in it, and how our behavior, rather than being motivated by ideals and heroism, is actually the result of baser and more trivial forces. Henry's survival at the end of the novel is the result of a little skill, some heroism—and a great deal of luck, not a little coincidence, a lot of guilt, and a fake wound. Henry, of course, fails to recognize this. Instead, he feels "a flash of astonishment" after the first skirmish to see the blue, pure sky and the sun gleaming on the trees and fields. It was surprising that Nature had gone tranquilly on with her golden process in the midst of so much devilment. (89)

Henry wants to get assurance that nature is his ally in this mighty struggle. Instead, as in Crane's famous short story, "The Open Boat" (1899), nature seems oblivious to man's noble goals and heroic acts. Our fates, Crane suggests, are more clearly in the hands of other mortals—officers who are as concerned with cigars, perhaps, as with battle plans. Henry Fleming is part of a "mighty blue machine" (128); his personal aims and ideals hardly matter. The callow youth seems truly "insignificant," whether or not he recognizes this naturalistic truth in the end. He is a victim of forces beyond himself, including his own false images of what war is really like. The absence of names reinforces this notion in the novel: war is the human condition, Crane argues, where we are all nameless and faceless.

But there is another, subtler message that Henry never learns. If he is insignificant, if all soldiers are actually just pawns and playthings of the universe, what, then, matters? Crane gives us a clear answer in the actions of the other characters. Every other soldier that Henry encounters ends up trying to help him: Jim Conklin, Wilson, the "tattered soldier," and the man "of the cheery voice" all aid Henry in various ways, with varying amounts of success. Jim Conklin, among other things, reassures Henry that others fear battle; the tattered soldier tries to befriend Henry; the cheery soldier leads Henry back to his regiment, where Wilson binds his wound. The only thing we *do* have in this world of war and wounds, Crane is saying, is human kindness, trying to make this life a little less painful for others. It is, however, a lesson that Henry barely hears: concerned throughout the novel with his own well-being and how he will appear to others, Henry hardly has the energy to help any of the soldiers that he encounters. When he returns the packet of letters to Wilson, he feels "generous" (154) about the act, but this is typical self-congratulation. Wilson *does* "'take keer'" of Henry, a promise that Henry fails to keep to Jim Conklin. Thus one of the most important themes of the novel—the crucial role of kindness and compassion in this bellicose world—may, in fact, be lost on the youthful protagonist.

Style and Language

As with most classic American novels, the power of *The Red Badge of Courage* comes in large part from its language and style. Crane has an almost painterly eye, and his scenes are rendered with rich and colorful brushstrokes.

The novel itself may give readers a little difficulty at first. It starts *in medias res* ("in the middle of things"), and the plot, while a chronological narrative with only one beginning flashback, is rather vague. Henry moves from place to place without clear explanation of why or where he is going. This structure, of course, not only captures Henry's psychological experience but reinforces the naturalistic lessons that Crane is giving us: we are the victims of forces outside ourselves and *motivation* is not always clear—and possibly beside the point. Similarly, the point of view is quite complex and can be confusing. While we enter only the mind of Henry Fleming (which is what makes the point of view limited omniscient), Crane himself comments on both the action and Henry's response to the action, and his *tone* can often be highly ironic, pointing up, as it does, contradictions in Henry's situation or in his thinking.

The novel's irony is both dramatic and linguistic. Dramatic irony is the result of reversed action; for example, the fact that they retreat only after winning is dramatic irony, as is Henry's "red badge of courage," which actually results not from heroism, but from flight. Linguistic irony is the play of words that points up the difference between appearance and reality: when Henry at the end feels he can look "back upon the brass and bombast of his earlier gospels and see them truly" (211), for example, the word *truly* is being used ironically by Crane.

The language and style of the novel are rich and colorful and often poetic. Below is a typical description, here of Henry before he enters his first battle. Notice how closely Crane renders the immediacy of Henry's psychosensory experience:

> He lay down in the grass. The blades pressed tenderly against his cheek. The moon had been lighted and was hung in a treetop. The liquid stillness of the night enveloping him made him feel vast pity for himself. There was a caress in the soft winds; and the whole mood of the darkness, he thought, was one of sympathy for himself in his distress. (62)

Most of the qualities of Crane's prose are apparent in this short passage: the scene is very pictorial, two or more modes of sensation are being used at the same time (here of sight, sound, and touch), and the image of the moon "hung in a treetop" is a good example of Crane's use of metaphor. (Crane regularly describes events in terms of other actions: the sound of bullets in the trees, a few pages later, is described "as if a thousand axes, wee and invisible, were being wielded" [79].) Although such highly metaphorical prose is rare for a naturalist (who usually lets the world speak for itself), it obviously works for Crane, in whose symbolism natural facts often have reference beyond themselves.

Certain of the metaphors run throughout the novel and play a symbolic and thematic role. Several times Crane uses religious language: early in the novel "the brigade was halted in the cathedral light of a forest" (72), and when Henry first stumbles upon the corpses in the woods, it is in a "chapel" where nature gives Henry "the religion of peace" (100–1). In the last two pages of the novel, Henry's earlier ideas are seen as "gospels" (211) and the sun breaks through the "hosts" (or communion wafers) of the clouds. Finally, in what is one of the most famous images in all of American literature, after the death of Jim Conklin the red sun is described as "pasted in the sky like a wafer" (alluding again to the element of communion). Crane's metaphorical language, in short, creates symbolic patterns that underscore the novel's ideas. Here, however, the use is ironic: nothing is *less* religious than war, Crane shows, and the religious imagery only works to point up the spiritual emptiness of this world. Heaven is indifferent, Crane says, and our only hope is each other. "J C" (Jim Conklin) is not able to save men; there is no God overlooking this battle scene—or, God overlooks but does not oversee (to use a Cranial irony). The world is "Hell—," as Henry says after Jim Conklin dies.

This metaphorical language, like the characterization, can sometimes be blurry. In just two pages of description, the marching columns of the regiment resemble "moving monsters," "crawling reptiles," and "two serpents crawling from the cavern of the night" (59–60). The animal imagery here clearly underscores the naturalistic themes of the novel— men in this army have been reduced to animal behavior—and the parallel will continue throughout the novel. But Crane later uses the word *monster* to refer to fear (65) and to the enemy (81). The point, perhaps, is not the lack of exactness (although in Crane's overblown and allegorical prose, that is sometimes a problem) but rather the fact that the image of "monster" refers to this whole war experience—soldiers on both sides, and the fear they all experience.

Finally, few novels are as *colorful* as *The Red Badge of Courage*— even its title hints at the color schemes of the novel. Here is a typical passage:

> It was a blind and despairing rush by the collection of men in dusty and tattered blue, over a green sward and under a sapphire sky, toward a fence, dimly outlined in smoke, from behind which spluttered the fierce rifles of enemies. (202)

It is not hard to understand why Crane has been called our most painterly of novelists: like impressionist paintings, Crane's verbal canvases are full of light, color, action, and movement. His sentence structure is often simple, but he uses plenty of adjectives and adverbs, and the final picture is usually vivid, if blurry—like Henry's own inner experience. Reading *The Red Badge of Courage* can be likened to rushing through a gallery of pointillist paintings.

TEACHING THE NOVEL

Teaching Suggestions

One reason students enjoy reading Crane is because he exaggerates— his descriptions tend to be overwritten, as his irony is often heavy-handed—and the best way to start *The Red Badge of Courage* is reading aloud, pausing to point out what Crane is doing. In the first paragraph, for example, notice that the army is described as an animal—with eyes, resting, and so forth—and the enemy as some kind of dragon. This type of *personification* works perfectly to Crane's purposes. In paragraph two, why is Jim Conklin referred to as "a certain tall soldier," how does he act (*"pompously"*), and what characterizes Crane's *tone* (*sardonic? exaggerated?*)? By going through the first few chapters with this kind of help, students get used to Crane's painterly eye and his irony, as well as to the fact that individual scenes are visually rendered without clear transitions between them, like Henry's mind might operate. They are thus able to figure out for themselves that this is not a traditional narrative but comes close to rendering Henry's inner experience. (Another helpful way to start is to read a passage aloud and ask students to close their eyes and visualize the scene. This activity will help them both appreciate Crane's style and see how close Crane is getting to rendering Henry's psychosensory experience for us.)

The most important idea to learn from Crane is the classic literary lesson of the difference between appearance and reality, here between Henry's expectations of what war will be like and the brutal, boring reality of it. The *irony* in the novel often aims in the same direction. Again and again, Crane points out the gap: instead of "a beautiful scene" in which she talked of his "patriotism" when Henry enlisted, the youth's mother made mundane comments about being "'a good boy,'" which made him "suddenly ashamed of his purposes" (47–49). Henry imagines war as "one of the great affairs of the earth" (46), and as "a series of death struggles with small time in between for sleep and meals" (50), instead of the mix of tedium and terror it really is. Henry's *illusions* about war are constantly being punctured during the novel, as his internal struggles are being pictured as inconsequential: at the end of Chapter 2, for example, as Henry is being tormented by the "monster" of his fear, the other soldiers are calmly playing cards. Students should be pushed toward recognition of these kinds of ironies in the novel.

One does not need to have any complicated definition of *naturalism* in order to recognize what Crane is doing here: pointing out the importance of environment but the indifference of the universe to man's fate. Still, it is important to note that Henry has choices, even within this deterministic universe: he could, like the other characters, choose to help his comrades; he could confess to Wilson the source of his wound (ironic, since it comes from another fleeing soldier) or the fact that he ran from battle. But Henry does neither of these. He chooses, instead, to protect his own image in the eyes of the others. Henry's initiation, as I argue in the analysis above, is only partially complete. His free will may be limited—a basic tenet of naturalism—but he hardly exercises any at all in the novel.

Discussion and Writing Ideas

1. Pre-reading activity: describe an event you anticipated with *fear*. What finally happened? Was the actual event worth the dread? What did you learn from the experience?
2. Pre-reading activity: write about a time when you had *illusions* about a person or thing. What happened to them? Was the reality better or worse than your illusions? How did your illusions help or hinder you?
3. Reflect on an error or wrong that you committed in the past and the thoughts you used as rationalizations. How was your experience like Henry's?
4. Henry's story is in part about *peer pressure*. Write about a time when you did something because of the expectations of others. What did you learn?
5. Write a report as a staff psychologist evaluating how Henry handles the psychological effects of war. What can you write positively about his efforts? How are his fears and actions like those of other soldiers?
6. What does the novel say about fear? duty? luck? Write about one of these ideas as it is described in the novel.
7. What is the point of the scene between the fat soldier and the horse at the opening of the novel (pp. 61–62)?
8. What is the significance of a "house standing placidly" that Henry sees several times (p. 70, for instance)?

9. Do a character sketch of Henry Fleming. What is he like? What are his major qualities? What does he learn?
10. Do an analysis of the plot of the novel. How does it unfold? What are its characteristics?
11. What evidence can you find of *foreshadowing* in the novel? In particular, how is the death of Jim Conklin foreshadowed?
12. Analyze the references to "Nature" in the novel, and discuss what significance it has for Crane. Is nature "benign and indifferent"?

Bridging to Other Works

Nathaniel Hawthorne, *The Scarlet Letter* (1851). Compare Henry Fleming and Arthur Dimmesdale in terms of guilt.

Selected poetry of Emily Dickinson (for its irony) and Walt Whitman (Civil War poems).

Mark Twain, *Adventures of Huckleberry Finn* (1884); see Chapter 2. Compare the two protagonists in terms of heroism and self-knowledge.

———, *The War Prayer* (1923). This powerful antiwar parody was published only after Twain's death.

———, "The History of a Campaign That Failed" (1904). Twain's account of his own brief Civil War experiences is included in many high school literature anthologies.

Stephen Crane's short stories, especially "The Blue Hotel" (a story about false notions of the West), "The Bride Comes to Yellow Sky" (the changing West), and "The Open Boat" (naturalism, importance of setting), share similarities of theme and style with *The Red Badge of Courage*.

William Dean Howells, "Editha" (1905). This short story is also about war, heroism, and false ideals.

Erich Maria Remarque, *All Quiet on the Western Front* (1929). This novel of a German soldier in World War I is a classic statement about the horror and futility of war.

Ernest Hemingway, *A Farewell to Arms* (1929). Compare Hemingway's description of war (World War I) with Crane's.

———, short stories. "Soldiers Home" and "In Another Country" as well as several others, are also about World War I.

Anne Frank, *The Diary of a Young Girl* (1952). This diary of a young Jewish girl, in hiding with her family in Nazi-occupied Holland, is a true story of courage in wartime.

Kurt Vonnegut, *Slaughterhouse-Five* (1969). Compare the character of

Billy Pilgrim, in this black comedy about World War II, with Henry
Fleming.

Robert Cormier, *The Chocolate War* (YA, 1974); see Chapter 3. Compare Henry Fleming and Jerry Renault, in this other novel about
courage and fear, in terms of how much they learn and develop in the
course of their novels.

8 "Seems that only children weep"

TO KILL A MOCKINGBIRD

Author: Harper Lee (b. 1926)
Genre: historical and psychological realism
Time of novel: 1932–1935
Locale: Maycomb, a small town in southern Alabama
Point of view: first person
First published: 1960
Edition used: Warner paperback (1982); 284 pp.
Grade level: 7–10
Principal characters:
  Jean Louise ("Scout") Finch, the narrator
  Jeremy Atticus ("Jem") Finch, Scout's brother
  Atticus Finch, their widowed father, a lawyer
  Calpurnia, the black cook who runs the Finch household
  Charles Baker ("Dill") Harris, a boy a year older than Scout who visits Maycomb each summer from his home in Meridian, Mississippi
  Aunt Alexandra, Atticus's sister, who comes to live in the Finch house
  Arthur ("Boo") Radley, the mysterious man living in the house down the street
  Miss Maudie Atkinson, a neighbor and friend to Atticus and the children
  Tom Robinson, a black man accused of the rape of Mayella Ewell
  Mayella Ewell, the daughter of Bob Ewell
  Bob Ewell, a poor white living on the edge of Maycomb
  Judge John Taylor, the jurist who presides over the trial of Tom Robinson

ANALYSIS OF THE NOVEL

Story and Setting

To Kill a Mockingbird was both a popular and a critical success when it was first published in 1960 (it won the Pulitzer Prize for fiction

that year), and it has been a perennial favorite, especially in high schools
and junior highs, ever since. A novel about growing up in a small
Southern town, *To Kill a Mockingbird* has a great deal to tell readers
about courage and tolerance.

Maycomb, Alabama, is a quiet town at the bottom of the Depression
of the early 1930s, a small piece of the South where everyone knows
everyone else and a strong caste system still prevails. The Finches comprise one of the first families of Maycomb County (Maycomb is the
county seat), for ancestor Simon Finch was one of the region's pioneers,
and many of the Finch clan still live in Finch's Landing, some 20 miles to
the west. But Atticus Finch went off to study law and settled in Maycomb, married, and had two children before his wife died (when Scout
was 2 and Jem, 6). He has raised them alone, with a kind of "courteous
detachment" (10), as Scout describes it, but also with love and with the
careful help of Calpurnia, the Finch housekeeper.

The novel is narrated from the perspective of Scout Finch, looking
back from the distance of some years but describing events as if she were
aged 9 and they had just occurred over the past three years. This double
point of view is perfect for the dual story of growing up in this poor and
provincial town. The younger voice tells us what has just happened to the
Finch children, while the older voice fills us in on the historical background. Actually, Maycomb is no different from other Southern (or
Northern, for that matter) small towns in the Depression, but both its
strengths and its weaknesses are intensified in Scout's recital of these
crucial three years in her childhood, her first three years in school. It is a
town still suffering under the curse of slavery, with its heritage of racial
hatred and violence, but it is also a town where good people (like Atticus
Finch, Judge Taylor, and Miss Maudie) are helping to bring about
change, if only in attitude. It will be a better place, Harper Lee implies,
when Scout and Jem become its adults.

There are essentially two stories interwoven in the novel. The first,
which opens the book, is the story of Boo Radley, a slightly retarded man
who, 15 years earlier, had stabbed his father in the leg with a pair of
scissors and has been confined to the Radley house ever since. As recluses
often do, Boo has turned his house into a source of fear and mystery for
the children. The novel begins with Jem and Dill and Scout trying to
trick Boo into coming out. The mystery deepens as it becomes clear that
Boo *is* leaving his house (at least at night) and is trying to make contact
with the children. (At the end of the novel, it is because he is following
Jem and Scout that he is able to save their lives.) In part a victim of small
town prejudice and suspicion, Boo Radley becomes a "quiet hero" at the
novel's end.

The second story, which is slower in starting, concerns Tom Robinson, a black man accused of raping a young white woman, Mayella Ewell. In this region, and at this time, such an accusation amounts to almost certain conviction (and rape is a capital offense in Alabama), which is why Judge Taylor appoints Atticus Finch to defend Tom Robinson, knowing that Atticus will do everything in his power—and in the face of the racial fear and hatred of Maycomb—to see that justice is done and that Tom is given the best possible deffense.

The case, however, is almost decided by the first time we hear of it, and even Atticus knows what the outcome will be. Still, the story contains several scenes of high drama. Atticus—with the inadvertent help of Scout—saves Tom from almost certain lynching at the Maycomb jail and then dramatically proves in the courtroom that Tom could not have beaten Mayella (she has been hit—supposedly in the course of the "rape"—by someone left-handed, and Tom's left arm is crippled). But Tom Robinson is nevertheless found guilty, loses all hope for himself in an appeal, and commits suicide by trying to climb the fence at the prison camp in sight of armed guards, dying with 17 bullet holes in him. His death is a terrible blow in the novel, for racial injustice has again triumphed over human rights. But the children have also witnessed other lessons during this ordeal—like the lesson of Atticus working so hard to defend this man and the love of the black community for their heroic father.

The two plots converge in the novel as Bob Ewell, who swore revenge when Atticus showed him up at the trial (it is clear from Atticus's cross-examination that Ewell beat up his own daughter, if not worse), tries to kill Jem and Scout one dark night, but is killed himself by Boo Radley, who is following the children. In the end, Atticus agrees with Sheriff Heck Tate that it is better to say that Bob Ewell fell on his own knife than to reveal the truth and drag Boo Radley into the spotlight of publicity. The mysterious recluse has emerged to save the Finch children from the man who, indirectly, at least, caused the death of Tom Robinson, and the two stories flow together rather neatly. They are further connected because both teach us something about life in a small Southern town. The Boo Radley story concerns fear and the need for tolerance, while the Robinson/Ewell story is about racial conflict and what poverty and ignorance can do to people. Atticus Finch tries to draw the appropriate lessons from each story for his children.

This dual plot in *To Kill a Mockingbird* is strong and keeps readers interested and guessing until the very last page, but the novel is not difficult reading, which is why it has become an adolescent classic in little more than a quarter-century and is often taught, especially in junior high.

Younger teenagers can identify with Scout and Jem and Dill, children who, while still preteens, are going through the process of initiation into adulthood in a series of exciting adventures.

Characters

There are more than the usual number of important people in this popular novel, and while a few are two-dimensional, the main characters are complex and interesting. Scout, in particular, endears herself to readers. She is a tomboy, a female Huck Finn who wants to do everything with her older brother Jem and their imaginative friend Dill (who visits every summer from Mississippi and finds in the Finch family the love he does not get in his own). A subplot in *To Kill a Mockingbird* has Aunt Alexandra, Atticus's provincial and snobbish sister, arriving in the Finch household to help Scout become a "lady" and to do the job that she feels Atticus cannot do alone with his children. But she fails in her attempts to fire Calpurnia, and, in her struggles with Atticus, we come to understand something of his values and his strengths as a father: "'Sister, I do the best I can with them!'" (85), he argues early in the novel, and it is more than enough, we come to feel, especially for his children. While Scout learns and grows a great deal in the three years of the novel (from ages 6 to 9), she still remains the innocent, funny kid who would rather fight than apologize, our observant witness to most of the novel's main actions.

If Scout is one pole in this double initiation novel, Jem is the other. Because he is four years older than his sister, more happens to Jem than to Scout: he is the one who loses his pants going under a fence on a foray to the Radley place, just as he is the one who has his arm broken in the struggle with the drunken Bob Ewell. He is also the child who learns more and faster than Scout about the racial realities in this small town: "'It ain't right, Atticus,'" he cries to his father at the end of Tom Robinson's trial; "'No son,'" his father agrees, "'it's not right'" (215). In many ways, the significant actions of the novel, and thus its lessons, occur through Jem, as witnessed by Scout. Sometimes, for all her adoration of him, Scout has trouble sympathizing with the rapid changes that Jem's growth seems to produce. "Overnight, it seemed, Jem had acquired an alien set of values and was trying to impose them on me" (117), Scout complains. And it is not only the physical changes that he is going through (Jem at one point shows Scout the new hair on his chest) but also his loss of childhood simplicity (e.g., "Jem was the one who was getting more like a girl every day, not I" [241]). Sensitive to both his children, Atticus puts Scout on his lap and counsels her: "'don't let Jem get you down. He's having a rough time these days'" (250). Jem must face more fully the pains and problems of trying to enter adult life, but seeing him in bed with a broken arm at the end of the novel, readers will probably feel that he has successfully passed his major trial by fire and, with the continued and loving help of his father—whose name he carries—will become a good adult. Scout is the admiring, if confused, chronicler of this growth.

If Jem is making a successful transition to adolescence (from ages 10 to 13), he must give much credit for his growth to his father, who does not protect him and Scout from the real world but lets them see it and gives them the love and understanding necessary for navigating their perilous journey through it. It is not right for the children to attend Tom Robinson's trial, Aunt Alexandra begins to argue. "'This is their home, sister,'" Atticus answers, meaning Maycomb. "'We've made it this way for them, they might as well learn to cope with it'" (215). By the end of the novel it becomes clear that Atticus knew about most of the mischief the children got into in the past three years—and let them go (245).

Some of the meaning of the novel involves Jem and Scout's discovery of who and what their father is. They start knowing only that he is older than other fathers (he is nearly 50), but they learn so much more during the novel about his past, his character, and his principles. He does not drink, for example, and he never punishes his children physically. Instead, he teaches them by example—for instance, to treat any person (including Boo Radley) with respect and dignity. When Walter Cunningham (a classmate of Scout's whose father is working off his debt to Atticus in food stuffs) comes for dinner, "he and Atticus talked together like two men, to the wonderment of Jem and me" (28). Atticus Finch is a truly integrated man, who is no different in the courtroom than the dining room. And when a mad dog appears on the streets of Maycomb, it is Atticus who kills it with a single shot. (Miss Maudie explains: he "'was the deadest shot in Maycomb County in his time,'" and only "'put his gun down when he realized that God had given him an unfair advantage over most living things'" [102].) There are, in fact, few characters in modern fiction as human and heroic as Atticus Finch, a man of learning and courage, but also a man of humor capable of compromise. In the closing lines of the novel, Jem is in bed with his broken arm, and Atticus is in a chair next to him reading: "He would be there all night, and he would be there when Jem waked up in the morning" (284). As the supposed town drunk tells Scout, "'your pa's not a run-of-the-mill man'" (204). If anything, Atticus is *too* good: a crack shot, a state legislator—we are relieved the few times he is wrong (as about the likelihood of Bob Ewell's revenge). If his qualities seem larger than life, it is, perhaps, because we have not seen many such heroes in recent literature.

Atticus's qualities are revealed most dramatically in the trial of Tom Robinson. He defends the black man against the town's racial prejudice but knows what anger and hatred his children must face because of his actions. As he explains to Scout,

> "every lawyer gets at least one case in his lifetime that affects him personally. This one's mine, I guess. You might hear some ugly talk about it at school, but do one thing for me if you will: you just hold your head high and keep those fists down. No matter what anybody says to you, don't you let 'em get your goat." (80)

At the end of the trial, the Reverend Sykes asks the children to stand as their father passes below them. It is one of the most moving scenes in the novel, for it is the tribute of the oppressed black community to a man of courage and principle who is fighting intolerance and injustice in spite of the overwhelming odds and the danger to his own family. It is not only blacks, however, who recognize his role. As Miss Maudie explains to the children after the trial, "'there are some men in this world who were born to do our unpleasant jobs for us. Your father's one of them. . . . We're so rarely called on to be Christians, but when we are, we've got men like Atticus to go for us'" (218).

If the major characters in the novel are rich and varied, some of the secondary characters are stereotypes. Certainly the novel contains far too many characters for all of them to be drawn with individual brushstrokes. Still, one of the weaknesses of the novel is that too many of the minor characters are simply heroes or villains. Tom Robinson and most of the other blacks in the novel, for example, are rather idealized: although Atticus argues that, as in any race, there are good and bad black people, all the blacks that readers see are good. The one exception is Lula, the loud woman who tries to keep Calpurnia from bringing Jem and Scout into the black church; more common is the Reverend Sykes, who welcomes them there and later gets four blacks to give up their seats in the "colored balcony" so that Jem and Scout can watch their father at the trial. Even Calpurnia is somewhat idealized, the surrogate mother who fusses over their clothes ("'I don't want anybody sayin' I don't look after my children'" [120]) and who is "'a faithful member of this family'" (139), as Atticus argues to her opposite, Aunt Alexandra, who is trying to get rid of the black cook. Alexandra is an almost perfect example of provincial prudery and snobbery, but she is no match for her brother's principled actions, and by the end she has softened somewhat. The Ewells, finally, are particularly weak as poor whites (a cross between characters out of Faulkner and "L'il Abner"); they are made even weaker, perhaps, by the contrast with the Cunninghams, who are working off their "entailment" to Atticus and seem much more realistic. Thus, the novel depends to a certain extent on heroes and villains, and both tend toward the two-dimensional.

Themes

As in so many novels of initiation, the main theme of *To Kill a Mockingbird* is human growth, and the subthemes are what the young people learn in their journey toward maturity.

The "significant other" in Jem and Scout's lives is, of course, Atticus, and they learn the most about life from him. In one sense, the novel is an extended essay in Atticus's adage that the only way to learn about someone is to "'climb into his skin and walk around in it'" (34). Over the course of the novel, Jem and Scout do just that, gaining patience and tolerance for everyone from Aunt Alexandra to Tom Robinson, until the very end of the novel, when Scout stands on the Radley porch and comes to understand the world from Boo Radley's perspective: "Atticus was right. One time he said you never really know a man until you stand in his shoes and walk around in them" (282). This discovery is made even more poignant by Scout's statement about Boo: "I never saw him again" (281). The recluse retreats back into his hiding place after his brief and nearly anonymous moment of heroism.

"'I think I'm beginning to understand why Boo Radley's stayed shut up in the house all this time'" (230), Jem muses to his sister: the world outside is just too painful. The most important lessons that Jem and Scout learn revolve around the trial of Tom Robinson. It takes real courage to defend Tom Robinson, not only in the courtroom—perhaps the easiest venue—but in the streets of Maycomb as well, where Atticus must face the ignorance and hatred of his fellow townspeople, the potential violence of the mob, and the attacks of Bob Ewell. But Atticus knows why he is defending Tom Robinson and explains it clearly to Scout:

> "Sometimes we have to make the best of things, and the way we conduct ourselves when the chips are down—well, all I can say is, when you and Jem are grown, maybe you'll look back on this with some compassion and some feeling that I didn't let you down. This case, Tom Robinson's case, is something that goes to the essence of a man's conscience—Scout, I couldn't

go to church and worship God if I didn't try to help that man. . . . before I can live with other folks I've got to live with myself. The one thing that doesn't abide by majority rule is a person's conscience." (109)

The trial and death of Tom Robinson realistically reflect American racial attitudes and behavior in the 1930s; the words and actions of Atticus Finch point to a better day.

But the children have something else to learn from their father, for they, too, are the products of Maycomb. When Dill cries out at the treatment of Tom Robinson, Scout retorts, "'Well, Dill, after all he's just a Negro'" (201). (Compare the similar statement by Huck Finn, cited in Chapter 2.) Atticus's lessons of love and tolerance are needed by us all. And when Maycomb blacks fill the Finch kitchen with gifts of food in tribute to the lawyer's attempts to save Tom, we understand and can only wish there were more heroes like Atticus working for change in the world.

There are several complex parts to Atticus's lesson of tolerance. Scout must learn, for one thing, that her teacher, Miss Gates—who can hate Hitler and worry about European Jews—can also hold fiercely to her prejudice against Maycomb blacks. Jem and Scout learn from their encounters with Mrs. Dubose about the contradictions of human life: that Mrs. Dubose can be a racist—and courageous at the same time. Likewise, Atticus teaches his children that hatred cannot be answered with hatred, but only with love and understanding. Bob Ewell is a despicable human being, but in describing the Ewell family life—or lack of it—in the courtroom, Atticus helps us and his children to see the parts that poverty and ignorance play in Ewell's hatred. Environment looms large in *To Kill a Mockingbird* for *all* the characters: even Boo Radley is a product of his milieu, a misfit who would rather return to the cave of his anonymity than face the eyes of Maycomb. On one level, perhaps, the novel is *about* misfits: Boo, Adolphus Raymond, Tom Robinson. "'I always thought Maycomb folks were the best folks in the world, least that's what they seemed like'" (218), Jem confesses in a moment of disillusionment. More and more the misfits look admirable in contrast to the "normal" townspeople.

Misfits, in fact, are what are referred to in the novel's title: "'it's a sin to kill a mockingbird,'" Atticus warns Scout, and later Miss Maudie explains why:

"Mockingbirds don't do one thing but make music for us to enjoy. They don't eat up people's gardens, don't nest in corncribs, they don't do but one thing but sing their hearts out for us. That's why it's a sin to kill a mocking-bird." (94)

Scout shows that she has learned this important lesson when, at the end of the novel, she recognizes that to expose Boo Radley to publicity would be "'sort of like shootin' a mockingbird, wouldn't it?'" Scout has gained some of Atticus's view of the world, and not a little of his poetic expression of it. The title of the novel exemplifies this knowledge, as it refers to several mockingbirds within its pages (such as Tom Robinson [243]).

Style and Language

To Kill a Mockingbird is successful, in part, because all of its literary components work. The structure, for example, is nearly perfect: the novel opens, where it closes, with Scout aged 9 (Jem is 13), thinking back over the past three years (1932–1935). We are slowly brought back up to the fictional present through the interconnected stories of Boo Radley and Tom Robinson. (The division of the novel into two books seems rather arbitrary, by the way.) If there is a fault with this structure, it is one that characterizes most novels with a large legal element: the trial scenes seem too long and the novel's action almost halts during them. It is a novel, on the other hand, with a number of exciting scenes (the attempted lynching, for example, or the attack on Jem and Scout by Bob Ewell) and with true feeling breaking through constantly (as when the Reverend Sykes asks the children to stand in tribute to their father).

But what makes the novel most successful is the strength of Scout's narration. As with so many adolescent initiation stories, from *Huck Finn* through *The Catcher in the Rye*, the naive narrator fits perfectly here. Scout makes the action of the novel exciting to us because she does *not* know, at the time of telling, how the Tom Robinson trial is going to turn out or what will happen to Boo Radley. Of course, she gives us enough clues to figure out both stories ourselves and thus to feel slightly superior to her (as her brother does as he figures out both before Scout). At other times, the actions of the characters tell us things that Scout does not see—like Atticus crying after the confrontation with the lynch mob outside the Maycomb jail (157). The words of Atticus, to cite another example, tell us from the beginning, that he is going to lose Tom's case, long before Scout or Jem realize it.

If readers listen carefully, they can actually hear a second voice, the adult Scout who is giving us all the background information and history of Maycomb, Alabama. Only occasionally does this second voice intrude on the innocent, younger one. (See the fifth paragraph from the end of Chapter 25 [243] for one obvious example.) For the most part, Scout is reacting to events in an immediate present.

What makes Scout's voice so strong and the novel consequently so authentic is Harper Lee's use of language. More than most contemporary novels, either "popular adult" ones like this or YA novels, *To Kill a Mockingbird* is a novel in which every word has been chosen with care and where the study of the language, therefore, is a fruitful activity. Some of the humor in the novel is situational, of course—like Judge Taylor's having to leave the Halloween pageant because Scout's entrance as a ham is so badly mistimed. But much of the humor is verbal, and both Scout in her narration and Atticus in dialogue are capable of complex and subtle *irony*. The Maycomb missionary society ladies sit in the Finch parlor and agonize over the "Mrunas"—while poverty and ignorance are breeding all around them. "It is a sad thing that my father had neglected to tell me about the Finch family," Scout writes (134)—and we get exactly the opposite impression. Much of the meaning of the novel, in fact, turns on the subtle use of language. "'Do you really think so?'" Atticus asks a member of the mob trying to lynch Tom Robinson, and Scout lets us know how loaded that simple question is (154). Likewise, Scout saves this situation with a greeting—"'Hey, Mr. Cunningham'"—and these three words defuse the violent tension of the scene. Finally, much of the meaning of the novel is carried in words like *nigger, nigger-lover, trash, common*—and who uses them.

Similarly, the novel is marked by a keen sensitivity to various dialects and languages. Calpurnia, as Scout notices when she accompanies her to church, actually speaks two languages: the one she uses with her own people (a version of what we would today call black English) and the one she uses in the Finch house. Most of the characters in the novel are drawn as much by their language as by any physical description, and the careful reader (or *listener*) should be able to distinguish quite easily, say, the learned and laconic language of Judge Taylor from the priggish voice of Aunt Alexandra. Some of the characters in the novel are actually illiterate (such as the people in Calpurnia's church "linin'" a hymn because they have no books and could not read them anyway), but their language is richer than that of many characters in modern fiction. Harper Lee has recorded the life of a Southern community with all its pimples and prejudices, and one of the ways this community comes alive for us is through its varied, often musical, voices. It is no mean accomplishment.

TEACHING THE NOVEL

Teaching Suggestions

To Kill a Mockingbird is a nearly perfect answer to the question of why we read (and teach) novels: to make an extended journey into another world. Harper Lee's only novel reveals to us—better than most history books could—what it must have felt like to grow up in a small town like Maycomb in the early 1930s. *To Kill a Mockingbird* transports its readers out of their own lives and into the not-so-distant past, but into a scene that is light years away for most students today. We learn about Hitler, about the Depression (which hurt small Southern farmers, like the Cunninghams, as hard as anyone), about the process of "entailment." We witness the treatment of blacks, the threat of a lynch mob, Maycomb's caste system, and much, much more. To read this novel is to gain a kind of historical consciousness, to move imaginatively into another time and place. Readers who cannot make this kind of leap are locked into their own egocentric present.

The film of *To Kill a Mockingbird* is one of the most successful translations of American fiction to the screen, and showing it works well for most classes that have read the novel. But it is interesting to note what is missing in the movie, in particular a great deal of the local and national history that makes the novel such rich and rewarding reading and tells us so exactly about the Depression South. (Gone from the film are the histories of the Finch family and of Maycomb, most references to the international scene, and such.) So, while the film captures the *emotional* power of the novel, it ignores almost all its *historical* context.

The book reveals other pleasures of reading as well. Here is a novel full of humorous scenes and characters, a novel with a scary ghost (or "haint") story at its center and with a plot that involves both a murder and a mystery. A classroom analysis of *To Kill a Mockingbird* can show how these literary elements work and how they function to support the themes.

Finally, the novel is an appropriate place to explore the joys and complexities of language. *To Kill a Mockingbird* contains a number of interesting words and phrases that students can look up or figure out, like "down the country" (210) or "pot liquor" (229)—which, surprisingly, is not liquor at all! (Scout's narration is so realistic that students will not be able to find some of her words in any dictionary: *morphodite*, for example, or *Mruna*, or *Chambertous connivance*.) Harper Lee's language gives us access to its setting and ideas, and the verbal freshness and detail help prepare us for the pleasures of its story.

Discussion and Writing Ideas

AFFECTIVE TOPICS

1. How did you feel when the novel ended? Why?
2. Who was the most interesting character in the novel? What was the most exciting part?
3. Describe a very scary experience you had.
4. Describe a time when you ignored or were mean to someone before you knew them. What did you learn?
5. Describe someone you know and admire as a *hero*. What qualities make that person a hero to you?
6. Describe the *social class system* in which you live and your place in it.
7. Describe an experience in which you felt you grew and matured.

ANALYTICAL TOPICS

1. What is going to happen to Scout and Jem following the end of the story? Write a paragraph on one of them ten years later.
2. Who are the *heroes* in this novel? Choose one, describe his heroism, and explain its importance. (Besides Atticus, Boo Radley, Tom Robinson, and Heck Tate could all be considered heroes. The point here is to find the *evidence* for their heroism.)
3. What are the events that mark Jem's journey into adulthood? Select one such major event, describe it, and then explain how it shows Jem's passage to maturity.
4. Describe the ways that you think Scout learns and grows in the course of the novel. What is your evidence?
5. What is the role of women in the South as depicted in the novel? (Consider Scout, Calpurnia, Aunt Alexandra, and Miss Maudie; note the discussions about women on pp. 86, 124, 129, 149, 224, etc.) What is the point about Aunt Alexandra trying to turn Scout into a "lady"? (Consider pp. 228, 232.) Is this any different from the effort to make Jem a "gentleman"? Discuss.
6. Scout calls the events of Halloween night "our longest journey together" (256). Why? Explain the importance of the actions of that night.
7. Describe the social class system in Maycomb, noting at least one character from each major class (e.g., the Finches, Cunninghams, Ewells, Robinsons). What does the novel say about wealth and social class? Does wealth have anything to do with goodness? Consider Walter Cunningham (and Aunt Alexandra's words on him), Miss

Maudie and possessions (p. 78), the missionary society. What effect is the Depression having on social class in Maycomb?
8. The novel gives an accurate picture of the complexity of racial relations in the Deep South in the 1930s. (Consider the case of Tom Robinson: he must run to repulse the advances of Mayella Ewell— which just proves his guilt—but he is convicted perhaps as much because of his pity for a white woman.) Give a brief synopsis of the state of civil rights in the novel.
9. Write on the significance of one of the following incidents or ideas:

the knothole
the snowman (a caricature of Mr. Avery)
reading to Mrs. Dubose
the epigraph to the novel (from Charles Lamb)
Mrs. Gates and Hitler (p. 248)
shooting the mad dog

Bridging to Other Works

YA NOVELS

William Armstrong, *Sounder* (YA, 1969). Compare setting, racial tensions, and the role of parents.
Robert Newton Peck, *A Day No Pigs Would Die* (YA, 1972); see Chapter 11. Note the fathers in these two novels, both heroes who teach their children important lessons.
Bette Greene, *Summer of My German Soldier* (YA, 1973). Note the parallels of setting and themes.
Mildred D. Taylor, *Roll of Thunder, Hear My Cry* (YA, 1976); see Chapter 12. Compare the two young narrators viewing similar events at the same time in similar settings. How do Scout and Cassie differ? Notice how much each learns from her parents. Compare the notions of heroism, tolerance, self-respect, and injustice.

POPULAR ADULT AND CLASSIC AMERICAN FICTION

Mark Twain, *Adventures of Huckleberry Finn* (1884); see Chapter 2. Compare the two young narrators in terms of what they see and do not see in their societies and how much they change.
Carson McCullers, *The Heart Is a Lonely Hunter* (1940). Notice parallels of settings and themes (e.g., misfits).

————, *The Member of the Wedding* (1946); see Chapter 9. Compare setting, theme, character.

John Steinbeck, *The Red Pony* (1945); see Chapter 10. Contrast what Jody learns to Jem and Scout's lessons.

Richard Wright, *Black Boy* (1945). Wright's autobiography about growing up in the South helps to explain the racial tension and incidents in *To Kill a Mockingbird*.

Alan Paton, *Cry, the Beloved Country* (1948). This is a poignant depiction of racial problems in another culture (South Africa).

William Faulkner, "A Rose for Emily." This short story takes place in a small Southern town similar to Maycomb.

Truman Capote, "A Christmas Memory." Capote's touching and sentimental story is included in a number of anthologies.

9 "That green and crazy summer"

THE MEMBER OF THE WEDDING

Author: Carson McCullers (1917–1967)
Genre: psychological realism
Time of novel: the last weekend of August 1944; a few months later
Locale: a small Georgia town
Point of view: limited omniscient
First published: 1946
Edition used: Bantam paperback (1986); 153 pp.
Grade level: 7–10
Principal characters:
   Frankie Addams, a 12-year-old girl on the edge of adolescence
   Berenice Sadie Brown, the black cook in the Addams house
   John Henry West, age 6, Frankie's first cousin
   Royal Quincy Addams, Frankie's father, a widower and the owner of a
      jewelry store
   Jarvis Addams, Frankie's older brother, a soldier in the army about to
      marry
   Janice Evans, a young woman from Winter Hill
   Honey Camden Brown, Berenice's foster brother
   T. T. Williams, a man Berenice will later marry
   Big Mama, Berenice's mother and a psychic
   A red-haired soldier

ANALYSIS OF THE NOVEL

Story and Setting

   The Member of the Wedding takes place in a small Georgia town
during one hot August weekend and revolves around the plans for the
wedding of Frankie Addams's brother. Jarvis Addams and Janice Evans
visit his family home on Friday, and on Sunday they are married in her
home in Winter Hill, some 100 miles away. But these are just the bare

bones of the story, and we only witness them through the reports of the three main characters: 12-year-old Frankie; her cook and confidante, Berenice; and her 6-year-old cousin, John Henry. The focus of the novel, rather, is on Frankie's uncertain journey through this weekend as she navigates her path out of childhood and into adolescence. The wedding becomes Frankie's symbolic rite of passage, but not in a way that she or anyone else would ever predict—or want.

The novel is broken into three parts, and each represents a distinct, if symbolic, stage in Frankie's growth. In Part One, we see Frankie stuck on the edge of childhood—and about to fall over. "This was the summer when Frankie was sick and tired of being Frankie. . . . Things began to change and Frankie did not understand this change" (19–20). She has grown inches that summer and is afraid she is "almost a big freak," and everything around her feels peculiar and peevish as well. It is hot and humid, and she and John Henry and Berenice have spent the entire summer, it seems, sitting in their sultry kitchen talking and playing cards, surrounded by walls covered with John Henry's childish drawings. She wants to escape this town, and her preadolescent life, and when her brother and his fiancée pay a brief visit, she falls instantly in love with them and with the idea of their wedding, which then becomes the deliverance she has been seeking. Berenice claims that Frankie is just "jealous," but it is more than that to Frankie: "the wedding was bright and beautiful as snow and the heart in her was mashed" (15).

Certainly Frankie has been feeling a lot of rejection lately: her best friend, Evelyn Owen, has moved away; the older girls in the neighborhood say that she is too young to play with them and that she smells; even her cat, Charles, has left home (to find a "friend," Berenice says). "'It looks to me like everything has just walked off and left me'" (29). In April, her widower father decided that his "'great big long-legged twelve-year-old blunderbuss'" (22) was too big to sleep with him any more. Frankie knows "that everything was changed; but why this was so, and what would happen to her next, she did not know" (24). She longs to get away, to travel, to flee her prepubescent predicament and this small town where "the world seemed somehow separate from herself" (21).

The arrival of Jarvis and Janice presents Frankie with an escape plan: she will not come back after the wedding in Winter Hill but will travel with the couple. "*They are the we of me*," she decides. "All other people had a *we* to claim, all except her" (39).

> "I love the two of them so much. We'll go to every place together. It's like I've known it all my life, that I belong to be with them. I love the two of them so much."

And having said this, she did not need to wonder and puzzle any more.
. . . Her heart had divided like two wings and she had never seen a night so
beautiful. . . . At last she knew just who she was and understood where she
was going. She loved her brother and the bride and she was a member of the
wedding. The three of them would go into the world and they would always
be together. And finally, after the scared spring and the crazy summer, she
was no more afraid. (43)

Part One covers the Friday of the visit, while the longer Part Two
describes Saturday, or the day before the trip to Winter Hill for the
wedding. In this second part, Frankie speaks of herself as "the old
Frankie" of the day before. Now she is the exotic "F. Jasmine Addams,"
and with this transformation—she has become a third "Ja" person with
Jarvis and Janice—"the world seemed no longer separate from herself
and . . . all at once she felt included" and "all was natural in a magic way"
(44). Frankie has willed herself out of the prison of childhood and,
through the vehicle of the wedding, feels a "new unnameable connection"
(50) to the world. But now what is verbal must become dramatic, and
what the new F. Jasmine Addams has imagined must actually occur.

The young girl takes what she believes will be her last walk through
her hometown, going through a series of strange experiences on this
symbolic journey. Everywhere she goes she must tell people—even total
strangers—of her wedding plans, and in this action she feels that her
"need to be recognized for her true self was for the time being satisfied"
(59). She follows the music of an organ grinder into the Blue Moon, a bar
where she first sees the red-haired soldier "who at the very end would
twist so strangely that last, long day" (55). Then she is greeted at her
father's jewelry store with the news that old Uncle Charles, John Henry's
great-uncle, is dead. On her way home, she finds the organ grinder
quarreling with the red-haired soldier, who wants to buy the monkey,
which "skittered up her leg and body and was huddled on her shoulder"
(63). The soldier invites Frankie into the Blue Moon for a beer, and while
she has "an uneasy doubt that she could not quite place or name" (65), at
the very same time, "The world had never been so close to her" (66).
Sitting at a table in the bar, drinking a bitter beer with a soldier who
represents adventure and travel (if only from Arkansas!), Frankie is close
to the adult "world" she so envies and desires.

The soldier asks Frankie for a date later that night, but, back home,
Frankie learns indirectly from the more experienced Berenice that he was
probably drunk. In what Frankie imagines will be "this last meal that the
three of them would ever eat together at the kitchen table" (75), Frankie,
Berenice, and John Henry discuss love for the first time, and Berenice

tries to help Frankie's passage into maturity by suggesting she become more ladylike and get herself a "beau." Berenice then tells the stories of her own four marriages, particularly of her happy days with her first husband, Ludie Freeman, before he died. Frankie feels grown up (she smokes with Berenice for the first time, as she has earlier had her first drink) and searches for "some final thing she ought to say or do before she went away" (106). Frustrated by her inability to communicate her own "unknown," "unsaid words" about the changes she is undergoing, Frankie grabs a butcher knife and Berenice has to pull her into her lap to calm her. But Berenice *does* understand something of Frankie's dilemma: "'The point is that we all caught'" (114)—caught in sexual and familial roles, imprisoned by our fates as by our bodies. In a spiritual catharsis for all, "the three of them began to cry" (116).

Later that night, Frankie goes to Big Mama's house to have her fortune told. Big Mama sees only a short trip ("a departure and a return" [123]), which is, of course, disappointing to the F. Jasmine who still plans to go off with her brother and his bride right after the wedding the next day in Winter Hill. (Big Mama also tells her, "'You look like a regular grown girl'" [124], which is a more important prediction, but Frankie ignores it.) Frankie wanders to the Blue Moon to meet the soldier—although she has "the unexplainable feeling that there was a mistake" (126)—and, when he invites her up to his hotel room, she has neither the sense nor the social skills to refuse him. A "child no longer" (127), Frankie is hardly a woman. In his room, the soldier grabs her and Frankie knocks him out with a glass pitcher. She goes home but cannot tell John Henry what has happened—she no longer shares childhood with him, although she reverts briefly to childishness herself by scribbling a joke in a library book. She has had her own sexual initiation, but, like so much of her growth, it has been confused and almost unconscious. She has yet to act her way completely out of childhood.

The brief Part Three covers the wedding and its aftermath. As with the first visit of Jarvis and Janice, we only see the events indirectly through the stories and memories of our three central characters. Everyone in Winter Hill treated her nicely, and as a child—and she acted accordingly. She never had the chance to tell Jarvis and Janice, "I love the two of you so much and you are the we of me" (137), but after the ceremony came her humiliation:

> They are not going to take me, she was thinking, and this was the one thought she could not bear.
> When Mr. Williams brought their bags, she hastened after with her own suitcase. The rest was like some nightmare show in which a wild girl in the

audience breaks onto the stage to take upon herself an unplanned part that was never written or meant to be. You are the we of me, her heart was saying, but she could only say aloud: "Take me!" And they pleaded and begged with her, but she was already in the car. At the last she clung to the steering wheel until her father and somebody else had hauled and dragged her from the car, and even then she could only cry in the dust of the empty road: "Take me! Take me!" But there was only the wedding company to hear, for the bride and her brother had driven away. (138)

Berenice tries to soothe Frankie's hurt on the trip home by reminding her that school starts soon and by planning an adult party for her, but Frankie is even more determined now to "go into the world" by running away from home. That night she writes a note to her father, steals his pistol and wallet, and takes her third journey downtown. She contemplates but discards the idea of suicide and then decides to see if she killed the red-haired soldier—and perhaps to marry him! At this very moment, Frankie has an epiphany in which her "separate recollections fell together in the darkness of her mind . . . so that in a flash there came in her an understanding" (146). The understanding is sex: she suddenly grasps from the various fragments in her memory and experience what it is. She gives up the idea of the soldier but simultaneously realizes "she was too scared to go into the world alone" (146). In the Blue Moon, a policeman finds her and sends for her father. She has passed a significant symbolic point in her development: an understanding of sex and a simultaneous recognition of her necessary interdependence. Her new sexual adolescent identity comes linked with her need for others.

In the brief epilogue that concludes Part Three, it is several months later, Frankie is now 13, and everything is different. Her father has decided to move the two of them into a house on the outskirts of town with relatives. It is the last afternoon before the move, and Frankie (now calling herself "Frances") is in the kitchen with Berenice for the last time. The changes that Frankie dreaded in Part One have occurred. The childlike pictures that John Henry had drawn all over the kitchen are gone—and so is John Henry, dead at age 6 of meningitis. He has appeared to her a few times in nightmares, but otherwise Frankie seems untouched by his death. She has a new best friend, a precocious older girl named Mary Littlejohn, with whom she discusses art and literature, and Mary is part of the reason for the estrangement between Frankie and Berenice. Berenice has decided not to make the move with the Addamses but to marry T. T. Williams instead. And she and Frankie can no longer communicate about anything of significance. Frankie has made a successful passage to adolescence—certainly not without nearly drowning—

but at what a price. She has survived her humiliation at the wedding, as she has moved out of summer into fall. But the sensitive and frightened 12-year-old has become a somewhat smug and insensitive teenager. She has grown up, but she still has a lot of growing to do, readers may conclude.

Characters

While there are any number of exotic minor characters in this short novel—from Honey Camden Brown and Big Mama to the organ grinder and the Portuguese owner of the Blue Moon—the bright spotlight in the novel falls on the three main characters on center stage. (McCullers herself successfully adapted the novel into a play in 1950 and a few years later it was made into a film, with Julie Harris and Ethel Waters reprising the roles they had created on stage.) John Henry is hardly formed, of course, and plays almost a comic shadow to Frankie and Berenice—repeating their remarks or turning them into questions, following Frankie around the kitchen or around town—and yet his death at the end moves us. He has offered Frankie his love and affection, but she has moved beyond it without recognizing its importance to her.

Berenice is a much more complex character, and in many ways represents the mother figure Frankie can learn from and define herself against. If John Henry is Frankie's foothold in innocence, Berenice stands on the side of experience. She is herself a survivor and a symbol of endurance. It is to Berenice that Frankie turns and returns after all her adventures (at least until the epilogue), and it is from Berenice that Frankie learns about the world and about love. Berenice's vision is split (like her two eyes): she is partly a child herself (which is why she relates so well to the children), and at the same time she holds a tragic view of human life and history. She tries to help Frankie through this difficult period by suggesting she get a boyfriend (ironically naming Barney MacKean, a boy with whom Frankie has earlier shared some "unknown sin" in the McKean garage), and she plans a party for her after her humiliation. She understands "'the way when you are in love. . . . A thing known and not spoken'" (94). And she shares with Frankie the stories of her own sorrowful love for Ludie Freeman and her mistaken marriages since then (her blue glass eye is the reminder of one). Finally, she gives to the children her perspective on the world, a combination of Christian idealism and poetic naiveté.

But the world of the Holy Lord God Berenice Sadie Brown was a different world, and it was round and just and reasonable. First, there would be no separate colored people in the world, but all human beings would be light brown color with blue eyes and black hair. There would be no colored people and no white people to make the colored people feel cheap and sorry all through their lives. No colored people, but all human men and ladies and children as one loving family on the earth. And when Berenice spoke of this first principle her voice was a strong deep song that soared and sang in beautiful dark tones leaving an echo in the corners of the room that trembled for a long time until silence.

No war, said Berenice. No stiff corpses hanging from the Europe trees and no Jews murdered anywhere. No war, and the young boys leaving home in army suits, and no wild cruel Germans and Japanese. No war in the whole world, but peace in all countries everywhere. Also, no starving. (91–92)

It is also Berenice who gives us the right angle on Frankie. The novel's center of consciousness is this 12-year-old, and we view events through her sensibility, but it is Berenice who gives us a perspective with which to view the central character herself. She sees how awful this prepubescent girl can be—mean and jealous and at times "'the most selfish human being that ever breathed'" (72). Berenice also recognizes Frankie's silliness at the engaged couple's visit, her obsession with the wedding, and the disaster she is headed for in Winter Hill. But she still loves Frankie, and she takes the young girl onto her lap and soothes her, in perhaps the most touching scene in the novel, when all three central characters, for their own reasons, cry. The world is hard, Berenice knows, and all they have is each other.

It is Berenice, in fact, who gives shape and definition to Frankie's dreams, for without Berenice as mother figure and foil, Frankie's illusions would seem much more shallow and obsessive. And the relationship between the two women is one of incredible depth and richness—alternately harsh, loving, nasty, and affectionate. But it is Frankie who is at the center of *The Member of the Wedding*. She is that central female protagonist Carson McCullers was constantly wrestling with, from the young Mick Kelly in *The Heart Is a Lonely Hunter* (1940) to the troubled Miss Amelia of *The Ballad of the Sad Café* (1951), but here is her strongest expression of this adolescent in transit. And in this novel McCullers paints her with all the warts and incompletions that make her so perfectly realistic. She is afraid she is a freak (which is one reason she is so fascinated with the Half-Man Half-Woman at the House of Freaks at the annual Chattahoochee Exposition) and knows she is a criminal (she "stole a three-way knife from the Sears and Roebuck Store" [23] and thinks the police may be after her). She is half child, half adult; part woman, part man. (She wears her hair short and wants to "go to the war as a Marine" [21].) She is, in short, a perfect—in her mind, imperfect—

mix of sexes and ages at the brink of falling into her own sexual identity. And the key missing ingredient is sex. "One Saturday afternoon she committed a secret and unknown sin. In the MacKeans' garage, with Barney MacKean, they committed a queer sin, and how bad it was she did not know" (23). It is, in fact, her sexual innocence that seems to be keeping her back from the leap into adulthood. She witnessed a couple having a "fit" in the Addams' front bedroom, older girls tell "nasty lies about married people" (11), and Berenice stops in the middle of a story about her last husband—but Frankie is unable to recognize the sexual ingredient in each of these and to put them all together into her own knowledge and thus into a new identity.

Her obsession with the wedding provides an escape from this oppressive world of preadolescence and actually gives her, in ways she had not expected, a push toward adulthood. In this one three-day weekend, she successfully completes her symbolic journey out of childhood, not quite to adulthood, certainly, but beyond the door—through which she can now no longer return—to childhood. For after her encounter with the soldier in his hotel room, she looks into John Henry's "cold child eyes" and knows that she cannot explain. The next night, after her epiphany, she understands the dark knowledge that separates adolescence from childhood: an understanding of human sexuality, of that "'peculiar'" (Berenice) part of human existence.

She has wanted a connection to the world, to be a "member" of something. "But the old Frankie had had no *we* to claim, unless it would be the terrible summer *we* of her and John Henry and Berenice—and that was the last *we* in the world she wanted" (39). She chooses the fantasy world of love, travel, and adventure that Jarvis and Janice represent, but in so doing she must jettison the only real world she has—the circle of warmth of Berenice and John Henry and herself. She is bound to be disappointed, Berenice warns her, but Frankie must go through her disillusionment, her humiliation, alone. She comes out on the other side, a smug and fairly shallow Frances, but a 13-year-old who has finally left childhood behind. She has survived the difficult passage to adulthood but paid a price. We may love her less, but we understand her fully. Change, we know, is never without loss.

Themes

Readers familiar with Carson McCullers's other fiction—*The Heart Is a Lonely Hunter* or *The Ballad of the Sad Café*—will not be surprised at a certain oblique or elusive meaning to *The Member of the Wedding*. Like a number of Southern writers (William Faulkner and Flannery

O'Connor come immediately to mind), McCullers has a symbolic, spiritual strain that sometimes makes final interpretations difficult. Readers are more often left with feelings about the book than with words, or with questions rather than answers. What is Frankie's epiphany about? Why all the freaks? Why do the three of them cry? What does the monkey represent?

Of course, the subject of the novel—Frankie's passage from childhood to early adolescence—is itself a difficult theme and, in McCullers's subtle psychological depiction, not always conscious, rational, and clear. But this passage is surely the central meaning of *The Member of the Wedding*. The novel presents the growth of a young girl from childhood to early adolescence, and does it with numerous psychological insights. Frankie *does* gain her own sexual identity—or at least the beginnings of one—and starts her adult sexual life with new knowledge and a new sense of self. Few novels have depicted this rough transition in a young girl's life with as much poignant immediacy. At the same time that she is trying to break free from childhood, to gain a new, individual, and sexual identity, Frankie is moving in the opposite direction, to *join* with others, to find "connections" and the "we": "All other people had a *we* to claim, all other except her" (39).

If there is a label for the major subtheme that underscores her initiation story, it would be "illusion/reality." Throughout this short novel, Frankie takes the image for the fact, the gesture for the act, and she is wrong most of the time. The "fit" the roomer had was, of course, sexual; she thinks she sees Jarvis and Janice out of the corner of her eye, and it turns out to be two boys of similar shapes in an alley. Whatever romance and adventure she imagines with the red-haired soldier soon become drunken sexual violence. Even the organ grinder in the end does not provide music for her. Frankie must learn one of the secrets that adulthood holds: what appears to be often is not. Even love, unfortunately, has this possibility. Berenice found it briefly with Ludie Freeman, and then he died, and she kept pursuing pieces of him in other men, only to find madness and unhappiness. In the end, she settles for T. T. Williams, surely a compromise, for "'he don't make me shiver none'" (89). Even love can be an elusive illusion.

In fact, the portrait of the world that McCullers paints is fairly bleak. The war rages on around these three central characters with little relief, and life often seems out of their control. "'The point is we all caught'" (114), as Berenice knows, a black woman in a world with few favors for blacks. Mr. Addams, a widower, surely knows what kind of a world it is, and John Henry, dead of meningitis before he is 7, is tragically saved from the knowledge. It is a deterministic universe Frankie Addams is growing up into, with only glancing chances for happiness. Perhaps that is why we feel sympathy for Frankie's dreams and illusions. Certainly she feels that her situation is unbearable: trapped in this small town, in this kitchen, in this freakish body. Her dream of becoming a member of the wedding seems harmless in the face of life's true harshness, just as Berenice's philosophy appears naive but noble, given such a world.

The Member of the Wedding, in short, has a poignant and, finally, tragic perspective on life. While Frankie's difficult passage is successful— she *does* become 13, after all—it is mainly due to the power of her imagination, her readiness to chase her dreams. She tends to ignore reality and along the way discards some of the most important gifts she has (e.g., exchanging a real trio of friends for an imaginary one). Life is transitory and "queer," McCullers is telling her readers. We have little control over our lives, there is much disillusionment and disappointment, and love may turn out to be illusory. ("'The whole thing is a irony of fate,'" Frankie writes in her note to her father before running away from home, "'and it is inevitable'" [141].) It is not a terribly positive message for teenagers, but they keep reading the book on their own or in the countless junior and senior high school English classes where it is still assigned. There, perhaps, the subject is the complex psychological portrait of Frankie, and the focus is on her successful passage to early adolescence—a story of change and survival in an uncertain world.

Style and Language

Carson McCullers is one of the consummate artists in twentieth-century American literature, and the power of *The Member of the Wedding* is partly carried in the structure and poetry of its prose. There is a formal unity to the work that comes from its three-part organization. Each part has its own crucial story, a new name for Frankie, and a distinct flavor or mood, and the progress through the three parts is similar to that through a three-act tragedy (from fantasy to sexual awareness to disillusionment—and eventual recovery). What is unique about the story, or plot, of the novel is that McCullers barely touches on the main events in the lives of these characters; rather, she focuses on the effects of these events on the three, particularly on Frankie's thoughts and feelings. We never witness the visit of Jarvis and Janice, for example, but only see the impact of that visit on Frankie; the wedding is covered in two sentences, but its attraction beforehand is overwhelming and its consequences afterward, disastrous. The psychological realism of the novel is nearly overpowering, for the story demonstrates how thought and feeling really operate in human consciousness and how memory and desire often play larger roles in human life than any "reality" or "history" could ever play.

Besides its formal unity and psychological depth, the novel can be cited for its rich and musical language. From its opening line—"It happened that green and crazy summer" (1)—the novel is larded with lyrically poetic language: that Saturday afternoon "was like the center of the cake that Berenice had baked" (70); "the telling of the wedding had an end and a beginning, a shape like a song" (57). And:

> Berenice spoke in an unwinding kind of voice, and she had said that she was happier than a queen. As she told the story, it seemed to F. Jasmine that Berenice resembled a strange queen, if a queen can be colored and sitting at a kitchen table. She unwound the story of her and Ludie like a colored queen unwinding a bolt of cloth of gold. (96)

This prose-poetry is incredibly rich, filled as it is with images, colors, and sounds. (Few novels have so much music running through them—from the radio that is playing constantly in the background in the kitchen, to the organ grinder, to Mr. Schwartzenbaum, the piano tuner, playing his unfinished scale.) There is, in fact, a tension between the novel's bleak message and its musical prose. And the pathos of the novel is further alleviated by its verbal humor ("'my candy opinion'" [18] or "'I can still ministrate'" [79]) as well as by its visual comedy (John Henry buttering the foot of his "perfect little biscuit man," perhaps, or Frankie looking like "'a human Christmas tree'" in the dress she bought for the wedding).

The power and purpose of McCullers's prose can best be seen in the major metaphor running through the novel, that of *winter*. Jarvis has been stationed in Alaska, and Frankie shakes her "glass globe with snow inside" (9) and dreams of being there ("She walked up a cold white hill and looked on a snowy wasteland far below" [10]); Jarvis and Janice will be married in Winter Hill; people are constantly shivering (in August); and there are almost constant references to ice, blue, cold, frost, and similar images. In terms of Frankie's psychological development, the seasonal imagery works this way: childhood is like summer, like sitting hot and sticky and stuck in that kitchen with Berenice and John Henry; winter, on the other hand, stands for freedom and adulthood—getting away and growing up. (Frankie dreams of going north to the wedding; Berenice's happiest memories involve Ludie in the winter, north in Cincinnati.) The imagery, in short, comes to represent almost exact emotional states. While Frankie is fighting for growth and change, the metaphorical language of the novel is underscoring her real development. At the end, of course, it is fall, only halfway to the emotional maturity of winter but well out of the oppressive, childlike conditions of summer.

TEACHING THE NOVEL

Teaching Suggestions

It is an anomaly that *The Member of the Wedding* should be one of the most commonly taught novels in U. S. high schools, for it is also one of the most subtle and complex. In addition to its tragic perspective and metaphorical language noted above, the novel contains a symbolic and mythic power missing from most adolescent literature. In all three of Frankie's trips to town, for instance, there is a *surreal* quality to her encounters—with the monkey man, the Portuguese owner of the Blue Moon, the red-haired soldier—for she is entering a kind of "hell" or "underworld" that one finds more commonly in classical mythology (and in modern classics like Joyce's *Ulysses*). Encounters here have a symbolic import (as with the organ grinder and his monkey), and events appear as "signs" to Frankie (like Big Mama's forecasts). Frankie's passage to adulthood, in short, has a clearly mythic element, and her adventures may seem a little strange to readers unfamiliar with this kind of writing. At the same time, of course, it is this very symbolic, mythical element that gives depth and meaning to McCullers's prose: Frankie's passage to adulthood partakes of classical myth (like the wanderings of Odysseus, perhaps, or Orpheus in Hades).

Readers do not need to know all this, of course, to enjoy the novel, but they may sense the deeper structure of *The Member of the Wedding* through a certain oblique or distancing quality to its prose: "the summer was like a green sick dream, or like a silent crazy jungle under glass" (1). Students can note those passages where McCullers is pushing us toward a symbolic or mythic reading of the events of the novel. (Consider such language as Frankie's "'I am sick unto death'" [14], or John Henry's "'The show is over and the monkey's dead'" [135].) Similar language occurs in children's literature—in fables and fairy tales, for example—and students should not have any special difficulty with it.

Point of view should not give readers any undue difficulty either: *The Member of the Wedding* is narrated in the third person by some omniscient narrator, but the "focus" or "center of consciousness" (phrases coined by Henry James) is Frankie Addams. Students will recognize how rarely we get the thoughts and feelings of other characters and how often the actions of the novel are being filtered through Frankie's sensibility.

A full appreciation of *The Member of the Wedding* does require a recognition of the complex *characterization* of both Frankie and Berenice. Berenice is a survivor herself (which is perhaps why she is so helpful to Frankie), but she is also a philosopher, a nurturer, a seer, and more. Readers should note all the roles that Berenice plays by keeping track of the different things she says and does that reveal her diverse character. (For example, as *cook*, she prepares Saturday dinner; as *mother figure*, she alters Frankie's dress, holds her in her lap.) If Berenice can be apprehended vertically by listing all the roles she plays at any one moment, Frankie must be seen horizontally as she moves through stages in her psychosexual development. Students should pay attention to Frankie's words and actions, noting when they are childlike, adult, or a combination. Finally, the relationship between Frankie and Berenice is complex and varied, and students can observe what they say and do to each other and how their relationship shifts during the course of the novel. What, for example, do their words and actions reveal about their changing feelings for each other at different points in the novel? How has this relationship changed by the end? Readers who can see the shifting relationship between these two central characters are at the heart of the novel.

Discussion and Writing Ideas

Affective Topics

1. Select someone you know well or have observed at close range and write a *character sketch*, illustrating that person's more important physical and personality traits.
2. How does Frankie appear to you? Write a *character sketch* of her, noting her most important physical and personality traits.
3. Consider how you have changed in the last five years, and describe what you were then and what you are now. (You may want to focus on one area—on family relationships, for example, or school.)
4. Briefly describe an experience (a person, incident, or relationship) that changed you in some fundamental way and detail how it affected you.
5. Think about and describe the various roles you play in your life (brother or sister, friend, student, etc.). Do different people see you differently because they view you only in one or another of those roles (e.g., parents who see you as less responsible than a boss does)?

6. Think of a relationship you have shared with someone (a friend or relative) in which definite changes have occurred. Describe the relationship and those changes.
7. How did you feel when you read that John Henry had died? Why? What is the loss?
8. Describe something you wanted very badly (as Frankie wants to go off with Jarvis and Janice) and did not get. What did your disappointment feel like? How did you get over it?

ANALYTICAL TOPICS

1. Describe the relationship between Frankie and Berenice. What is it like and how has it changed by the end?
2. Frankie thinks that she would like "for her expression to be split into two parts" (105), as Berenice's is. Why? What does this split represent?
3. What is the role of the red-haired soldier? Write a letter from him to a friend, after this weekend. What would he say about what happened with Frankie?
4. Compare Frankie at the beginning and at the end of the novel. Is she different? How? Are the changes positive or not? Discuss.
5. Write a description of Frankie Addams ten years later. What is she doing? What is she like? What does she think now of her early adolescence? Did she learn anything from this period? What important incidents have occurred in the interim?
6. Discuss *setting*. What is important about where the novel takes place? (Consider the location, the season, and the time of day of different scenes.) What feeling does a particular scene give to us? How much of that feeling has to do with the setting?
7. Read the play version of *The Member of the Wedding* and compare the two. What does the play stress? Leave out?

Bridging to Other Works

Mark Twain, *Huckleberry Finn* (1884); see Chapter 2. Compare the two young Southern protagonists and such themes as illusion/reality.
Carson McCullers, *The Heart Is a Lonely Hunter* (1940). Note the parallels in the story of Mick Kelly.
Tennessee Williams, *The Glass Menagerie* (1945). Compare settings and themes—illusions, expectations—in this play from the same period.
Carson McCullers, *The Ballad of the Sad Café* (1951). This later novella has much of the symbolic, mythic element found in *The Member of the Wedding*.

J. D. Salinger, *The Catcher in the Rye* (1951); see Chapter 1. How are Frankie Addams and Holden Caulfield similar?

James Agee, *A Death in the Family* (1957). Compare settings, characters, and themes.

Harper Lee, *To Kill a Mockingbird* (1960); see Chapter 8. Compare setting (a small Southern town), characters, moods, and themes (initiation, etc.).

Bette Greene, *Summer of My German Soldier* (YA, 1973). Compare subjects (parents and kids, friendship, etc.).

Mildred D. Taylor, *Roll of Thunder, Hear My Cry* (YA, 1976); see Chapter 12. Note similarities in setting, characters, and themes.

Cynthia Voight, *Come a Stranger* (YA, 1987). The setting is contemporary and the protagonist is a bright, self-reliant black girl, but the subjects are similar.

10 "The gain of new and unfamiliar things"

THE RED PONY

Author: John Steinbeck (1902–1968)
Genre: psychological realism
Time of story: early 1900s
Locale: a ranch in California's Salinas Valley
Point of view: third-person limited omniscient
First published: 1937/1938
Edition used: Penguin paperback (1986) of *The Long Valley*, which includes *The Red Pony* (pp. 199–304)
Grade level: 7–10
Principal characters:
Jody Tiflin, a young boy (from age 10 to 12) growing up on an isolated California ranch
Carl Tiflin, Jody's "tall stern" father
Mrs. Tiflin, Jody's mother
Billy Buck, the Tiflins' middle-aged ranch hand
Gitano, an old *paisano* who returns to the ranch to die
Jody's grandfather (Mrs. Tiflin's father), who led a wagon train west in the late 1800s

ANALYSIS OF THE NOVEL

Story and Setting

The Red Pony is a short, episodic novella held together by setting, character, and theme. While each of its four parts is really a short story that can stand on its own (which is how each was originally published and how the fourth story, "The Leader of the People," at least, is still anthologized), together they form an incremental narrative concerning the education of Jody Tiflin. As originally published in 1937, *The Red Pony* contained only the first three stories, but the fourth was added the following year when *The Red Pony* was included in *The Long Valley*, a collection of Steinbeck's short stories, and again when *The Red Pony* was republished separately in 1945. In all subsequent editions of these two volumes, *The Red Pony* has appeared as a four-part novella, which is how it is considered here.

The first part, "The Gift," contains most of the elements of all four and, in some ways, is the best story in the book. It is late summer when Carl Tiflin and Billy Buck drive six old milk cows into Salinas and return with the red pony, a gift for the 10-year-old Jody. The boy is overwhelmed: "'Mine?'" is all he can ask, "shyly" (209). He names the colt Gabilan (meaning "hawk"), after the mountains that border one side of the Tiflin ranch, and begins the slow process of training the pony. Most of what he learns he picks up from the Tiflin ranch hand; "the whole country knew that Billy Buck was a fine hand with horses" (215). Time drags for Jody, and he cannot wait for Thanksgiving, when his father has told him he can first try to ride the pony and thus test himself—will he be able to ride Gabilan?

But nature and human fallibility intervene. One bright day Jody leaves Gabilan in the corral when he goes to school. Billy assures him that it is not likely to rain, that "'a little rain didn't hurt a horse,'" and that he'd "'watch out'" for the colt if he gets back in time.* The rain does come, however; Billy Buck does not get back in time, and Gabilan catches cold. Billy reassures Jody that the horse will get better, but it only gets worse. Billy "steams" the horse, opens its swollen glands with a knife to drain the pus, and finally has to perform a tracheotomy. Jody looks at Gabilan after this last operation and knows "at last that there was no hope for the pony" (235). Jody has been sleeping in the barn with his horse, and one night had awakened to find the barn door blown open and Gabilan wandering weakly in the dark. Now, on this last night, the barn door blows open again, and Jody wakes in the morning to find Gabilan gone. When he finally locates the pony, over the ridge, the buzzards have already attacked it. Jody dives into the middle of the black birds, catches one, and kills it. "He was still beating the dead bird when Billy Buck pulled him off and held him tightly to calm his shaking." His father lectures him: "'the buzzard didn't kill the pony.'" Of course he knows this, Billy Buck "said furiously. 'Jesus Christ! man, don't you see how he'd feel about it?'" (238). Jody has learned something about the fallibility of human beings—his own (the barn door blew open twice while he

---

*Billy and Carl Tiflin are "'going back on the hill to clean the leaves out of the spring,'" an annual ranch event—compare Robert Frost's poem, "The Pasture," with its inviting lines, "I'm going out to clean the pasture spring. . . . You come too."

was caring for Gabilan) as well as that of his hero, Billy Buck—but also about the natural order of life and death. His attack on the buzzards is a human protest against this knowledge.

In "The Great Mountains," the second part of *The Red Pony*, Jody's education into matters of life and death continues. It is a hot midsummer afternoon (probably a year after the start of the first story), and Jody is again a restless boy out of school. In his boredom, he kills a bird with his slingshot and must wash "the bird's blood from his hands in cold water" (240) where the spring-pipe runs into the round tub, and the scene is a modest recapitulation of the violent scene with the buzzards at the end of the previous story (alternatively, the two stories are woven together by the repeated image). Then Jody lies down in "a stretch of fine green grass, deep and sweet and moist," where the water from the tub spills over, and studies "the great mountains," the second range circling the ranch (opposite the Gabilans), "where they went piling back, growing darker and more savage" (240). There is "something secret and mysterious," both inviting and frightening, locked in "the Great Ones" for Jody, and neither his father nor his mother can explain the secret to him.

And then Gitano, an old *paisano* with "large and deep and dark" eyes, returns to the ranch where he was born (in an old adobe house now gone) in order to die. Carl Tiflin reluctantly lets him stay for the night but cruelly reminds him that, like the old horse Easter that wanders up for water, "'Old things ought to be put out of their misery'" (249). For Jody, Gitano holds "some unknown thing" (252), just as the mountains do. At the first opportunity, Jody asks Gitano if he has ever gone into "'the big mountains back there?'" and Gitano answers that, yes, once, when he was a boy, his father took him there, and it was "'quiet'" and "'nice.'" Jody also discovers Gitano's sword, "a lean and lovely rapier with a gold basket hilt" (253) that was a gift from Gitano's father. Jody realizes that he "must never tell anyone about the rapier" (254), and he does not.

The next morning, Gitano and Easter and the rapier are gone, and a neighbor (Jess Taylor) comes by to say that he has seen the old man "'heading straight back into the mountains'" (255) on a horse with what looked like a gun: "'At least I saw something shine in his hand'" (255). The old man has apparently ridden into the mountains with his sword to die. "Jody thought of the rapier and of Gitano. And he thought of the great mountains. A longing caressed him, and it was so sharp that he wanted to cry to get it out of his breast" (256). Jody has experienced the cycle of life and death again; the secret that Gitano shares with the mountains is *death*. Jody feels the loss; he lies down again "in the green grass near the round tub at the brush line. . . . and he was full of a nameless sorrow" (256).

The third part of *The Red Pony*, "The Promise," returns us to the concerns of the first story. It is spring, and Carl tells Jody that because he took good care of Gabilan before the pony died, and because "'Billy says the best way for you to be a good hand with horses is to raise a colt'" (260), Jody is to get a new one. First he must take the mare Nellie to a neighbor's ranch to get it bred; then follow the slow 11 months during which Jody must wait for the colt to be born. (Jody worries that before the colt appears, "'I'll be grown up.'") Billy warns the boy that things can go wrong, that sometimes you have to "'tear the colt to pieces to get it out, or the mare'll die'" (267), but Jody still insists on reassurance that nothing will happen to the colt.

> And Billy knew he was thinking of the red pony, and of how it died of strangles. Billy knew he had been infallible before that, and now he was capable of failure. This knowledge made Billy much less sure of himself than he had been. (268)

Jody's worst fears are confirmed: at the moment of birth, Billy Buck discovers that the colt is turned wrong inside the mare, and he must kill Nellie with hammer blows to the forehead and cut the colt out of her.

> Billy's face and arms and chest were dripping red. His body shivered and his teeth chattered. His voice was gone; he spoke in a throaty whisper. "There's your colt. I promised. And there it is. I had to do it—had to." (279–80)

But the reader is not so sure. Would Billy Buck have killed Nellie if he had not promised the colt to Jody, or would he, instead, have killed the colt to save the mare? In either case, Jody has again been witness to the pain and violence of ranch life (in the second brutally realistic scene in the novella), has been put in touch again with the natural cycle of death and birth, and has been reminded again of human fallibility—or at least of the difficult choices adults often face.

The last part of *The Red Pony*, "The Leader of the People," is almost a reprieve from the violence of the preceding parts, for it is the first story that does not involve death. Here, in fact, the focus is not even primarily on Jody; rather it is on his grandfather, who comes to the ranch for a visit. (Its oblique relation to the central themes of the others stories is, perhaps, the reason Steinbeck did not include it when *The Red Pony* was first published, only adding it later.) The grandfather is a garrulous old man, but he holds "a granite dignity." He loves to tell his stories of leading a wagon train west, and he has a willing audience in Jody and Billy Buck (who, like Jody, admires the old man). Carl, however, is tired

of the oft-repeated tales and sarcastic about them, and one morning the
old man accidentally overhears his cruel criticism. Carl apologizes, but
his father-in-law is clearly hurt.

Later, his grandfather tries to explain to Jody why he keeps telling
these old stories. "'It wasn't Indians that were important, nor adventures,
nor even getting out here. It was a whole bunch of people made into one
big crawling beast. And I was the head. It was westering and westering'"
(302–3). But that time has gone. "'Westering has died out of the people.
. . . Your father is right. It is finished'" (303). Earlier, Jody had wished
"he could have been living in the heroic time, but he knew he was not of
heroic timber" (298). Yet he also risked the displeasure of his father and
"arose to heroism" by asking his grandfather to "'Tell about Indians'"
(296). Now he offers to make his grandfather a glass of lemonade. When
he asks his mother for a lemon, she realizes the significance of his gesture
and is touched. Jody has learned about history and about different
attitudes toward the past. But he has also apparently learned civility and
human compassion. The reader, like Jody's mother, feels warmly toward
the boy. He has risen to some small heroism himself.

Characters

Because *The Red Pony* is essentially a collection of four related short
stories, its structure is rather static and there is little character development. Unlike a novel, which unfolds as a movie might, *The Red Pony*
strikes us as a slide show of four fairly fixed photographs. We see
characters at four stages and watch them act and interact at those stages,
but only in the character of the protagonist, Jody Tiflin, do we see any
real growth.

Jody is a normal young boy growing up in the isolation of a rural
California ranch in the early part of this century. In the first story, he
smashes "a green muskmelon with his heel"; on his way home from
school in the third story, he fills his lunch pail with toads and lizards—
and lets his mother discover the surprise; at the opening of the last story,
Jody is scuffing his shoes "in a way he had been told was destructive to
good shoe-leather" (283) and looking forward to hunting mice in an old
hay mound.

We do not enter Jody's mind a great deal, but we see events from his
perspective; very little happens in the novella outside of Jody's conscious
line of sight. We are at what critic T. K. Whipple calls "the middle
distance" in Steinbeck (quoted in Lisca 100–1), witnessing the action of
the stories with Jody as our touchstone. And Jody *does* react to events,
for he is a dreamy and sometimes sensitive young boy who wants a horse

of his own, loves his parents and grandfather and Billy Buck, and wants to be loved by them. ("It was a bad thing to do," smashing the musk-melon, "he knew perfectly well. He kicked dirt over the ruined melon to conceal it" [205].) From each of the characters here, Jody appears to take something: practical sense from his father, sensitivity from his mother, courage and caring from Billy Buck, and a feeling for the past from his grandfather. He does not change radically over the course of the four stories, which take him from the ages of 10 to 12, but his gestures to his grandfather in "The Leader of the People" hint that his remaining development will be successful.

The other characters in *The Red Pony* are much more fixed foils for Jody and show little change within themselves. Carl Tiflin is a disciplinarian who "insisted upon giving permission for anything that was done on the ranch" (285). He can be both "cruel" and "mean," he gives presents "with reservations," he hates "weakness and sickness, and he held a violent contempt for helplessness" (224). But he is not without saving graces: he tells stories to Jody one night to keep the boy's mind off his sick pony, his feelings are "badly hurt" when Billy Buck turns on him "angrily" about the boy, and he is "embarrassed" by his own displays of emotion. Carl Tiflin's limitations are clearly derived from the harsh environment he is trying to control, for, like most of the people here, his character has been determined by the world he inhabits.

Jody's mother is much more sensitive and sympathetic: in the first scene of the novella, she tells Jody to hurry into breakfast because she is aware that Billy Buck does not like to sit down to a meal before the family he works for is seated. In "The Leader of the People," she defends her father to her husband: "Her voice had become soft and explanatory" (288). Jody is often witness to the discussions of adults around him, but it is not until this last story (perhaps a sign of his maturity) that he becomes aware of the tension between his parents.

Billy Buck is the "significant other" in Jody's life, a "broad, bandy-legged little man with a walrus moustache" (201) who teaches Jody a great deal, both by what he does (getting angry at Carl, for example, for his insensitivity to Jody's feelings) and what he says (that the only way to learn something is "'to start at the start'" [272], to note one instance). Billy does everything he can, first to save Gabilan and then to make sure that Nellie's colt lives, but in both cases he is only human: in the first he fails, and in the second he has to sacrifice the mare for the colt. Jody learns from Billy Buck's fallibility, and this knowledge is an important part of his development.

Jody's grandfather is a talkative old man who nonetheless teaches the boy something about heroism and history. Gitano is an old man with a body "as straight as that of a young man" (250) who shows Jody a part of the mystery of life—and the "secret" that is death. Jody's small gestures at the end of "The Leader of the People" are perhaps symbolic of other changes going on inside the boy, changes caused, in large part, through his interactions with these other characters.

Themes

The main theme of *The Red Pony* is Jody's education about life and death, his (obviously incomplete) initiation into adulthood. At the opening of "The Gift," Jody feels "an uncertainty in the air, a feeling of change and of loss and of the gain of new and unfamiliar things" (205). He is right, and his feeling is a preview of events that will happen to him over the next two years. If at the beginning of the novella Jody is an innocent 10-year-old capable of little besides mischief, by the last story he has grown into a sensitive 12-year-old capable of heroic acts.

Many of the lessons Jody learns are small ones (about patience, adult behavior, etc.), and many are learned from Billy Buck. But the larger lessons that Jody learns are the other themes of *The Red Pony*. The major idea is death, its role in the life cycle, and its different faces. In the first story, Gabilan's death seems merely a waste. Nothing is gained from it—except the incidental knowledge of how human carelessness and fallibility are tied up in all of life—and Jody's violent attack on the buzzards seems a frustrated protest against this meaningless loss. But the death of Gitano in "The Great Mountains" is different, almost peaceful, and Jody's "nameless sorrow" at the end is the result of real loss: he has discovered the "secret" of death that Gitano and the mountains held in common, and he grieves for his discovery as well as for the old man. Finally, in "The Promise," the mare's death produces life, and Jody is granted a new "gift," a new colt born out of Nellie's death. Thus Jody moves from death as empty pain, through death as human sorrow, to death as producing life.

This theme of death as a necessary part of the life cycle is conveyed most graphically in the image of the "mossy tub" that sits on the hill above the ranch buildings. It is here that Jody goes when he wants to get away and from here that he gets a perspective on his life. When he first realizes just how sick Gabilan is, he walks up to the tub and looks down on the ranch. "The place was familiar, but curiously changed. It wasn't itself any more, but a frame for things that were happening" (235). And it is from this "patch of perpetually green grass" in the second story that Jody notices the contrast between the "jolly" Gabilan mountains and "the great mountains." This is the contrast between life and death; both surround the ranch, and both exist in Gitano, as in all life.

By the time Jody goes to "the old green tub" in the third story, "This place had grown to be a center-point for Jody. When he had been punished the cool green grass and the singing water soothed him" (268–69). The place is a symbol for life, or for rebirth, for the grass is perpetually green here. But it is on this visit that Jody also notices in more detail "the black cypress tree by the bunkhouse . . . as repulsive as the water-tub was dear"; it is there that the pigs are slaughtered. As the black cypress stands in contrast to the "deep and sweet and moist" spot by the tub, so death stands in relation to life; so, in this story, the death of Nellie stands in relation to the birth of the colt. Both poles—"opposites and enemies" (269)—are natural, and both are part of the education of Jody Tiflin in this rough, sometimes violent, life on the ranch.

"The Leader of the People" is almost a coda to the novella, for there is a dramatic, thematic shift in this last story. If the first three stories are about death (or about birth/life/death as a cycle), the last is more about the past and about our attitudes toward it. Jody has learned the lessons death can teach him in the first three parts of the novella; now he is moving on in the school of life. For his father, the past is the past, and he wishes Grandfather would stop repeating stories about it. But Jody learns from his grandfather that the past is more than that, a time of possibility and, perhaps, of heroism. Even though westering is "finished," as Carl argues, it still represents another important cycle. As Grandfather says in the last scene in the novella, "'We carried life out here and set it down the way those ants carry eggs'" (303). Jody's gestures at the end indicate that he shares his grandfather's reverence for history as a living thing, a cycle of past and future that we are all inextricably caught up in (and that is represented, perhaps, by the grandfather and grandson themselves).

Earlier in "The Leader of the People," Jody remarks to Billy Buck that the mice he's about to hunt "'don't know what's going to happen to them today.'" "'No, nor you either,' Billy remarked philosophically, 'nor me, nor anyone'" (299). Jody "knew it was true," though he is still "staggered" by this knowledge. Through the course of *The Red Pony*, Jody is being given a set of skills, attitudes for dealing with the unpredictable future, which—like the bad weather that surprised Gabilan in his corral—constantly threatens to engulf human life. By the end of "The Leader of the People," we feel more confident about Jody's future, for the values he has gained should help him to survive and grow in this environment.

Style and Language

The themes in *The Red Pony* are simple and natural, but that is because they are part of the very fabric of Steinbeck's prose; form and content are woven subtly together in the novella. No moral is affixed (as is the case in some YA fiction); rather, the ideas emerge organically from the language and imagery of the stories.

The best example of this organic style of *The Red Pony* is its descriptions. The exposition of the novella is clear, and Steinbeck only describes things that Jody sees or notices, which are objects that occur as necessary parts of farm life, such as the two farm dogs, Doubletree Mutt and Smasher; Gabilan's red leather saddle; and the old bunkhouse. Thus the *imagery* of the novella is natural to this life. When Gabilan is sick, for example, Jody notices two blackbirds chasing a hawk and the clouds "moving in to rain again" (229) and, the next day, "how the young grass was up and how the stubble was melting day by day into the new green crop" (230). The green tub and the black cypress indicate that the struggle for life goes on in a natural world, which Steinbeck describes in both outline and detail.

The Red Pony is loaded with animal imagery—from the title through the many references to snakes, hawks, toads—and what this imagery should alert us to is Steinbeck's philosophical view of life. Man is an animal, in Steinbeck's view, like other animals, merely part of a very impersonal nature. This view of man as both part of nature and subject to its forces is central to literary *naturalism*. (See Stephen Crane's "The Open Boat" for a similar view.) The grandfather's talk of the westward migration as "one big crawling beast" and his reference to humans as ants, Billy Buck's comparison of humans to mice—these are part of Steinbeck's naturalistic philosophy. Like the real pain and violence of life on the ranch (the death of both Gabilan and Nellie, for example), the animal imagery reminds us of the insignificance of human decisions in the face of greater forces, a clearly Darwinian view of reality.

At the same time, these natural objects in Steinbeck often stand for ideas: they are *symbols*. The green tub symbolizes life and rebirth, just as the old cypress tree stands for death. Similarly, the two chains of mountains stand in symbolic opposition to each other. This symbolism is not superimposed onto the novella but, again, comes out of the natural fabric of its language and imagery.

If there is a weakness in the narrative of *The Red Pony* it is in its structure. The four stories alternate: animal/old man/animal/old man. The animal stories are the most violent and dramatic, and the rhythm of the novella is thus, to use the language of poetry, *trochaic*, with the emphasis falling on the first and third beats of this work. Put another way, *The Red Pony* is most exciting in its first part, and then in its third; there is a falling energy in the novella, instead of a rising one. It is not a terrible fault, and it clearly comes from yoking together four stories that started life as separate creations, rather than writing a book from start to finish. Still, the novella does not have the structure or momentum we expect in most novels, and readers may find it a little choppy.

TEACHING THE NOVEL

Teaching Suggestions

Steinbeck's ideas in *The Red Pony* are serious, and younger readers especially may not be able to articulate them at once. On the simplest level, the lessons that Jody learns are *psychological*, giving us insight into how humans act and react, or behave. (Like any normal boy, for example, Jody worries about the consequences of grabbing the saddlehorn in learning to ride Gabilan; would his parents be ashamed of him?) On another level, the stories here have a certain *mythic* power, for Steinbeck, like some contemporary Native American writers, is in touch with a deeper knowledge of human life. When Jody attacks the buzzards, when his grandfather talks about "'the one big crawling beast,'" or when Gitano rides into the mountains, Steinbeck is recapitulating basic patterns of human history, cycles of struggle, migration, and death that underlie the development of the human species. Teachers need not dwell on this mythic level of the novella, but it is clearly there. Probably the best way to start *The Red Pony*, as with other literary works that have elements students are not familiar with, is through the affective writing topics in the next section that ask students about their own experience; then use these parallels as bridges into the novel itself.

Of course, there is always sentimentality in Steinbeck—as there is in most writers who deal with such emotional and primal situations—but what is remarkable in *The Red Pony* is how unobtrusive that sentimentality is. The most potentially emotional scenes—the deaths of two horses, the scenes of Jody with the two old men—are usually described so sparely that the reader does not feel any authorial manipulation. On the other hand, Steinbeck is sometimes guilty of personification (attributing human qualities to nonhuman objects), as when he describes the two ranch dogs at the opening of "The Gift" as "hunching their shoulders and grinning horribly with pleasure" (204). Dogs cannot grin—except, perhaps, in a child's eyes, and Jody is not narrating this story. (Ironically,

Steinbeck said in an interview in 1969: "What can you tell 'em about writing except putting things down honestly, precisely? 'I looked at the dog. The dog looked at me.' You can try 50 different ways but you'll never be able to say it any better than that" [Schulberg 14]. Thus we see something of the gap between theory and practice.)

   Point of view in the novella is limited omniscient: we watch events with Jody in the center of our field of vision. A helpful concept here is Whipple's notion of "the middle distance" in Steinbeck, which keeps us at arm's length from the thoughts and feelings of all his characters (instead of inside their heads). As Peter Lisca notes, it is through this distancing technique "that the stories about Jody escape both the infantilism and the excessive psychological distortions which are the usual literary pitfalls of these stories' subject matter" (101). Students can learn about point of view in the novella by keeping track of how the actions are usually viewed from Jody's perspective, how rarely we see things he could not see or get into the thoughts and feelings of other characters. But students should also look for the values that Jody is observing in the other inhabitants of his world and developing on his own.

Discussion and Writing Ideas

AFFECTIVE TOPICS

1. Parents play different roles in different families. Briefly describe the role of your parent(s) in relation to your growth and development.
2. Recall and briefly describe an event or person (parent, grandparent, other adult) that influenced the way you view history and the past.
3. Select a person from whom you have learned a valuable lesson through his/her words/deeds; describe the lesson and how you have applied it to your life.
4. Write about Jody Tiflin 20 years after the end of the novella. Where is Jody at age 32, and what is he doing?
5. If you were in Jody's shoes (and had the power to do it), what would you change on the Tiflin ranch? Why?
6. Describe an experience you had that taught you *responsibility*. Be specific in your description.
7. His grandfather tells Jody, in "The Leader of the People," that the westward migration is "finished." If you were Jody today, and wanted to emigrate to a different place, where would you go? Why?
8. *Teacher:* Play excerpts from Aaron Copland's score for the 1949 film version of *The Red Pony*. Have students write down the scenes they imagine from the novella or free-write to the music.

ANALYTICAL TOPICS

1. What specifically does Jody learn about *death* in the first three stories of *The Red Pony*? Does he get a similar message in each story? What is it?
2. What does Jody learn about history (or about attitudes toward the past) in "The Leader of the People"? What does he learn from his grandfather in this story? From the other characters?
3. Describe the roles that Jody's parents play in *The Red Pony*. What does Jody learn from them? How important are they in his growth? Who is more important in this development, his mother or father?
4. Describe the role of Billy Buck, the Tiflins' ranch hand and Jody's mentor, or teacher. What does Billy teach Jody, both by what he says and what he does?
5. Describe the roles that Gitano and Jody's grandfather play in the novella. What does Jody learn from each man? Are there any similarities in these lessons?
6. Write about *responsibility* and *human fallibility* in *The Red Pony*. Who or what is responsible for the deaths of Gabilan and Nellie? What could have been done to save them? What does Jody learn from their deaths, if anything?
7. Describe the influence of *setting* in this novella. Could the stories here have taken place somewhere else? Where? Why or why not?

Bridging to Other Works

WORKS BY STEINBECK

The other 11 stories in *The Long Valley*, although not having Jody Tiflin as a character, are related to *The Red Pony* by setting—the Salinas Valley—and theme—survival, death, initiation. Consider especially the following two stories:

"The Crysanthemums" has a rural, isolated setting and powerful imagery. In this story, a farm wife, Elisa, learns about sexual/social roles and their limitations.
"Flight" concerns a young boy (Pepé Torres) who kills a man and must flee into the mountains. The animal imagery in the story is very close to that of *The Red Pony*.

Other Steinbeck novellas (a length of narrative well suited to young readers) that reflect the ideas and style of *The Red Pony* are:

The Pearl (1947). This is a short parable about a Mexican fisherman who finds a huge pearl that brings tragedy to his family.

Of Mice and Men (1937). This is a short novel (also made into a play, a film, and several TV versions) about two itinerant farmhands, Lennie and George, that replicates the animal imagery, the violence, and the naturalistic setting of *The Red Pony*.

NOVELS WITH YOUNG PROTAGONISTS

Harper Lee, *To Kill a Mockingbird* (1960); see Chapter 9. Compare the fathers in these two novels.

Richard Bradford, *Red Sky at Morning* (YA, 1968). Josh's search for values in New Mexico echoes some of the moods of *The Red Pony*.

William Armstrong, *Sounder* (YA, 1969). Note the parallels of rural life, relation to animals, and so forth.

Robert Newton Peck, *A Day No Pigs Would Die* (YA, 1972); see Chapter 11. Compare what the two young protagonists learn about death, responsibility, etc.

Theodore Taylor, *The Maldonado Miracle* (YA, 1973). This novel recounts the adventures of a young Mexican boy and his dog on a ranch near Salinas.

WORKS DEALING WITH VIOLENCE, DEATH, AND INITIATION

Stephen Crane, *The Red Badge of Courage* (1895); see Chapter 7.

Edith Wharton, *Ethan Frome* (1911).

Ernest Hemingway, *The Old Man and the Sea* (1952) and *The Nick Adams Stories* (1972).

William Golding, *Lord of the Flies* (1955).

James Agee, *A Death in the Family* (1957).

ANIMAL STORIES FOR YOUNGER STUDENTS

Marjorine Kinnan Rawlings, *The Yearling* (1938).

Scott O'Dell, *Island of the Blue Dolphins* (YA, 1960).

Wilson Rawls, *Where the Red Fern Grows* (YA, 1961).

Sheila Burnford, *The Incredible Journey* (1961).

Jean Craighead George, *Julie of the Wolves* (YA, 1972).

11   "Every man must face his own mission"

A DAY NO PIGS WOULD DIE

Author: Robert Newton Peck (b. 1928)
Genre: historical fiction (YA)
Time of story: mid-1920s
Locale: rural Vermont
Point of view: first person
First published: 1972
Edition used: Dell Laurel-Leaf paperback (1977); 139 pp.
Grade level: 6–9
Principal characters:
    Robert (Rob) Peck, the 12-year-old narrator
    Haven Peck, Rob's father, a 60-year-old farmer and hog butcher
    Lucy Peck (Mama), Rob's mother
    Aunt Carrie, Mama's oldest sister (nearly 70), who lives on the Peck
      farm
    "Aunt" Mattie, a friend of Mama and Aunt Carrie
    Benjamin Tanner, the Pecks' "near" neighbor
    Iris Bascom, another neighbor
    Ira Long, the Widow Bascom's hired man and, later, her husband

ANALYSIS OF THE NOVEL

Story and Setting

A Day No Pigs Would Die is a semi-autobiographical novel about growing up in a Shaker family in Vermont in the 1920s. (The novel is dedicated "To my father, Haven Peck . . . a quiet and gentle man whose work was killing pigs".) By the end of the novel, Rob Peck has learned enough to take over responsibility for his economically poor but spiritually rich family. Along the way, readers witness the pain, hardship, and violence of actual farm life in an earlier part of this century.

Rob narrates his story in a leisurely manner, and the structure of the novel is very episodic: events follow each other naturally, but without any compelling plot line. In fact, chapters are often separable short stories in the life and adventures of this young boy. Chapter 1 tells how Rob skips school—"I should of been in school that April day" (7), the novel opens—and, wandering in the woods above his family's farm, comes across Apron, a neighbor's cow, struggling to give birth to a calf. The quick-thinking Rob takes off his pants, ties one leg around the calf's head and the other to a dogwood tree, hits the cow, and thus aids in the birth. Then, when the cow is still in obvious pain, Rob reaches down her throat to remove a "goiter" the size of an apple and is badly bitten. Rob is found unconscious by the cow's owner, Mr. Tanner, and taken home.

This first chapter is exciting and "hooks" the reader at once with its drama. (I suggest that teachers start the novel by reading Chapter 1 aloud to a class.) But even in this dramatic chapter, we are learning a great deal, not only basic information about Rob (that he is a young Shaker living near Learning, Vermont) but also about his character (that he is brave, stubborn, and commonsensical). The novel is carved out of little more than a year of Rob's adolescence (his 12th to 13th year), but it is probably the crucial year of his young life, for it is the year when his father dies and Rob must become a man.

Many of the actions and incidents in the novel are connected to this central initiation story. In reward for helping Apron, Rob is given a piglet by Mr. Tanner, his very first "possession." During this year he raises his pig, and in one of the climactic scenes of the novel, Pinky wins a blue ribbon for "best-behaved pig" at the annual Rutland Fair. Many of the other stories in the novel revolve around the Peck farm and Rob's increasing maturity as he learns about life and death there through such activities as building a crib for Pinky, "weaseling" the neighbor's dog, and slaughtering the pig. Even the scenes when Rob wanders away from the farm repeat these lessons: he witnesses a crow eating a frog, then a hawk killing a rabbit, and later he kills a squirrel himself. The novel is steeped in the rural, sometimes primitive, life of Vermont in the 1920s, when the Pecks are barely making a living out of their farm. Poverty is close, self-sufficiency is necessary, and birth and death are natural parts of the life cycle.

Along the way, the younger reader will learn a great deal of incidental information, not only about rural farm life in Vermont in the 1920s but also about "the Shaker way," a religious culture that was once a small but important part of American life and that is now completely gone. Rob Peck not only becomes a man in the novel; he learns what it means to be a Shaker man and neighbor and begins to model his life on his

father's. At the end of the novel, after Pinky is slaughtered and his father
dies, Rob begins to assert himself as the new head of this small Shaker
family.

Characters

Most of the characters in *A Day No Pigs Would Die*—naturally
enough in such a short YA novel for younger readers—are two-dimensional, but both major characters—Rob and his father—are well developed.

The women and neighbors in the novel play only bit parts and act
mainly to support the development of the two protagonists. Rob's mother
stays in the background most of the time, and Aunt Carrie is an even more
shadowy figure. (Rob has four married sisters who do not figure in the
story at all.) Neighbors appear now and then, but their roles generally call
for them to act as foils for Haven Peck and as agents in Rob's growth.

But Rob and Haven Peck are fully fleshed out by the end of the
novel, which is quite an accomplishment for such a short work. Haven
Peck is a heroic figure and was clearly meant to be so by the author. He is
old and, by the end of the novel, sick, but he holds his family together by
the strength of his hands and the power of his spirit. He tends his farm
and, since that is not enough to support them, he also works as a local
slaughterer of hogs. (The smell of pig is always on him, but his wife
"'never complains'"; "'She said I smelled of honest work, and that there
was no sorry to be said or heard,'" he tells Rob [112].) He has the
reputation as the best butcher in the region. The title of the novel refers to
the day of his death—the only day no hogs would die, since the men he
worked with will attend his funeral. He is also illiterate, but the author
allows us to see the dignity that this poor, unschooled man has.

His values are clear and strong, and we see them both in his actions
and in key conversations with his son. In Chapter 8, for example, he
helps Sebring Hillman rebury his illegitimate child. In another scene, he
reveals to Rob that he cannot vote because he cannot write his name.
Rob asks if that makes him "'heartsick.'"

"No, I take what I am. We are Plain People, your mother and aunt, and your
sisters, you and me. We live the Book of Shaker. We are not worldly people,
and we suffer the less for not paining with worldly wants and wishes. I am
not heartsick, because I am rich and they are poor."

"*We're* not rich, Papa. We're . . ."

"Yes we are, boy. We have one another to fend to, and this land to tend.
And one day we'll own it outright. . . . We have Daisy's hot milk. We got rain

to wash up with, to get the grime off us. We can look at sundown and see it all, so that it wets the eye and hastens the heart. We hear all the music that's in the wind, so much music that it itches my foot to start tapping." (38–39)

Haven Peck is a man who has lived his life with principle, and there are few figures of such heroic size in contemporary YA fiction.

Rob Peck begins almost as a child, but, in the course of the novel, he acts and learns and, by the end, is able to shoulder many of the responsibilities previously carried by his father. (His growth in the last chapter is rather abrupt, but the author has a great deal to say or imply in those last ten pages and thus condenses.) In particular, Rob's own actions—like raising and showing Pinky—have taught him self-reliance; his interactions with the Tanners and the Widow Bascom and Ira Long have taught him neighborly interdependence; and his relationship with his father has taught him lessons that will reach well beyond the limits of the book. He will certainly grow up to be a different man from his father; among other things, he is going to school and will be able to vote. Also, he recognizes his father's limitations: as he tells Benjamin Tanner, Haven Peck has been "'trying all his life to catch up to something. But whatever it is, it's always ahead of him, and he can't reach it'" (121). And in the weaseling scene he actually asserts himself against his "elders." ("'Kill her,'" he says with authority about the crippled Hussy.) By the end of the novel, Rob Peck has come of age, has passed into adulthood. And, as Ben Tanner reminds Rob at his father's funeral, "'The way you said that . . . you sort of sounded like your father'" (137). He will always, we hope, sound like his father.

Themes

As is true in many YA novels, where the didactic strain is strong, *A Day No Pigs Would Die* contains quite a few ideas. The central one is initiation: Rob Peck learns and grows and moves quickly from childhood into adulthood. At the beginning of the novel, he is a normal 12-year-old, skipping school; by the end of the novel, and with the death of his father, he has been pushed into early adulthood, and both Mama and Aunt Carrie look to him for leadership. This is a patriarchal society, and when Rob is called, he proves ready. (It is also a provincial and sexist society, as it proves in its treatment of the Widow Bascom, but few small towns are not.)

Many of the crucial incidents in this initiation theme revolve around Pinky. Mr. Tanner gives Rob the pig in thanks for helping Apron with her Holstein calves Bob and Bib (Bob has been named for Rob, since the boy assisted in the birth; Bib was born after Rob passed out). But he must find another excuse for the gift, since, as Haven Peck holds, "'it's not the Shaker Way to take frills for being neighborly'" (24). (A subtheme here is possessions: the family has few, and Pinky is "the first thing I had ever really wanted and owned" [25].) His pride in the pig, his responsibility in taking care of her, and his final sacrifice in helping slaughter her are all part of Rob's passage to manhood. At the Rutland Fair, he "shows" Bob and Bib for Mr. Tanner and feels a "sinful" pride: "I wanted the whole town of Learning to see me just this once" (90). A few minutes later, Pinky wins a blue ribbon for "best-behaved pig" (appropriately, for Haven Peck has stressed "manners" in his son's trip away from home), and Rob's getting sick on the judge's shoe does not detract from a scene that sits at the moral center of the novel. When Rob sees that Pinky has rolled in manure at the last minute before the judging, he does not hesitate to spend his only dime (his aunt's secret present for a treat) on a piece of soap to clean the pig. It is a sacrifice that his father never learns about but which would make him proud. Rob is fulfilling his "mission."

A major part of the initiation story is the death of Rob's father, an event that caps his journey to adulthood. Like the animals he works so closely with, Haven Peck knows when he is about to die, and he moves to the barn and tries to prepare Rob for his new responsibilities. "'Come spring, you aren't the boy of the place. You're the man. A man of thirteen'" (115). And then the two men mark Rob's passage into manhood in a painful scene: they slaughter the barren Pinky to provide the family with meat for the winter. "'That's what being a man is all about, boy,'" Haven Peck says to his sobbing son. "'It's just doing what's got to be done.'"

> I felt his big hand touch my face, and it wasn't the hand that killed hogs. It was almost as sweet as Mama's. His hand was rough and cold, and as I opened my eyes to look at it, I could see that his knuckles were dripping with pig blood. It was the hand that just butchered Pinky. He did it. Because he had to. Hated to and had to. And he knew that he'd never have to say to me that he was sorry. His hand against my face, trying to wipe away the tears, said it all. His cruel pig-sticking fingers so lightly on my cheek.
>
> I couldn't help it. I took his hand to my mouth and held it against my lips and kissed it. (129)

This scene symbolizes both Rob's initiation and his undying love for his father. And Haven Peck is not unmoved; he cries as well. "It was the first time I ever seen him do it" (130). In the next chapter, Haven Peck dies.

Even in death, his father remains a presence for Rob. Wandering in their barn before the funeral, he notices the handles of his father's tools.

> Most of the tools were dark with age, and their handles were a deep brown. But where Papa's hands had took a purchase on them, they were lighter in color. Almost a gold. The wear of his labor had made them smooth and shiny, where his fingers had held each one. I looked at all the handles of his tools. It was real beautiful the way they were gilded by work. (133–34)

Beneath the tools, Rob finds a box with a piece of paper on which, long ago, Haven Peck had practiced his signature. "One of the 'Haven Pecks' was near to perfect" (134). And then all the neighbors in this small farm community arrive.

> I was glad they came. Some of them were dressed no better than I. And some not even as well, but they came. They came to help us plant Haven Peck into the earth, and that was all that counted. They'd come because they respected him and honored him. As I looked at all them, standing uneasy in our small parlor, I was happy for Papa. He wasn't rich. But by damn he wasn't poor. He always said he wasn't poor, but I figured he was just having fun with himself. But he was sober. He had a lot, Papa did. (135–36)

The character of Haven Peck, his death, and his son's journey into adulthood are all tied together here at the touching end of *A Day No Pigs Would Die.*

A subsidiary theme in the novel is what we can call, as Haven Peck does, "'the Shaker Way.'" The Pecks are part of one of the last Shaker settlements in America. (In 1826 there were 18 Shaker communities in 8 different states, but by the 1970s, when Robert Newton Peck wrote this account, they were all but extinct.) The novel does not talk about the more distinctive Shaker qualities (Shaker furniture, meetings, or celibacy) but about Shaker values as they are embodied in the Peck family, and especially in Haven Peck. "'No, I cannot read. But our Law has been read to me. And because I could not read, I knew to listen with a full heart. It might be the last and only time I'd learn its meaning'" (33). Among other rules, Haven Peck tells his son, Shaker law "'forbids frills on any day. And that goes double on Sunday'" (34). But in "the Book of Shaker it says to do a good turn and neighbor well" (80), and much of the novel concerns these activities.

For us as for Rob, the Shaker theme translates into the importance of *tolerance.* Rob has cut school in Chapter 1 because a schoolmate "pointed at my clothes and made sport of them" (7). But Rob himself must learn acceptance of others: in the course of the novel he comes to discover that Aunt Matty and the Tanners, "the three people who probably loved me more than anyone in the whole world" (outside his immediate family), are not Shakers but "good shouting Baptists" (123). In his gentle way, author Peck describes a culture that is sadly gone but whose values—hard work, self-sufficiency, tolerance—we can still admire and emulate.

A major part of the Shaker Way is *neighborliness*. In Chapter 3, Rob and his father mend fences, and Haven Peck remarks (in a line reminiscent of Robert Frost's poem, "Mending Wall") that "'A fence sets men together, not apart'"; and much of the novel details the ways in which the families in this community *are* together. When Benjamin Tanner carries Rob home in Chapter 2, he jokingly sacrifices the blanket that wraps the bloody boy. "'Ain't mine. Belongs to my horse'" (14). And it is the Widow Bascom's good word to Mr. Tanner that gets Rob to the Rutland Fair. At Rob's suggestion, Haven Peck "weasels" Ira Long's terrier (in what may be the most painful scene in the book); that the good deed misfires is the fault of custom, not neighbors. In Chapter 9, Mama and Aunt Carrie discuss the Widow Bascom and her hired man, and we recognize how much of neighborliness demands tolerance. Benjamin Tanner, in one of the many domestic images that underpin the novel, "'will stand without hitching,'" Haven Peck says of his "near" neighbor (97). And at the funeral, Tanner acts it: "'Robert, my name is Benjamin Franklin Tanner. All my neighbors call me Ben. I think two men who are good friends ought to front name one another'" (135). Neighborliness is what defines a community like Learning, Vermont. Some of the people here are not terribly well off (when Rob needs stitches, it is not a doctor but his mother who does the sewing), but they can count on each other. It is a quality that many Americans have lost—and a value that most students can still afford to learn—but one of the mainstays of this foreign but important Shaker culture.

Style and Language

The most noticeable thing about the plot of *A Day No Pigs Would Die* is its casual, episodic structure. Many of the incidents in the book do not work to further the plot but function, rather, as set pieces of humor or information (and can often be removed without seriously damaging the novel's major themes—a real test of organic structure). The conversation between Haven and Rob about baseball and Ethan Allen in Chapter 4 is but one example; the subjects are being milked for their comic possibilities. (Is it possible that Haven Peck could spend 60 years in Vermont and know so little about Ethan Allen and the Green Mountain

Boys?) Similarly, the scene in Chapter 6 between Rob and Aunt Mattie, when she tries to teach him grammar, could be removed with no loss of meaning to the book as a whole.

If *A Day No Pigs Would Die* reminds readers of Mark Twain's *Huckleberry Finn* in its lazy, riverlike structure and its innocent humor (as in the scene between Rob and Aunt Mattie), the novel also resembles that nineteenth-century American classic in its point of view. The story is told from the perspective of a 12-year-old boy, and we witness only the scenes he could see. We view Rob's world through his eyes, and the exciting incidents in the novel (like the opening scene and the weaseling) are vivid because of the fresh language and perspective this innocent young boy brings to his narration. (Conversely, the weakest scenes are the "set" pieces where the language is not his—the bits about "rest rooms" and "perverts" in Chapter 10, for example.)

Much of the figurative language Rob Peck uses in telling his story is natural and domestic, for it comes out of the experience of rural people in the 1920s. A hill yellow with goldenrod, for instance, looks to Rob "Like somebody broke eggs all over the hillside" (108), a light snow like "the way Mama would flour her cake board" (126), while a muddy Rob appears to his mother like a "'potato dug up on a rainy day'" (75). The language of the novel is clear and laconic but can be vivid and poetic at the same time: an exacting job can become, in Haven Peck's folksy analogy, "'a longtail cat in a room full of rocking chairs'" (26).

Two other elements that must be mentioned in any analysis of the style and structure of this short work are its *humor* and its *sentimentality*. The comedy in the novel is obvious and often reminds us of situations in *Huck Finn*, where a naive narrator is describing events just beyond his ken. Such humor, when it is not self-directed (as when Rob compares Rutland to London [85]), often pokes gentle fun at the rustic life. (Rob tells the story of a rube from Learning who went to New York City but reports back that "There was so much going on at the depot, I never got to the village" [87].) The weaker humor in the novel comes out of the set pieces.

The sentimentality of the novel is equally obvious. The situations in *A Day No Pigs Would Die*—the death of a major character, the slaughter of a pet pig, the rapid maturity of the narrator—are intrinsically emotional, and at times it appears that the author, rather than downplaying these situations, is pulling out all the emotional stops. The language in the novel is often understated, but the feelings are sometimes exaggerated. It is not a terrible defect. Many YA novels are sentimental and didactic, but few have the strengths of this short but powerful work.

TEACHING THE NOVEL

Teaching Suggestions

A Day No Pigs Would Die is another good example of why we read—and teach—novels: to enter, to experience, and to share a world unlike the one we presently inhabit. Here is a novel that most 12- to 15-year-olds can read easily—and it may be as distant from their own lives as if it were a work of science fiction set in the twenty-first century. The Pecks are a family living light years away, in a rural religious community in the 1920s, and abiding by values that may seem alien to contemporary mores. A class that has gone through this novel has *experienced* another way of life and been enriched by that journey.

The important situations and themes in the novel are self-explanatory, but students may need to know a little about the Shakers, a small religious sect in the nineteenth and earlier twentieth centuries with strong values and even stronger rules of conduct. (Some students may have seen *Witness*, a 1984 film centering on a similar religious community, the Amish, or Pennsylvania Dutch.) Picture books or slides of Shaker life, available in most libraries, can give graphic illustrations of the story. Likewise, students may need to learn something about rural farm life in the mid-1920s during Calvin Coolidge's presidency (another Vermonter, as we learn in the novel), but the essential information on these subjects can come out of a careful reading of the book itself. In fact, that is one of the attractions of this novel: a student who reads *A Day No Pigs Would Die* carefully will learn how a calf is born or how animals in the wild mark off their territory, about Ethan Allen and Major Robert Rogers, and dozens of other bits of folklore and history. Students can be asked to keep lists of such information in their Reading Logs and to share them in groups; it is one good way to teach reading for content.

Much of the charm of *A Day No Pigs Would Die* comes from the language the characters use, language that has its roots in rural nineteenth-century America. Students may not recognize a number of the words and expressions used in the novel (*quern*, for example, or *feathered*, or *Gosh 'em Moses*), although a few can be figured out by context (*sorry him good*, perhaps, or *a yoke of times*). Students should look up words and expressions with which they are not familiar and record both the words and the definitions in their Reading Logs.

A Day No Pigs Would Die is a good illustration of the delicate task teachers are constantly performing with regard to language in literature. Here is a novel that teaches the best possible values—discipline, respect for elders, the importance of hard work, and neighborliness—and also contains, for example, earthy language that could be troublesome for younger readers. (Think of the first chapter, for example—which I urge teachers to read aloud—with its descriptions of Rob being dragged by Apron through the woods, with "my own bare butt and privates catching a thorn with every step" [9] and hitting Apron and yelling, "'you move that big black smelly ass, you hear?'" [101].) Obviously, the sensible and sensitive teacher presents the novel so that younger readers come to see such language as part of the authentic voice of this 12-year-old growing up in this historically accurate environment. If students have this kind of experience with the novel and its language, their own worlds will be immensely broadened.

Discussion and Writing Ideas

AFFECTIVE TOPICS

1. How did you like the novel? What were your reactions? What did it make you think of? (Reading Log entries)
2. Who was your favorite character in the novel? Why? What was the most vivid scene?
3. What would you have done differently from what Rob Peck did in the novel? Describe.
4. Have you ever been in a situation like Rob Peck's at the Rutland Fair, where you had to sacrifice something you really *wanted* to do for something that you knew you *had* to do? Describe a similar situation and your feelings afterwards.
5. Pinky is Rob's first "possession." Write about something you have owned and lost—and how you felt after it was gone. Did you change as a result of your loss?
6. What does it mean to be a "good neighbor"? Briefly describe the qualities that you think go into neighborliness—and judge yourself as a neighbor.
7. Write about how someone's death affected you.
8. In what ways are you similar in values and attitudes to your mother or father or another adult? How do you feel about these similar traits?
9. Briefly describe a personal experience that helped you grow up in some way, and comment on the effects of the experience on your later values and behavior.
10. Describe a family or community you have encountered that lives by a

different value system from your own. Which of their attitudes or
behaviors do you admire? Why?

ANALYTICAL TOPICS

1. What will Rob Peck be doing 15 years after the end of the novel? Will
   he still be a farmer? Will he be living in Learning? Will his father still
   be a major influence on his life? Explain.
2. Is Haven Peck a *hero*? Why or why not?
3. Write about whether or not Rob Peck reaches adulthood by the end
   of the novel. What is your evidence?
4. List all the incidents in the novel that involve death. What are the
   attitudes toward death of different characters?
5. Write about the idea of possessions. How does Rob deal with his new
   possession, Pinky, and how does Pinky contribute to Rob's development?
6. Analyze Shaker Ways as they are practiced in the Peck household.
   What are the values that the Pecks live by? How are their values
   reflected in their daily lives?
7. Describe the Rutland Fair. What importance does this event have in
   Rob Peck's life? How is it a climax or major point of Rob's development?
8. What is unique or important about the *setting* of the novel? Could
   the events have taken place in another time or place? Where or when?
9. Name the scene in the novel that most clearly portrays the novel's
   central meaning to you, and explain (in terms of character, plot,
   and/or themes) why the scene is so important.
10. Mr. Tanner tells Rob that there's no "'higher calling'" than being a
    farmer "'and making things live and grow. We farmers are stewards.
    Our lot is to tend all of God's good living things, and I say there's
    nothing finer'" (122). Do you agree? Explain, with references to the
    novel.

Bridging to Other Works

Robert Frost, poems. Compare the attitudes in "Mending Wall" to
    Haven Peck's ideas on neighbors on p. 22 of the novel.
Mark Twain, *Adventures of Huckleberry Finn* (1884); see Chapter 2.
    Compare character, point of view, humor, and structure.
John Steinbeck, *The Red Pony* (1938); see Chapter 10. Note the parallels
    of setting, character, and themes.

Harper Lee, *To Kill a Mockingbird* (1960); see Chapter 8. Compare such elements as the two fathers and the theme of tolerance.

Chaim Potok, *The Chosen* (1967). Another novel about minority religious life in the United States, this one deals with Hasidic Jews in an urban New York City setting.

William Armstrong, *Sounder* (YA, 1969). Compare such facets as character and rural setting.

Bette Greene, *Summer of My German Soldier* (YA, 1973). Compare themes, setting, character.

Mildred D. Taylor, *Roll of Thunder, Hear My Cry* (YA, 1976); see Chapter 12. Note the parallels of character, rural setting, themes (tolerance, self-respect, etc.).

Robert Cormier, *I Am the Cheese* (YA, 1977). This mystery is set in contemporary, rather than 1920s, New England.

12 "Things they need to hear"

ROLL OF THUNDER, HEAR MY CRY

Author: Mildred D. Taylor
Genre: historical and psychological realism (YA)
Time of novel: October 1933 to August 1934
Locale: rural Mississippi
Point of view: first person
First published: 1976
Edition used: Bantam paperback (1984); 210 pp.
Grade level: 6–9
Principal characters:
  Cassie Logan, age 9, the narrator
  Stacey, her 12-year-old brother
  Christopher-John, another brother, age 7
  Clayton Chester ("Little Man"), the youngest Logan, age 6
  David Logan (Papa), who works on the railroad in Louisiana for part of each year
  Mary Logan (Mama), the seventh-grade teacher at the Great Faith Elementary and Secondary School the four children attend
  Big Ma, Cassie's grandmother (Papa's mother), in her 60s
  Uncle Hammer, Papa's older brother, who lives in Detroit
  Mr. Morrison, the man Papa brings back from Louisiana to help protect the family against the night riders
  T. J. Avery, a friend of Stacey's who is repeating the seventh grade and who is responsible for Mrs. Logan's being fired
  Jeremy Simms, a poor white boy trying unsuccessfully to befriend the Logan children
  Lillian Jean Simms, Jeremy's nasty older sister
  Mr. Jamison, a liberal white lawyer
  Harlan Granger, the owner of the Granger plantation surrounding the Logan land
  The Wallaces, a white family that runs the crossroads store the Logans are boycotting

ANALYSIS OF THE NOVEL

Story and Setting

The Logan family lives in Spokane County, Mississippi, on 400 acres of land that Cassie Logan's grandfather, a former slave, purchased years ago. Harlan Granger, whose family originally owned the Logan property and who owns all of the farms around it (now sharecropped by poorer black families), wants the Logan parcel back, and it is a struggle—especially here in the bottom of the Great Depression—for the Logan family to hold onto their land.

The Logans live 22 miles from the nearest town, Strawberry, and the children must walk several miles to the shabby school that educates black children from October to March, the months when they are not expected to be working the cotton crop. On this first day of school, when the novel opens, the Logan children are forced off the dirt road by the schoolbus taking white children to the Jefferson Davis County School. This is rural Mississippi in the early 1930s, and conditions for blacks could hardly be worse. But just how bad, Cassie Logan must still learn.

Cassie, who narrates the novel, is a bright and rebellious girl who loves her parents—but especially her Papa, now off in Louisiana working on the railroad in order to make the money for the mortgage on the 200 acres they are still paying off and the taxes on the entire 400 acres they own. (The cotton crop plus Mama's salary barely give the Logans enough to live on.) When Mr. Logan appears in Chapter 2, walking up the road, he is accompanied by Mr. Morrison, a huge "human tree" who has been fired from his railroad job for fighting with whites and whom Papa is bringing home to help protect the family against a recent wave of vigilante terrorism; distant neighbors have just been visited by the dreaded night riders, and one man has already died of his burns.

Several plot lines grow out of this opening situation. Papa tells the children to stay away from the Wallaces' crossroads store, knowing the Wallaces are involved in the recent terror, and organizes a boycott of their store. The children plan their own act of retaliation against the white schoolbus that deliberately sprays them with the red mud the late October rains turn the road into: they dig a trench and the bus lurches into it and breaks an axle. "Oh, how sweet was well-maneuvered revenge!" (41), crows Cassie to herself. When the "night men" appear again, the children are afraid it is because of what they have done to the bus. It is not, but the vigilantes tar and feather another black man, Sam Tatum, that same night.

When T.J. Avery, Stacey's supposed friend, lets Stacey get caught with T.J.'s "cheat notes," Stacey chases him to the Wallace store to get his revenge. Mr. Morrison takes the children home and promises not to tell Mama that they defied their father's orders—"''Cause I'm leaving it up to you to tell her'" (66). But Mama does not punish them; instead, the next Saturday she takes the kids on her charity call to Mrs. Berry, and they see the horribly burned Mr. Berry. "'The Wallaces did that, children. They poured kerosene over Mr. Berry and his nephews and lit them afire'" (74). On the way home, Mama rallies other black families to the boycott of the Wallace store.

The following Saturday, Cassie and Stacey and T.J. ride into Strawberry—Cassie's first trip to town—where Big Ma sells her dairy products at the weekly market. Cassie has much to learn about the real world—like why Big Ma parks her wagon at the back of the field—and her education really begins on this day. Shopping in the Barnett store, Cassie cannot understand why Mr. Barnett waits on white customers first, and she is thrown out when she complains. Worse, she bumps into the obnoxious Lillian Jean Simms, whose father throws Cassie off the sidewalk and forces *her* to apologize. "No day in all my life had ever been as cruel as this one" (87). Cassie wants fairness and justice in this world, but she is instead learning about the injustice and discrimination that prevail. As Stacey says to his sister, "'There's things you don't understand'" (89)—yet. When Uncle Hammer shows up from Detroit in his new silver Packard (the same model that Harlan Granger owns, but newer), only Mr. Morrison is able to keep him from punishing Mr. Simms for his abuse of Cassie.

And now, as the momentum of the novel builds, the two stories coalesce: the fight to save the land from Harlan Granger and the fight against the racism and brutality of the Wallaces are intertwined, because the Wallace store is on Granger land. When Harlan Granger comes by to warn the Logans that he will get their land if they continue the boycott, David Logan responds, "'You plan on getting this land, you're planning on the wrong thing'" (129). But not all whites here are racists: Mr. Jamison aids the boycott by backing the credit of black families shopping in Vicksburg and by transferring the Logan land from Big Ma to her sons, so that the title is clear in case of trouble. "'I'm a Southerner born and bred,'" Mr. Jamison explains, "'but that doesn't mean I approve of all that goes on here, and there are a lot of other white people who feel the same'" (122). Meanwhile, Cassie gets her own revenge on Lillian Jean, and does it in such a way that the adults never get involved.

The real crisis, however, is precipitated when T.J. Avery, caught cheating on his exams by Mrs. Logan, tells the Wallaces that Mrs. Logan has pasted over the names of white children on the inside covers of the

12-year-old textbooks she is forced to use. When the school board members pay a surprise visit to her classroom, they find her teaching a lesson on slavery not in the book and promptly fire her. (The real reason for her firing, of course, is her active role in the boycott.) With one salary gone, the Logans must tighten their belts still further. Granger puts pressure on the families that tenant-farm his land, and many drop out of the boycott. When Papa and Mr. Morrison next go into Vicksburg for supplies, they are attacked by vigilantes, Papa is shot, and his leg is broken when the wagon runs over it. Mr. Morrison saves Papa—and nearly kills two of the attackers doing it—but another income has been lost. Papa gets better, but when the bank calls in the mortgage, Uncle Hammer is forced to sell his new car to make the payment.

The climax comes when T.J. Avery—a prime instrument of so much of the novel's action—arrives at the Logan house one night badly hurt. When the Logan children abandoned him because he got Mrs. Logan fired, T.J. was befriended by the white Simms boys, R.W. and Melvin, who used T.J. to rob the Barnett store, injuring Mr. Barnett in the process and then beat up T.J. The children help T.J. get home, but then the night riders arrive (led by the two Simmses, who say that they saw three "black boys" coming out of the Barnett store) and drag the Avery family from their house, beat them, and are about to lynch T.J. when Mr. Jamison and the sheriff arrive. But even these two cannot hold back the mob. Stacey acts quickly, sending the other children home to warn the Logans that the crowd will come to their house next. The resourceful David Logan sets fire to his own cotton field, which borders on Harlan Granger's land, and the mob rushes to put it out. Black and white, men and women, the community fights the fire through the night.

But the crisis is not over. Mr. Barnett dies from his wounds, and T.J., says Mr. Logan, will probably die for his part in the robbery. The land has been saved, the Logans have survived as a family and are probably even stronger, and two of the children—Cassie and Stacey—have learned more about the world of cruelty and injustice and how to maneuver in it safely. But the novel does not end on a note of false optimism: the Logans are still poor, and racism and violence are still everywhere about them. "I cried for T.J.," Cassie says in the last line of the novel, "For T.J. and for the land" (210).

Characters

Characterization is one of the real strengths of *Roll of Thunder, Hear My Cry*. The characters are believable and, for the most part, sympathetic, and younger readers can easily identify with them.

The narrator and central character of the novel is 9-year-old Cassie Logan, a bright (some might say precocious) rebel who, in the course of the novel, comes to learn a great deal about the sacrifices her family is making to keep their land, about their struggle for equality, and about their pride in themselves and their heritage. She is, of course, no blank slate when the novel opens (she knows, for example, "that punishment was always less severe when I poured out the whole truth to Mama on my own before she had heard anything from anyone else" [19]), but she still cannot understand why Mr. Barnett will not wait on them at his store. Through the actions of the novel, Cassie learns that—as Mama puts it— "'in the world outside this house, things are not always as we would have them to be'" (95). Her treatment of Lillian Jean Simms is an indication that the strong, independent Cassie will be able to operate in this racist society after the novel closes, but her tears at the end are also a sign of sadness for this loss of innocence.

As much as from anyone else, Cassie learns from her family; the Logans overwhelm us with their warmth and mutual support. Big Ma tells Cassie about the importance of the Logan land and, by the lesson of her hard work in the Logan household, how much she is willing to do to hold onto it. Cassie's mother is, like her daughter, a real rebel: although she has been teaching for 14 years, she is still considered a "disrupting maverick" by her fellow teachers. Children may have to learn the realities of race relations, she tells a colleague early on, "'but that doesn't mean they have to accept them'" (21–22). She is eventually fired for this principle. She is also sensitive and loving; when Papa surprises her by arriving with Mr. Morrison, she graciously accepts him: "'Welcome to our home, Mr. Morrison'" (27). There is a strong physical and spiritual bond between Cassie's parents, and their love spills over onto others beyond the circle of the family. David Logan is a man of compassion who "always took time to think through any move he made" (109) but whose quick thinking at the end of the novel saves the Logan family. It is no wonder that Mr. Morrison chooses to stay with this family when the trouble gets intense.

One of the unique qualities of *Roll of Thunder, Hear My Cry* as an initiation novel is that it has not one but two protagonists. While Cassie is learning about the world and moving from innocence and naiveté, she is also telling us about her older brother Stacey's taking more responsibility and growing into maturity himself. At the opening of the novel, with his father away working on the railroad, Stacey is itching to become the man of the family, and he resents the arrival of Mr. Morrison. He is already a young man with several clear Logan traits: it is his loyalty to his brother Little Man (humiliated when the school bus muddies him) that

leads to his plan of revenge, and he refuses to betray his friend T.J. when
he gets caught with T.J.'s "cheat notes." But he is still learning. When he
gives away his new coat to T.J. because the other boy ridicules him for
wearing it, Uncle Hammer warns him: "'You care what a lot of useless
people say 'bout you you'll never get anywhere, 'cause there's a lot of
folks don't want you to make it'" (108). In the attack on the wagon,
Stacey is unable to hold the horse, his father's leg is broken, and Stacey
feels responsible. But in his actions at the end of the novel, Stacey
demonstrates that he has become his own man. "'That boy's gotten
mighty grown'" (197), Papa complains, but his assessment is correct in a
number of ways. When T.J. shows up hurt, Stacey responds with loyalty
to his old friend, and his later actions help to save the Logan family.

Even minor characters play important roles in this novel. Uncle
Hammer is "a tall, handsome man" who is more hot-tempered than his
younger brother and an interesting contrast to him for the children.
Jeremy Simms is a poor, sad boy who wants to do the impossible—
befriend the Logan children—but whose actions underline the important
theme of friendship in the novel. Only the adult whites, liberal
(Mr. Jamison) or racist (the Wallaces and the Simmses), seem two-
dimensional and stereotypical here.

Themes

There are a number of complex ideas at work in *Roll of Thunder*.
The overriding theme, of course, is the initiation of the two oldest Logan
children into the real world of Depression Mississippi, and there are a
number of lessons they learn along their road to self-discovery, both from
what people say and from what they do. Stacey, for example, benefits
from Uncle Hammer's "principle that a man did not blame others for his
own stupidity; he learned from his mistake and became stronger for it"
(110). When Stacey gets a flute from Jeremy for Christmas, he complains
to his father that he has not given Jeremy anything. "'Not even your
friendship?'" (119) his father replies. And both children learn that
"'there'll be a whole lot of things you ain't gonna wanna do but you'll
have to do in this life just so you can survive'" (133), as Papa tells Cassie.

There are two major subthemes within this general framework of
initiation, two areas of adult life that Cassie and Stacey must learn about
"'just so you can survive.'" One is the negative pole: injustice and discrimination—what they do to people and the cruelty that follows from
them. The other is almost the antidote to the first: the pride and self-
respect and dignity that come from the Logan land and heritage.

Roll of Thunder is historically accurate and psychologically realistic—and brutal. The uneasy relations between the races established in rural Mississippi since Reconstruction are coming apart under the multiple pressures of the Depression (which began in the South *before* the 1930s), and the "night men" are riding again. While Mr. Jamison may be correct in saying that not all Southerners are bigots, characters like the Wallaces and the Simmses predominate in this world of poor whites and blacks, and the novel is filled with incidents of discrimination and violence (the white school bus, the trip to Strawberry, Papa being shot, T.J. nearly being lynched, etc.). It is an ugly, violent world that the Logan children are growing up into, but their parents try to give them the skills and support to make their journey a little less hazardous. Mr. Simms is "'one of those people who has to believe that white people are better than black people to make himself feel big,'" Mama explains to Cassie after he has knocked her down. But what we give to such people "'is not respect but fear. What we give to our own people is far more important because it's given freely'" (96–97). "'Maybe one day whites and blacks can be real friends,'" Papa later explains to his daughter, "'but right now the country ain't built that way'" (119–20). Mama concludes her speech to Cassie with the notion of self-respect: while we have no choice over our color or whether we are born rich or poor, "'What we do have is some choice over what we make of our lives once we're here'" (97). When Mr. Morrison tells the horrible story of how night riders killed his family when he was a child, Papa says to Mama of their own children, "'These are things they need to hear, baby. It's their history'" (112). And when Mr. Jamison argues with Papa that he cannot win the boycott, Papa agrees. "'Still,' he said, 'I want these children to know we tried, and what we can't do now, maybe one day they will'" (125).

Thus the theme of discrimination is from the beginning set against its opposites: self-respect, black pride, and the struggle to overcome prejudice and injustice. The physical embodiment of this positive pole is the Logan land. "'You ain't never had to live on nobody's place but your own and long as I live and the family survives, you'll never have to,'" Papa explains to Cassie early in the novel. "'That's important. You may not understand that now, but one day you will'" (4). This link to their land runs through the novel and becomes one of the major lessons Cassie learns. "'If you remember nothing else in your whole life, Cassie girl, remember this: We ain't never gonna lose this land'" (115). Cassie's tears for "the land" at the end of the novel symbolize her double recognition of how much this struggle costs—but how much it is worth.

Their land gives the Logans freedom and a sense of their own worth, and it helps them hold themselves up in a world of white power and discrimination. Early in the novel, Big Ma takes Cassie out to the Logan forest and explains its history, as well as how the family's values and blood are tied to this land. When Stacey complains that other families, pressured by whites, are dropping out of the boycott, Papa reprimands him: he should have more tolerance; these other men do not own their land. "'You were born blessed, boy, with land of your own. . . . It's hard on a man to give up, but sometimes it seems there just ain't nothing else he can do'" (155–56). And when Cassie asks her father, in this same scene, whether the Logans will have to give up, he points at a small tree overshadowed by larger ones:

> "That fig tree's got roots that run deep, and it belongs in that yard as much as that oak and walnut. It keeps on blooming, bearing good fruit year after year, knowing all the time it'll never get as big as them other trees. Just keeps on growing and doing what it gotta do. It don't give up. It give up, it'll die. There's a lesson to be learned from that little tree, Cassie girl, 'cause we're like it. We keep doing what we gotta, and we don't give up. We can't." (156)

What this struggle finally gives the Logans is self-respect, as Papa explains:

> "There are things you can't back down on, things you gotta take a stand on. . . . You have to demand respect in this world, ain't nobody just gonna hand it to you. How you carry yourself, what you stand for—that's how you gain respect. But, little one, ain't nobody's respect worth more than your own." (133–34)

The Logans are historically realistic and overwhelmingly positive in their love and their pride. These values are grounded in the land, Mildred D. Taylor is telling us: give all the other families here—white and black—land of their own, and we would not witness all the bloodshed and humiliation we see now. In her "Author's Note," Ms. Taylor dedicates the novel to the memory of her father, "a master storyteller" who gave her countless oral histories "of great-grandparents and of slavery and of the days following slavery; of those who lived still not free, yet who would not let their spirits be enslaved" (vii). *Roll of Thunder, Hear My Cry* is a novel woven out of that history, a story not only of economic survival, but also of the survival of the human spirit in the face of incredible obstacles.

Style and Language

David Logan's story of the fig tree, quoted above, is typical of the style of this book. The figurative language is local and natural: Big Ma is "the color of a pecan shell" (23), Mr. Morrison's voice is "like the roll of low thunder" (27), and Mama always "smelled of sunshine and soap" (99). When Papa explains to Christopher-John why Mama's firing is so hard on her, he says, "'she's born to teaching like the sun is born to shine'" (142). The first-person narration by Cassie is easy and consistent (if often adult in its vocabulary) and, like the conversations she quotes, captures beautifully the black dialect of rural Depression Mississippi. When Mama calls on the Turner family to encourage them to join the boycott, Mr. Turner explains his reluctance:

> "I sho' sorry, Miz Logan. I'm gonna keep my younguns from up at that store, but I gots to live. Y'all got it better'n most the folks 'round here 'cause y'all gots your own place and y'all aint gotta cowtail to a lot of this stuff. But you gotta understand it ain't easy for sharecroppin' folks to do what you askin'." (76)

One of the distinctive characteristics of this novel is the richness of its detail. Domestic life on this Southern Depression farm is rendered sensuously: we watch Big Ma ironing (with a second iron always heating in the fireplace); we see Cassie churning, picking cotton, lying under her patchwork quilt; we feel the red Mississippi mud oozing through the children's toes on their way to school; and we get hungry at the descriptions of food at the family get-togethers. (Notice, incidentally, that people here do not have to drink to have fun or share love, and that their humor—like Papa's story of switching the watermelon—is genuine and shared.)

The action of the novel is relatively fast-paced: there are several stories here, and they build to an exciting climax. Further, the actions are interdependent: the fight for the land, for example, is connected both to the boycott and to the children's struggles. There are few, if any, superfluous scenes here. (*A Day No Pigs Would Die* could be contrasted as one example of a less organic structure.)

Finally, the novel is noteworthy for its unforced symbolism. Objects and incidents in the novel are important for their narrative value, and at the same time they often represent something larger. The Logan land, for instance, is a motivating force in the story, but it also symbolizes the Logan history in slavery and freedom. The Logan forest, in particular, has this symbolic quality: as in many novels, it is a place of refuge and escape. (When Mama wants to nurse the hurt of getting fired, she walks into the woods; when the children witness the beating of the Avery family, they are safe in the protection of the forest.) And the trees in the woods, as in Papa's story of the fig tree, have "roots," just as this family does. Weather, likewise, has this double meaning: the title's "roll of thunder" (see the verse that Mr. Morrison sings at the opening of Chapter 11) is not only a presage of rain but also the heavenly response to a cry of anguish. Finally, even manmade objects can have this symbolic import: Uncle Hammer's silver Packard is an assertion of his own worth against the power of whites, while the gun that T.J. Avery hungers for is a sign of his need for that power but a clue to his ultimate weakness.

The style and language of *Roll of Thunder*, in short, work against the didactic or preachy qualities of this fine novel and help to underscore subtly its significant themes.

TEACHING THE NOVEL

Teaching Suggestions

Roll of Thunder, Hear My Cry won the 1977 Newbery Medal for "the most distinguished contribution to American literature for children," and Mildred D. Taylor's acceptance speech (reprinted in the August 1977 *Horn Book*) gives a number of insights into what she was trying to do in the novel and the difficulties she had doing it. Teachers may want to read or otherwise share that speech (particularly its last three pages) with their classes. Students hearing it can begin to see writers as people "just like us" who somehow manage to get their own stories down.

Roll of Thunder, Hear My Cry lends itself perfectly to use of the Reading Log, for students enjoy the novel and its rich detail gives them much to write about. One practical activity is to ask different students (or groups of students) to keep Reading Log entries on one or another secondary character (Jeremy or Lillian Jean Simms, Harlan Granger, etc.) in order to watch how they further the plot of the novel. T.J. Avery, for example, is not only himself a prime mover of the action but is the means by which Stacey establishes his beginning adulthood. Big Ma, who has so many household duties here, also teaches Cassie the importance of the Logan land. Other characters have equally important roles in propelling the action of this organically unified novel.

Likewise, students can keep a Reading Log entry on the plot of the novel, in particular the role that *conflict* plays in furthering the action. We are told, in most standard discussions of fiction, that there can be four kinds of conflict in a novel: conflict within a character, between one character and another, between a character and nature, and finally, between a character and the larger society. Readers can easily find all four kinds of conflict in *Roll of Thunder*, but it may be most valuable, as a follow-up to the focus on a secondary character suggested above, to look for conflict from the perspective of the central protagonist, who manifests all four kinds. What is an example of a conflict that Cassie has within herself, for example? Cassie's conflicts with other characters— with Miss Crocker, her teacher, perhaps, or with Lillian Jean Simms— abound here. Does she have conflicts with nature? (The rain at the end is really the answer to Logan prayers, as in the novel's title.) Finally, Cassie's conflicts with her society get to the heart of such themes as discrimination and self-respect. Through this focus on conflict, younger readers can begin to see the crucial relationship between the development of the central characters and the action of the novel, for it is the conflicts within and between the characters, as well as the conflicts with their environment, that help propel *Roll of Thunder, Hear My Cry* forward.

Discussion and Writing Ideas

AFFECTIVE TOPICS

1. How did you like the novel? What characters did you like best? Why? (Reading Log entries)
2. Choose either Cassie or Stacey. What did you like about this character? How does this character change and grow during the course of the novel? What are his/her outstanding characteristics? Cite specific examples.
3. Briefly describe a friendship or a feeling of loyalty you share(d) with another person, giving the details of that relationship and its meaning for you.
4. Select a family (perhaps your own), and describe what you think are its key values. Give one example of behavior for every value you list.
5. Describe an instance in which you were discriminated against (because of race, sex, age, friends, etc.), and detail how you felt, both then and now.

ANALYTICAL TOPICS

1. How would the novel be different if it were narrated by Stacey Logan? What stories would he tell differently? What might he tell us about Cassie that we don't learn from her point of view?
2. What is the significance of the novel's title? (See the text of the hymn verse at the beginning of Chapter 11, on p. 84.)
3. Discuss the theme of friendship and loyalty. What are the major instances of this theme in the novel, and what do they add up to?

4. What are the specific values of the Logan family and how are they expressed—by thoughts, words, acts?
5. Compare the Logan and Avery families. How are they similar, and how are they different? What accounts for the differences?
6. Compare David Logan and his brother Hammer. How are they similar, and how are they different? What accounts for the differences?
7. Describe the actions of the white characters in the novel (Mr. Jamison, Jeremy and Lillian Jean Simms, the Wallaces), and analyze what these actions represent.
8. What does *Roll of Thunder, Hear My Cry* say about roots, about the Logans' pride in their heritage (in slavery and beyond) and their mutual respect. Compare what happens to T.J. when he denies his black identity.
9. What are the different ways that the Logan children deal with racial prejudice and discrimination? What ways work most effectively and last longest?

Bridging to Other Works

Richard Wright, *Black Boy* (1945). This is an autobiography about growing up black in the South during the same period.

Harper Lee, *To Kill a Mockingbird* (1960); see Chapter 8. Note the parallels of Southern setting, character, and themes of racial injustice and initiation. Compare the young narrators of these two novels, viewing similar events in similar settings. How do Scout and Cassie differ in what they learn? Note such ideas as those of heroism, parental influence, tolerance, and self-respect.

William Armstrong, *Sounder* (YA, 1969). This novel, too, has parallels of setting, character, and theme. Compare what the young protagonist of *Sounder* learns with Cassie's growth. How are the two characters similar? How do the parents differ?

Ernest J. Gaines, *The Autobiography of Miss Jane Pittman* (1971). This popular adult novel (and TV film) gives a poignant view of black history.

Robert Newton Peck, *A Day No Pigs Would Die* (YA, 1972); see Chapter 11. Although this novel has parallels in its rural setting and young protagonist, its structure is quite different, as noted above in "Style and Language."

Mildred D. Taylor, *Song of the Trees* (YA, 1973). This is a long short story with the same characters and setting (the story concerns the time when the forest was partially cleared) as well as similar themes (the land, self-respect, etc.).

———, *Let the Circle Be Unbroken* (YA, 1981). This sequel to *Roll of Thunder* continues the story of the Logan family the next year (and the trial of T.J. Avery).

Virginia Hamilton, *Sweet Whispers, Brother Rush* (YA, 1982). This novel has similar characters and addresses such similar themes as black history and self-esteem.

Cynthia Voight, *Come a Stranger* (YA, 1987). This novel concerns a contemporary black girl and the conflicts she goes through on her way to adulthood.

Ernest J. Gaines, *A Gathering of Old Men* (1983). This is another novel about black strength through pride.

Appendixes

Glossary

Bibliography

Index

About the Author

Appendix A

SAMPLE THEMATIC UNITS

As the introduction to this book argues, the best way to teach literature in high school is thematically. Listed below are nine suggested thematic units with some of the novels that fit them. Teachers can add appropriate plays, poems, essays, and short stories to these units as they see fit.

MY BODY, MY SELF: Individual Psychology and the Search for Self

Green, *I Never Promised You a Rose Garden*
Kesey, *One Flew over the Cuckoo's Nest*
Plath, *The Bell Jar*
Salinger, *The Catcher in the Rye*
Wharton, *Birdy*

FAMILY CIRCLE: Focus on Family Relationships

Armstrong, *Sounder* (YA)
Guest, *Ordinary People*
Hamilton, *Sweet Whispers, Brother Rush* (YA)
Lee, *To Kill a Mockingbird*
Peck, *A Day No Pigs Would Die* (YA)
Steinbeck, *The Red Pony*
Taylor, *Roll of Thunder, Hear My Cry* (YA)

THE INDIVIDUAL AND SOCIETY

Crane, *The Red Badge of Courage*
Fitzgerald, *The Great Gatsby*
Hemingway, *The Nick Adams Stories*
Kosinski, *The Painted Bird*
Mason, *In Country*

The "Bridging to Other Works" section of the chapter on *The Chocolate War* (Chapter 3) provides additional suggestions for a thematic unit on this topic.

169

YOUNG LOVE

Blume, *Forever* (YA)
Davis, *Vision Quest* (YA)
Guest, *Ordinary People*
Head, *Mr. and Mrs. Bo Jo Jones* (YA)
Hinton, *That Was Then, This Is Now* (YA)
Kerr, *Dinky Hocker Shoots Smack* (YA)
———, *Night Kites* (YA)
Koertge, *When the Kissing Never Stops* (YA)
Mazer, *Someone to Love* (YA)
Naylor, *Unexpected Pleasures*
Wharton, *Ethan Frome*
Zindel, *The Pigman* (YA)

FRIENDSHIP

Guest, *Ordinary People*
Hinton, *That Was Then, This Is Now* (YA)
Knowles, *A Separate Peace*
Peck, *Princess Ashley* (YA)
Taylor, *Roll of Thunder, Hear My Cry* (YA)
Twain, *Adventures of Huckleberry Finn*
Wharton, *Birdy*
Zindel, *The Pigman* (YA)

DEALING WITH DEATH

Agee, *A Death in the Family*
Armstrong, *Sounder* (YA)
Craven, *I Heard the Owl Call My Name*
Guest, *Ordinary People*
Hamilton, *Sweet Whispers, Brother Rush* (YA)
Paterson, *The Bridge to Teribithia* (YA)
Peck, *A Day No Pigs Would Die* (YA)
Steinbeck, *The Red Pony*
Zindel, *The Pigman* (YA)

THE NEED FOR OTHERS

Beagle, *The Last Unicorn*
Brancato, *Winning* (YA)

Head, *Mr. and Mrs. Bo Jo Jones* (YA)
Kerr, *Dinky Hocker Shoots Smack* (YA)
McCullers, *The Heart Is a Lonely Hunter*
Mason, *In Country*
Zindel, *The Pigman* (YA)

Survival

Brancato, *Winning* (YA)
Cormier, *I Am the Cheese* (YA)
————, *After the First Death* (YA)
George, *Julie of the Wolves* (YA)
Golding, *Lord of the Flies*
Hogan, *The Quartzite Trip* (YA)
Kosinski, *The Painted Bird*
O'Dell, *Island of the Blue Dolphins* (YA)
Taylor, *The Cay* (YA)
Twain, *Adventures of Huckleberry Finn*

Courage and Heroism

Childress, *A Hero Ain't Nothin' But a Sandwich* (YA)
Crane, *The Red Badge of Courage*
Frank, *The Diary of a Young Girl*
Gaines, *The Autobiography of Miss Jane Pittman*
Lee, *To Kill a Mockingbird*
Peck, *A Day No Pigs Would Die* (YA)
Schaefer, *Shane*
Taylor, *Roll of Thunder, Hear My Cry* (YA)

Appendix B

SELECTIVE LISTS OF OTHER AMERICAN NOVELS OF INITIATION

CLASSIC AND POPULAR ADULT TITLES

James Agee, *A Death in the Family* (1957). This poetic Southern novel concerns young Rufus Follet and the death of his father.

Sherwood Anderson, *Winesburg, Ohio* (1919). The short stories here are connected by the character of George Willard, who is learning about life and love before leaving his hometown.

Peter S. Beagle, *The Last Unicorn* (1968). This is a delightful medieval fantasy, complete with witches, harpies, and a love story. (F)

Margaret Craven, *I Heard the Owl Call My Name* (1973). A young Anglican priest is sent into the wilds of British Columbia to learn about the meaning of life and death from Indians.

William Faulkner, *The Bear* (1942). This novella involves the initiation of a young boy into the mysteries of life and death, history and wilderness.

Ernest Gaines, *The Autobiography of Miss Jane Pittman* (1971). The life of this former slave involves multiple lessons about American history and human endurance. (F)

Hannah Green (Joanne Greenberg), *I Never Promised You a Rose Garden* (1964). This realistic novel about life in a mental hospital recounts Deborah's struggles with schizophrenia.

Ernest Hemingway, *The Nick Adams Stories* (1972). Nick Adams learns about love, social castes, and war in these Hemingway stories drawn from different collections. (F)

John Knowles, *A Separate Peace* (1960). Two boys at an exclusive Eastern boys' school grow up together. (F)

Jerzy Kosinski, *The Painted Bird* (1965). A young boy wanders wartorn Europe and experiences many of the cruelties that humans can inflict on each other.

(F) = also a film

Carson McCullers, *The Heart Is a Lonely Hunter* (1940). This novel is less about the young Mick Kelly, perhaps, than about the mute John Singer and the characters from the small town who come to see him. (F)

Larry McMurtry, *Horseman, Pass By* (1961). This is a modern Western about a boy growing up on an isolated ranch. (F—*Hud*)

———, *The Last Picture Show* (1966). This novel recounts life in a small Texas town for two young men coming of age. (F)

Bobbie Ann Mason, *In Country* (1985). Sam Hughes, the 18-year-old heroine, finds out about her country and herself as she searches for information on her father, killed in Vietnam before she was born.

Kemm Nunn, *Tapping the Source* (1984). A murder mystery with a Southern California surfing setting, this novel also involves a search for identity.

Charles Portis, *True Grit* (1968). A Western set in the nineteenth century, this novel has a young girl as the protagonist and much Twain-like humor. (F)

Chaim Potok, *The Chosen* (1967). This novel is about a young man growing up in an urban community of Hasidic Jews. (F)

Marjorie Kinnan Rawlings, *The Yearling* (1938). This is a classic story of a young boy and his pet fawn, of love and growing up. (F)

Danny Santiago (Daniel James), *Famous All over Town* (1983). This is a delightful coming-of-age novel about a young Chicano boy learning about love, sex, and his own family history.

Jack Schaefer, *Shane* (1949). This classic American Western is also a story of a young boy learning about life, love, and his family's values. (F)

John Steinbeck, *The Pearl* (1947). This classic tale of greed and love is set in rural Mexico. (F)

Walter Tevis, *Queen's Gambit* (1983). A young girl becomes a chess champion but nearly loses herself in the process.

Will Weaver, *Red Earth, White Earth* (1987). A novel about Native Americans and white farmers struggling over land in rural Minnesota. (F)

William Wharton, *Birdy* (1979). A young man's adolescence prepares him for his experiences in war. (F)

YOUNG ADULT TITLES

Rudolfo A. Anaya, *Bless Me, Ultima* (1972). A young Chicano boy's first adventures with school, religion, and friends are aggravated by the split he feels between his parents but aided by the magical powers of his *cundera* grandmother.

*William Armstrong, *Sounder* (1969). A young black boy comes of age in the rural South at the turn of the century in an almost allegorical short novel. (F)

Judy Blume, *Forever* (1975). This is a serious and sensitive treatment of initiation into sexuality from the perspective of a young girl.

Richard Bradford, *Red Sky at Morning* (1968). This humorous novel is set in rural New Mexico, where a young boy is trying to grow up. (F)

*Robin Brancato, *Winning* (1977). A young man must learn life anew after he is crippled in an accident. Themes include friendship, loyalty, family, courage, and handicaps.

Alice Childress, *A Hero Ain't Nothin' But a Sandwich* (1973). This is a realistic novel about black urban street life, with a 13-year-old junkie as the central character.

Robert Cormier, *After the First Death* (1979). A young girl shows real courage when terrorists hijack a busload of children she is driving.

————, *The Bumblebee Flies Anyway* (1983). This is another morbid, compelling Cormier tale: Barney is trying to discover why he is in a hospital with terminally ill young people.

————, *I Am the Cheese* (1977). In this mystery thriller, a young boy tries to figure out his family's history and fate. (F)

*Terry Davis, *Vision Quest* (1979). Loudon Swain narrates this tale of high school wrestling and first love. (F)

Lois Duncan, *Stranger with My Face* (1981). In this exciting novel of the occult, Laurie Stratton describes her adventures with out-of-body experiences.

Paula Fox, *The Slave Dancer* (1973). A young fifer shanghaied onto an eighteenth-century slave ship finds out the reality of this life.

Jean Craighead George, *Julie of the Wolves* (1972). A young Eskimo must use all her skills to survive on the ice alone for a period of time.

Bette Greene, *Summer of My German Soldier* (1973). A young girl learns about prejudice and her family when she harbors a German POW in her small southern town. (F)

*Virginia Hamilton, *Sweet Whispers, Brother Rush* (1982). This is an occult novel about ghosts, time travel, and a young black girl learning her family history and her own identity.

Ann Head, *Mr. and Mrs. Bo Jo Jones* (1967). July narrates this novel about a young couple's decision to drop out of school and try to raise the baby they accidentally created.

---

* = highly recommended

*S. E. Hinton, *The Outsiders* (1967). This early realistic YA novel describes Ponyboy Curtis's attempt to find his own identity amidst the gang rivalry of the "Socs" and the "Greasers." (F)

——, *Rumble Fish* (1975). A young man looks back on his earlier life with gangs and motorcycles. (F)

——, *Tex* (1979). Two brothers try to stay together at home and in school, in spite of numerous problems. (F)

——, *That Was Then, This Is Now* (1971). Even though they have grown up together as brothers, Bryon turns Mark in when he finds out that Mark has been dealing drugs. (F)

*William Hogan, *The Quartzite Trip* (1980). Teacher P. J. Cooper takes a group of his seniors to the desert to learn about life and themselves, but more takes place on this annual trip than anyone had expected.

*M. E. Kerr, *Dinky Hocker Shoots Smack* (1972). This is a novel about the relations between parents and children, and among kids, and the importance of self-esteem.

——, *Night Kites* (1986). A young boy finds out about love at the same time that he must deal with the fact that his brother has AIDS.

Jamaica Kincaid, *Annie John* (1985). This novel is about a young girl growing up in the West Indies—her relations with her family and with other girls.

Ronald Koertge, *When the Kissing Never Stops* (1986). Walker, a high school student, narrates this mature and sensitive novel of male sexual initiation.

Ray Maloney, *The Impact Zone* (1986). This is a novel about sex and surfing for younger readers. (Winner of the Delacorte Press Prize for Outstanding YA novel.)

Norma Fox Mazer, *Someone to Love* (1983). This is a YA problem novel about "living together" that also addresses such related issues as jealousy.

Phyllis Naylor, *Unexpected Pleasures* (1986). An adult book (with adult sexuality), but with a compelling adolescent character, this novel has been marketed for the YA audience.

Scott O'Dell, *Island of the Blue Dolphins* (1960). This novel is about an Indian girl who spends 18 years on a deserted island. Themes include isolation, survival, and relations to nature. (F)

*Katherine Paterson, *The Bridge to Teribithia* (1977). In this poignant novel for younger readers, a 10-year-old boy in rural Virginia must deal with the sudden death of a friend.

——, *Jacob Have I Loved* (1980). Louise begins to find her own identity in spite of her struggles with her twin sister and herself.

*Richard Peck, *Princess Ashley* (1987). This is a novel about teenage

romance and alcoholism and what it is like to be in troubling relationships with both peers and parents.

Wilson Rawls, *Where the Red Fern Grows* (1961). This is a sentimental,
romantic novel about dogs as much as people.

Sandra Scoppettone, *The Late Great Me* (1976). This is a YA problem
novel about teenage alcoholism.

Mildred D. Taylor, *Let the Circle Be Unbroken* (1981). A sequel to *Roll
of Thunder, Hear My Cry*, this novel picks up the Logan family a
year later.

*Theodore Taylor, *The Cay* (1969). This is an exciting survival novel
about a young boy who is cared for by an old black man on a
deserted cay (or small island). (F)

——, *The Maldonado Miracle* (1973). José, a "wetback," and his dog,
Sanchez, cross the U.S.-Mexican border to the problems of a Salinas
ranch.

*Cynthia Voight, *Come a Stranger* (1987). A coming-of-age novel about
a young, bright black girl who learns about self-reliance and love.

——, *Dicey's Song* (1982). Dicey Tillerman must deal with the death of
her mother, a new life with her grandmother, and school. (Winner of
the 1983 Newbery Medal.)

——, *A Solitary Blue* (1983). Another novel in Voight's Chesapeake
series, this one concerns Jeff Greene, who grows up with his father
and then must deal with his mother.

*Paul Zindel, *The Pigman* (1968). One of the first YA novels, this
concerns the triangle between a young boy and girl and the old man
they befriend. It treats such themes as old age, loneliness, children
and parents, and nonconformity.

——, *The Pigman's Legacy* (1980). A sequel to *The Pigman*.

Glossary of Literary Terms

affective writing topics: questions that ask students to write about their own experiences and then use these connections as bridges into the novels themselves; see, for example, the affective writing topics on *A Day No Pigs Would Die* in Chapter 11.

Bildungsroman: a "novel of education" (German) that focuses on the youthful development of a central character, such as Huck Finn (Chapter 2).

characterization: the ways in which major and minor characters in a novel are developed by an author. Major protagonists or heroes are usually "full," or three-dimensional, in characterization—Esther Greenwood in *The Bell Jar* (Chapter 5), for example, or Conrad Jarrett in *Ordinary People* (Chapter 4). Minor characters are often flat, stock, stereotypical, or two-dimensional and rarely act out of the internal motivation that typically propels a major character. See **conflict** and **motivation** for fuller descriptions of two important aspects of characterization.

conflict: a struggle or opposition within one character, between one character and another, between a character and nature, or between a character and his/her society; see the discussions of different kinds of conflict in the "Teaching Suggestions" to *Roll of Thunder, Hear My Cry* (Chapter 12) and *The Chocolate War* (Chapter 3).

figurative language: "deliberate and intentional departure from normal word meanings or word order so as to gain freshness and strength of expression" (Shaw 114), for example, similes and metaphors. See the discussions in the "Style and Language" sections of the chapters on *A Day No Pigs Would Die* (Chapter 11) and *Roll of Thunder, Hear My Cry* (Chapter 12). Some examples of figurative language are:

image: "a physical representation of a person, animal, or object" or "the mental impression or visualized likeness summoned up by a word, phrase, or sentence" (Shaw 142); see, for example, the discussions of imagery in *The Bell Jar* (Chapter 5) and *The Red Pony* (Chapter 10).

metaphor: "a figure of speech in which a word or phrase is applied to a person, idea, or object to which it is not literally applicable. . . . an implied analogy which imaginatively identifies one thing with

179

another" (Shaw 171). For example, cars and driving in *The Great Gatsby* (Chapter 6) and images of winter in *The Member of the Wedding* (Chapter 9) are both used metaphorically.

symbolism: writing in which objects or actions come to represent things or ideas beyond themselves; see, for example, the discussion of ducks and mummies in *The Catcher in the Rye* (in the "Teaching Suggestions" section of Chapter 1) and the religious symbolism in *The Chocolate War* (in the "Style and Language" section of Chapter 3).

foreshadowing: a plot device in which something that will happen later is suggested earlier; the death of Jim Conklin, for example, is foreshadowed in *The Red Badge of Courage* (Chapter 7).

image: see **figurative language**

in medias res: "the middle of things" (Latin), meaning to begin a narrative after the start of the actual story, as Crane does in *The Red Badge of Courage* (Chapter 7).

irony: "a device by which a writer expresses a meaning contradictory to the stated or ostensible one" (Beckson & Ganz 99). There are basically two kinds of irony:

dramatic irony: opposition in meanings is pointed up by the action of the work; see, for example, the discussion of irony in the "Style and Language" section on *The Chocolate War* (Chapter 3).

linguistic (or verbal) **irony:** the contradiction in meaning is indicated by the language of the work, as in *To Kill a Mockingbird* (Chapter 8).

metaphor: see **figurative language**

motivation: the causes for the actions or behavior of a character; see, for example, the discussion of character motivation in the "Teaching Suggestions" section to *The Chocolate War* (Chapter 3).

mythic: referring to classical myths that contain stories "of the origin of the world, the creation of mankind, the feats of gods or heroes, or the tragedies which befell ancient families" (Beckson & Ganz 131), as Carson McCullers does in *The Member of the Wedding* (Chapter 9).

naturalism: a literary movement (and an extension of realism) in the late nineteenth century that holds that "man's existence is shaped by heredity and environment, over which he has no control and about which he can exercise little if any choice" (Shaw 185). Both *The Red Badge of Courage* (Chapter 7) and *The Red Pony* (Chapter 10) contain naturalistic elements.

personification: attributing human qualities to nonhuman objects, as Steinbeck does in *The Red Pony* (Chapter 10) or Crane does in *The Red Badge of Courage* (Chapter 7).

picaresque: referring to an episodic and generally satirical novel about a "rogue" (or *picaro*, Spanish); *Adventures of Huckleberry Finn* (Chapter 2) is a picaresque novel on the basis of its structure.

plot: the structure of a novel's actions, as they are arranged by the author to achieve a certain effect; see, for example, the discussion of the plot of *A Day No Pigs Would Die* in the "Style and Language" section of Chapter 11.

point of view: the "way a story gets told—the perspective or perspectives established by an author through which the reader is presented with the characters, actions, setting, and events which constitute the narrative in a work of fiction" (Abrams 133). There are essentially three points of view in fiction:

> **first-person narration:** a character within the novel narrates the story, as Holden Caulfield does *The Catcher in the Rye* (Chapter 1); such a narrator can be either a major or minor character, and either unreliable, like Nick Carraway in *The Great Gatsby* (Chapter 6), or naive, like Scout Finch in *To Kill a Mockingbird* (Chapter 8).

> **third-person omniscient:** the author is above the action and can choose to go into the heads of any or all characters, as Robert Cormier does in *The Chocolate War* (Chapter 3).

> **limited omniscient:** the author tells the story in third-person but focuses on the thoughts of one or two characters, as Carson McCullers does with Frankie Addams in *The Member of the Wedding* (Chapter 9) and Judith Guest does with Conrad and Calvin Jarrett in *Ordinary People* (Chapter 4).

quest novel: a form of romance in which the hero experiences trials and tests but ultimately achieves success, as Holden Caulfield does in *The Catcher in the Rye* (Chapter 1).

reading log: a journal or notebook that students regularly carry to English classes and use for journal ideas, responses to literature, etc. To see how it can be used, read the "Teaching Suggestions" for *Roll of Thunder, Hear My Cry* in Chapter 12.

realism: "A theory of writing in which the familiar, ordinary aspects of life are depicted . . . to reflect life as it actually is" (Shaw 228–29). Both *Huck Finn* (Chapter 2) and *Ordinary People* (Chapter 4) strive for realism.

romance: in opposition to realistic fiction, a romance or romantic fiction presents life as "we would have it be, more picturesque, more adventurous, more heroic than the actual" (Abrams 140). Tom Sawyer, in *Huck Finn* (Chapter 2), has gotten many of his ideas (like about how to free Jim) from romantic fiction.

sentimentality: an author's attempt to arouse an exaggerated emotional response in readers, beyond what the situation in the novel actually demands, as in *The Red Pony* (Chapter 10) or *A Day No Pigs Would Die* (Chapter 11).

setting: the time and location in which a story takes place

structure: plot, or the events of the story, as organized by the writer for an intended effect on readers; see, for example, the discussions of narrative structure in the "Style and Language" sections of the chapters on *Huckleberry Finn* (Chapter 2) and *The Red Pony* (Chapter 10).

symbolism: see **figurative language**

tone: the author's attitude toward his or her material; note the ironic tone, for instance, in Crane's *The Red Badge of Courage* (Chapter 7).

Bibliography

THE TWELVE NOVELS

Note: The first date given in each entry is the original date of publication. The additional publication information is for the edition referred to in this text.

Cormier, Robert. *The Chocolate War.* 1974. New York: Dell, 1985.
Crane, Stephen. *The Red Badge of Courage.* 1895. New York: Penguin, 1983.
Fitzgerald, F. Scott. *The Great Gatsby.* 1925. New York: Collier, 1980.
Guest, Judith. *Ordinary People.* 1976. New York: Ballantine, 1977.
Lee, Harper. *To Kill a Mockingbird.* 1960. New York: Warner Books, 1982.
McCullers, Carson. *The Member of the Wedding.* 1946. New York: Bantam, 1986.
Peck, Robert Newton. *A Day No Pigs Would Die.* 1972. New York: Dell, 1977.
Plath, Sylvia. *The Bell Jar.* 1963 (U.K.); 1971 (U.S.). New York: Bantam, 1979.
Salinger, J. D. *The Catcher in the Rye.* (1951). New York: Bantam, 1980.
Steinbeck, John. *The Red Pony.* In *The Long Valley.* By Steinbeck. 1938. New York: Penguin, 1986. 199–304.
Taylor, Mildred D. *Roll of Thunder, Hear My Cry.* 1976. New York: Bantam, 1984.
Twain, Mark. *Adventures of Huckleberry Finn.* 1884. Ed. Walter Blair and Victor Fischer. Berkeley: University of California Press, 1985.

PRIMARY LITERATURE CITED

Agee, James. *A Death in the Family.* New York: McDowell, Obolensky: 1957.
Alther, Lisa. *Kinflicks.* New York: Knopf, 1976.
Anaya, Rudolfo A. *Bless Me, Ultima.* Berkeley: Quinto Sol, 1972.
Anderson, Sherwood. *Winesburg, Ohio.* 1919. New York: Viking, 1960.
Armstrong, William H. *Sounder.* New York: Harper & Row, 1969.
Atwood, Margaret. *Surfacing.* New York: Simon & Schuster, 1972.
Beagle, Peter S. *The Last Unicorn.* New York: Viking, 1968.
Blume, Judy. *Forever.* New York: Bradbury, 1975.
Bradford, Richard. *Red Sky at Morning.* Philadelphia: Lippincott, 1968.
Brancato, Robin. *Winning.* New York: Knopf, 1977.
Burnford, Sheila. *The Incredible Journey.* Boston: Little, Brown, 1961.

Capote, Truman. *Selected Writings*. Ed. Mark Schorer. New York: Random House, 1963.

Childress, Alice. *A Hero Ain't Nothin' but a Sandwich*. New York: Coward, 1973.

Cormier, Robert. *After the First Death*. New York: Pantheon, 1979.

———. *Beyond the Chocolate War*. New York: Pantheon, 1985.

———. *The Bumblebee Flies Anyway*. New York: Pantheon, 1983.

———. *I Am the Cheese*. New York: Pantheon, 1977.

Crane, Stephen. *The Portable Stephen Crane*. Ed. Joseph Katz. New York: Viking, 1969.

Craven, Margaret. *I Heard the Owl Call My Name*. New York: Doubleday, 1973.

Davis, Terry. *Vision Quest*. New York: Viking, 1979.

Dickinson, Emily. *Complete Poems*. Ed. Thomas H. Johnson. Boston: Little, Brown, 1960.

Dreiser, Theodore. *Sister Carrie*. 1900. New York: Penguin, 1981.

Duncan, Lois. *Stranger with My Face*. Boston: Little, Brown, 1981.

Eliot, T. S. *The Waste Land and Other Poems*. New York: Harcourt, 1962.

Ellis, Brett Easton. *Less Than Zero*. New York: Penguin, 1985.

Faulkner, William. *The Faulkner Reader*. New York: Random House, 1942.

Fitzgerald, F. Scott. *The Fitzgerald Reader*. Ed. Arthur Mizener. New York: Scribner's, 1963.

Fox, Paula. *The Slave Dancer*. New York: Bradbury, 1973.

Frank, Anne. *The Diary of a Young Girl*. Garden City, N.Y.: Doubleday, 1952.

Franklin, Benjamin. *The Autobiography of Benjamin Franklin*. Ed. Leonard W. Larabee *et al*. New Haven, Conn.: Yale, 1964.

French, Marilyn. *The Women's Room*. New York: Summit, 1978.

Frost, Robert. *The Poems of Robert Frost*. New York: Random House, 1946.

Gaines, Ernest. *The Autobiography of Miss Jane Pittman*. New York: Dial, 1971.

———. *A Gathering of Old Men*. New York: Knopf, 1983.

George, Jean Craighead. *Julie of the Wolves*. New York: Harper & Row, 1972.

Golding, William. *Lord of the Flies*. New York: Coward, 1955.

Green, Hannah (Joanne Greenberg). *I Never Promised You a Rose Garden*. New York: Holt, Rinehart & Winston, 1964.

Greene, Bette. *Summer of My German Soldier*. New York: Dial, 1973.

Guest, Judith. *Second Heaven*. New York: Viking, 1982.

Hamilton, Virginia. *Sweet Whispers, Brother Rush*. New York: Putnam, 1982.

Hawthorne, Nathaniel. *The Scarlet Letter*. 1850. New York: Bobbs-Merrill, 1963.

Head, Ann. *Mr. and Mrs. Bo Jo Jones*. New York: Putnam, 1967.

Heller, Joseph. *Catch-22*. New York: Simon & Schuster, 1961.

Hemingway, Ernest. *A Farewell to Arms*. New York: Scribner's, 1929.

———. *The Fifth Column and the First Forty-Nine Stories*. New York: Scribner's, 1938.

———. *The Green Hills of Africa*. New York: Scribner's, 1935.

———. *The Nick Adams Stories*. New York: Scribner's, 1972.

———. *The Old Man and the Sea*. New York: Scribner's, 1952.

————. *The Sun Also Rises.* New York: Scribner's, 1926.

Hinton, S. E. *The Outsiders.* New York: Viking, 1967.

————. *Rumble Fish.* New York: Delacorte, 1975.

————. *Tex.* New York: Delacorte, 1979.

————. *That Was Then, This Is Now.* New York: Viking, 1971.

Hogan, William. *The Quartzite Trip.* New York: Atheneum, 1980.

Howells, William Dean. *Between the Dark and the Daylight.* New York: Harper, 1907.

Ibsen, Henrik, *The Complete Major Prose Plays.* New York: Farrar, Straus & Giroux, 1978.

Jackson, Shirley. *The Lottery.* New York: Farrar, Straus, 1949.

Joyce, James. *The Dubliners.* New York: Modern Library, 1954.

Kerr, M. E. *Dinky Hocker Shoots Smack.* New York: Harper & Row, 1972.

————. *Night Kites.* New York: Harper & Row, 1986.

Kesey, Ken. *One Flew over the Cuckoo's Nest.* New York: Viking, 1962.

Kincaid, Jamaica. *Annie John.* New York: Farrar, Straus & Giroux, 1985.

Knowles, John. *A Separate Peace.* New York: Macmillan, 1960.

Koertge, Ronald. *When the Kissing Never Stops.* Boston: Atlantic Monthly, 1986.

Kosinski, Jerzy. *The Painted Bird.* Boston: Houghton Mifflin, 1965.

Lawrence, Jerome, and Robert E. Lee. *The Night Thoreau Spent in Jail.* New York: Hill & Wang, 1970.

Lewis, Sinclair. *Babbitt.* 1922. New York: Signet, 1961.

McCullers, Carson. *The Ballad of the Sad Café.* Boston: Houghton Mifflin, 1951.

————. *The Heart Is a Lonely Hunter.* Boston: Houghton Mifflin, 1940.

————. *The Member of the Wedding, a Play.* New York: New Directions, 1951.

McKay, Claude. *Selected Poems.* New York: Bookman Associates, 1953.

McMurtry, Larry. *Horseman, Pass By.* New York: Harper & Row, 1961.

————. *The Last Picture Show.* New York: Dial, 1966.

Maloney, Ray. *The Impact Zone.* New York: Delacorte, 1986.

Mason, Bobbie Ann. *In Country.* New York: Harper & Row, 1985.

Mazer, Norma Fox. *Someone to Love.* New York: Delacorte, 1983.

Melville, Herman. *The Portable Melville.* Ed. Jay Leyda. New York: Viking, 1962.

Miller, Arthur. *The Crucible.* New York: Bantam, 1959.

Naylor, Phyllis. *Unexpected Pleasures.* New York: Putnam, 1986.

Neufeld, John. *Lisa, Bright and Dark.* Chatham, N.Y.: S. G. Phillips, 1969.

Nunn, Kemm. *Tapping the Source.* New York: Dell, 1984.

O'Dell, Scott. *Island of the Blue Dolphins.* Boston: Houghton Mifflin, 1960.

Paterson, Katherine. *The Bridge to Teribithia.* New York: Crowell, 1977.

————. *Jacob Have I Loved.* New York: Crowell, 1980.

Paton, Alan. *Cry the Beloved Country.* New York: Scribner's, 1948.

Peck, Richard. *Princess Ashley.* New York: Delacorte, 1987.

Plath, Sylvia. *Collected Poems.* Ed. Ted Hughes. Boston: Faber and Faber, 1981.

Potok, Chaim. *The Chosen.* New York: Simon & Schuster, 1967.

Porter, Katherine Anne. *The Collected Stories*. London: Virago, 1985.

Portis, Charles. *True Grit*. New York: Simon & Schuster, 1968.

Rawlings, Marjorie Kinnan. *The Yearling*. New York: Scribner's, 1938.

Rawls, Wilson. *Where the Red Fern Grows*. Garden City, N.Y.: Doubleday, 1961.

Remarque, Erich Maria. *All Quiet on the Western Front*. Boston: Little, Brown, 1929.

Salinger, J. D. *Nine Stories*. New York: Signet, 1954.

Santiago, Danny (Daniel James). *Famous All Over Town*. New York: Simon & Schuster, 1983.

Schaefer, Jack. *Shane*. Boston: Houghton Mifflin, 1949.

Scoppettone, Sandra. *The Late Great Me*. New York: Putnam, 1976.

Steinbeck, John. *Of Mice and Men*. New York: Viking, 1937.

———. *The Pearl*. New York: Viking, 1947.

Taylor, Mildred D. *Let the Circle Be Unbroken*. New York: Dial, 1981.

———. *Song of the Trees*. New York: Dial, 1973.

Taylor, Theodore. *The Cay*. Garden City, N.Y.: Doubleday, 1969.

———. *The Maldonado Miracle*. Garden City, N.Y.: Doubleday, 1973.

Tevis, Walter. *Queen's Gambit*. New York: Random House, 1983.

Thoreau, Henry David. *Walden and Other Writings*. Ed. William Howarth. New York: Random House, 1981.

Townsend, Sue. *The Adrian Mole Diaries: A Novel*. New York: Grove, 1986.

Twain, Mark. *The Adventures of Tom Sawyer*. 1876. New York: Bantam, 1981.

———. "The Art of Composition." In *Life As I Find It*. Ed. Charles Neider. Garden City, N.Y.: Hanover House, 1971.

———. "The History of a Campaign That Failed." In *The American Claimant and Other Stories and Sketches*. By Twain. New York: Harper, 1904.

———. *Life on the Mississippi*. 1883. New York: Signet, 1961.

———. *The War Prayer*. 1923. New York: Harper & Row, 1970.

Updike, John. *Pigeon Feathers and Other Stories*. New York: Knopf, 1962.

Voight, Cynthia. *Come a Stranger*. New York: Atheneum, 1987.

———. *Dicey's Song*. New York: Atheneum, 1982.

———. *A Solitary Blue*. New York: Atheneum, 1983.

Vonnegut, Kurt. *Slaughterhouse-Five*. New York: Delacorte, 1969.

Ward, Mary Jane. *The Snake Pit*. New York: Random House, 1946.

Weaver, Will. *Red Earth, White Earth*. New York: Simon & Schuster, 1987.

Wharton, Edith. *Ethan Frome*. 1911. New York: Scribner's, 1939.

Wharton, William. *Birdy*. New York: Knopf, 1979.

Whitman, Walt. *Complete Poetry and Selected Prose*. Ed. James E. Miller, Jr. Boston: Houghton Mifflin, 1959.

Williams, Tennessee. *The Glass Menagerie*. New York: Random, 1945.

Wright, Richard. *Black Boy*. New York: Harper & Row, 1945.

Zindel, Paul. *The Pigman*. New York: Harper & Row, 1968.

———. *The Pigman's Legacy*. New York: Harper & Row, 1980.

SECONDARY SOURCES CITED

Abrams, M. H. *A Glossary of Literary Terms.* 3rd ed. New York: Holt, Rinehart & Winston, 1971.

Beckson, Karl, and Arthur Ganz. *A Reader's Guide to Literary Terms.* New York: Farrar, Straus, 1960.

Bleifuss, Joel. "In Short." *In These Times* 25 November-8 December 1987: 5.

Gottlieb, Anne. "A New Cycle in 'YA' Books." *The New York Times Book Review* 17 June 1984: 24-25.

Lisca, Peter. *The Wide World of John Steinbeck.* New Brunswick, N.J.: Rutgers, 1958.

Model Curriculum Standards: Grades Nine Through Twelve. Sacramento: California State Department of Education, 1985.

Nilsen, Alleen Pace, and Kenneth L. Donelson. *Literature for Today's Young Adults.* 2nd ed. Glenview, Ill.: Scott, Foresman, 1985.

Probst, Robert E. "Adolescent Literature and the English Curriculum." *English Journal* 76.3 (1987): 26-30.

———. *Adolescent Literature: Response and Analysis.* Columbus, Ohio: Merrill, 1984.

Reed, Arthea J. S. *Reaching Adolescents: The Young Adult Book and the School.* New York: Holt, Rinehart & Winston, 1985.

Schulberg, Budd. "John Steinbeck: Discontented Lion in Winter." *West Magazine, Los Angeles Times* 23 February 1969: 12-15.

Shaw, Harry. *Concise Dictionary of Literary Terms.* New York: McGraw-Hill, 1972.

Smith, Henry Nash. *Mark Twain: The Development of a Writer.* Cambridge: Harvard, 1962.

Taylor, Mildred D. "Newbery Award Acceptance." *The Horn Book Magazine* 53 (1977): 401-9.

Trelease, Jim. *The Read-Aloud Handbook.* Rev. ed. New York: Penguin, 1985.

Index

Note: Page numbers in boldface indicate definition of a term, major discussion of a work, or listing of a theme.

About the Author

DAVID PECK is professor of English and American Studies at California State University at Long Beach, the author of numerous articles and bibliographies, and the coauthor of *A Guide to the Whole Writing Process* (Houghton Mifflin, 1984; with Jack Blum, Carolyn Brinkman, and Elizabeth Hoffman) and *Guide to Marxist Literary Criticism* (Indiana, 1980; with Chris Bullock). Professor Peck lives in Laguna Beach, California.